SONOMA COUNTY LIBRARY
3 7565 00061 7067
S0-ACX-165

SONOMA COUNTY
LIBRARY
OFFICIAL
DISCARD

A HISTORY OF SHOE FASHIONS

A HISTORY OF SHOE FASHIONS

A study of shoe design in relation to costume
for shoe designers, pattern cutters, manufacturers,
fashion students and dress designers, etc.

by Eunice Wilson

With shoe drawings by the author
Costume drawings by Gay Lloyd

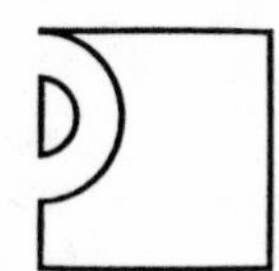

PITMAN PUBLISHING

First published 1969
Reprinted 1970

SIR ISAAC PITMAN AND SONS LTD.
Pitman House, Parker Street, Kingsway, London, W.C.2
P.O. Box 6038, Portal Street, Nairobi, Kenya
SIR ISAAC PITMAN (AUST.) PTY. LTD.
Pitman House, Bouverie Street, Carlton, Victoria 3053, Australia
PITMAN PUBLISHING COMPANY S.A. LTD.
P.O. Box 9898, Johannesburg, S. Africa
PITMAN PUBLISHING CORPORATION
6 East 43rd Street, New York, N.Y. 10017, U.S.A.
SIR ISAAC PITMAN (CANADA) LTD.
Pitman House, 381–383 Church Street, Toronto, 3, Canada
THE COPP CLARK PUBLISHING COMPANY
517 Wellington Street, Toronto, 2B, Canada

ISBN: 0 273 40094 0

MADE IN GREAT BRITAIN AT THE PITMAN PRESS, BATH
G0—(G.3313)

Foreword

by Martin Miller

Norvic Shoe Co. Ltd., Norwich

LET'S face it. . with a cliché. . fashion, like history, repeats itself. In this, as in all clichés, there is a modicum of truth. There are those who would deny that fashion repeats itself, as though to admit it would detract from the creative genius of pure design. This line of thinking belongs to the creation of great works of art, of occasional great buildings. The designers who "create" fashion, however, are working within the discipline imposed on all commercial artists, that of producing a commonly-used article that is going to be currently acceptable to a sizeable number of people. The permutations of "treatment" are countless. The commercially-successful designer is the one who can interpret, divine and foresee the delineation suggested by time and assess the receptivity of the public, and this we know as the interpretation of trends. Trends do tend to repeat themselves, although sometimes separated by a considerable lapse of time.

This is a book about the history of shoe fashions. The actual, original, functional shoe design is long since lost in the mist of time. Within the restrictions of the functional nature of footwear, the fashions of shoes have see-sawed around the shape of the toe from point to cow-mouth and the height of the heel from nothing to six inches. What lie between these two fundamentals are the countless permutations of "treatment." The toe shape and the heel height are the two most important facets of shoe fashion and are the disciplines imposed on shoe designers. The very nature of the article itself determines the necessity of a return of past shapes. The creative shoe designer is the person who leads with a "new" shape, having determined correctly that the public is ready for it, or can be persuaded to wear it.

Sometimes a trend in shoe fashion is directly co-ordinated with dress fashion and line, but the exciting shoe fashions through the ages are those that have leapt to the forefront for their own intrinsic daring. It is an unequivocal fact that the lower the *per capita* consumption of shoes in any age, the more functional they have been at that time, and therefore deadly dull. Fashion feeds on success and on the limit of daring and fashion consciousness to which a receptive public can be attuned. There are two important reasons for the rapidity with which fashion changes today compared with past ages. The first is the infinitely greater number of people who can afford to indulge in fashion and secondly the mass media available through which fashion can be promoted. In the past all new fashions permeated down from the top of society. Today it often leads in through the teenager with an altogether new conception of couture design.

At no time could it be more apposite to bring out a history of shoe fashions when all, in our virtually classless society, have the opportunity to participate in fashion changes. There are many volumes devoted to the history of costume in general, awarding to shoes but a cursory glance. At last, a professional designer focuses on shoes the historical regard they deserve. Miss Wilson traces the varied pattern of the shoemakers' art, establishing it as an influential necessity of fashion.

MARTIN MILLER

Preface

THIS is a book about shoes. It is a product of many years of collecting historical fashion information in sketch form, and of scouring museums and picture galleries for evidence. It does not claim absolute accuracy for there are too few early examples and these are not always complete. There is not always sufficient evidence for what one says, so I must ask for tolerance from those who prefer historical accuracy, and for those technical authorities who might have means of knowing more and better.

My collection has been made from books, from paintings, from sculpture and statuary, from contemporary records, from the evidence in museums, in other words from anything that shows a shoe. There is not space here to catalogue every reference or to mention every place from which the sketch might have come. This is the reason for listing the books, the museums, the galleries, that have helped, so that the enthusiastic student might look for himself.

My grateful thanks are due to very many people, in and out of the shoe trade, and it is not possible to list them all. I hope all those who have met me in the course of its collection will therefore remember my visits, and accept my deep gratitude for their help.

In particular, however, I should like to thank the following: Robert Jellinek of the Bally Shoe Company; James Ayres of the John Judkyn Memorial, Bath; Mrs. Doris Langley Moore of the Museum of Costume, Bath; Professor Janey Ironside of the Royal College of Art; John Thornton of Northampton College of Technology; James Laver, who was at the Victoria and Albert Museum when I began collecting; Barbara and Martin Miller for their interest in Norwich History; Mrs. Gay Lloyd who drew the fashion illustrations and for her early help in collecting shoes; and my parents (who also caught the collecting bug) for their encouragement.

Most of this book was written at the Saint Deiniol's Library, at Hawarden near Chester, to whose warden the Rev. Dr. Stewart Lawton, his wife and staff, I should like to give particular thanks. This is a residential library where students may study and work. It grew out of Mr. Gladstone's own library and is made available for students of all kinds and nationalities by the generosity of members of the Gladstone family who still live in Hawarden Castle. Although it is not a library with a particular bias towards costume, I was able to find here many valuable references to people and places.

May I say finally that I shall be very pleased to receive any suggestions for additions or improvements that might be made to this book in the event of its being reprinted, as well as any information regarding sources for shoe sketches and photographs.

EUNICE WILSON

Contents

Illustrations

Plates

(between pages 288 *and* 289*)*

Introduction

WE ARE APT TO FORGET that our civilization is the product of innumerable influences, histories, cultures, and fashions. We forget that our today was yesterday's future and is tomorrow's past. To those who have studied their trade's evolution it is not surprising when fashions come round again, but those who do not have the opportunity to spend time in study are frequently shocked by the directions of new fashion trends.

Whilst it is not yet possible to forecast accurately which fashions are going to be the ones which will influence next year's shoe styles, it is possible by the study of history to foresee something of the direction they will take. Fashion works in cycles and spirals, and whilst it is a fact that some ideas do come round again in their due time they never come back exactly as they were. Instead, they in turn are influenced by the way of life and the technical developments of the period into which they are re-introduced.

Mr. James Laver, who has given many lectures on the subject of fashion, has expounded these theories so much better than I can, and so often, that there cannot be a student of fashion who has not read his books and articles. I will therefore not attempt to re-echo what he has said so well on this subject. It is, however, an essential item in the shoe design student's programme to make a study of fashion in shoe history. This is difficult to do without spending a great deal of time travelling and making notes, so I have tried to put together some of my own findings in order to lessen the task.

Mr. Laver has suggested that it takes about twenty years for a fashion to return; in other words, when it comes back there is a younger generation who do not remember its first appearance. This generation finds it new and fresh, instead of a revival, and so interprets it in a new idiom, in the way most suitable to a changed way of life. The more one studies history the more one finds this to be true, though it is truer of recent generations than in earlier periods. And all these theories apply as much to shoe fashions as to clothes.

The further we go back the less consistent we find fashion to be. In the Saxon period, for instance, we find jewellery designs differing from region to region, far more than they differ in our present century. This is because communications have speeded up so much that nowadays there is little time-lag between country and country. Neither is there such marked social difference these days, and, apart from intricate detailing which is always expensive and rare, it is difficult to tell by looking at a shoe from which social strata it has come. In past ages this was not difficult because sumptuary laws limited the number of those who could wear certain kinds of garments, and even colour had a class distinction.

This book cannot cover all aspects of shoe fashion, for it is far too large a subject. Neither can it incorporate the full technical reasons for shoe development as this would require a separate book more than twice the size. Many technical books have been written on this subject, however, and it is hoped that the fashion aspect explained in the present book will supplement the very essential information given in them.

Shoe designers are increasing in numbers and there are many more of them than when I first started in the trade; there will be more as the industry develops and increases. There are also many more women coming into the trade so that it is almost as common to find women designing in the factory as it is to find men. And, since well-designed shoes of high quality are no longer the prerogative of the upper and wealthy classes, there is far more scope for the designer than ever before.

Even if one is not actively engaged or interested in the making of shoes, they become more interesting if one knows a little of the background.

In his book, *The Age of Chivalry*, Sir Arthur Bryant, one of our most eminent historians, makes a statement which could be quoted on many occasions: "Unless those responsible for a nation's policy. .in a parliamentary democracy, the electors. .can climb that tower, they cannot see the road along which they have come or comprehend their country's continuing destiny."[1] The tower referred to bears the name by which he first wanted to call his book, *The Tower of Memory*.

If Sir Arthur will forgive me for linking him with an art as transient as fashion, I would like to suggest that those interested in fashion, and those in the shoe trade in particular, would derive infinite benefit from erecting their own tower and using it to remind themselves of past developments and future possibilities where their trade is concerned.

This book is an attempt to lay the foundation for such a tower, and it is hoped that it will help those who are responsible for the new designs of our shoes to increase their knowledge of their industry's fashion history. No trade can achieve the success it desires without a knowledge of the past on which to build its future. In the pages that follow is a gathering-up of a little of that past, in which I hope the wearers as well as the makers of shoes will be interested.

[1]Quoted by permission of Sir Arthur Bryant and A. D. Peters & Co.

I

The Affinity of Shoes with Clothes

THERE IS a strong relationship between shoes and the clothes with which they are worn, although this is not always instantly recognized. Through the ages this has been so, but at no time is it more clearly perceptible than in our own day when shoes and legs are a major part of fashion.

To generalize, initially we can say that the height or shape of the heel is the part of the shoe which renders it more noticeably different from fashion to fashion, and therefore heels are particularly important. Heels are closely related to hems because their height varies with the length of the skirt. Making allowance for the ins and outs of current trends, one can say that the shorter the skirt the lower is the height of the heel. And conversely, the longer the skirt the higher must be the heel.

Although this applies only from the Tudor period, when heels were first worn, and applies much more to our own century than to any other, it can be said that this is a fairly infallible rule. Even when hem lengths varied but little, it can be seen that the difference between ground-length and ankle-length made many heels vary between being completely flat and lifting to a height of one inch.

In the year of 1968, when mini-skirts were at their shortest, heels showed a tendency to rise from the accepted low and flat shapes, which were more proportionately suitable, to a higher shape. This was because when the skirt almost totally disappears into a tunic it has the same effect on heels as the obliterating ground-brushing hemline of other eras, rendering them variable.

In more detail, shoes of every period tend to echo the fashion of that period, both in colour and shape, so that when we have an elongated shape in clothes, such as at the vertical Plantagenet period, shoes also extend their toes to match. On the opposite and contrasting side, that of the Tudors, whose fashions were square and broad, and whose clothes were horizontal rather than vertical, toe shapes followed the same directions and were broad and square also. Decorative details of rosettes and ribbons were found on shoes as well as on clothes, a matching-up which was to be echoed in the 'sixties by the "Op Art" fashion, which cut every shape into black and white geometrics.

There are periods when fussy clothes call for the same fussiness in shoes. These are generally followed by periods of restraint when the simplicity of clothes, which rely on

2—(G.3313)

cut and colour alone, needs the same undecorated theme in shoes. But there are periods in between—the transitional period of one trend to another, when shapes and styles are undecided and there is a mixture of both until the style settles. This is no less true of our own period than of any other, and this is why there are often years in costume history when the fashion for one style overlaps with the next, and the scene appears confusing.

To clarify some of this confusion in our own years one must study costume in other eras. From them we can find without too much difficulty which is the waning fashion which has passed its peak, and which is the growing fashion slowly coming to acceptance. In a single book it is possible to map out the big changes only, but a closer study of each period, especially of those fashions which link the changes of direction, should make this clearer and more easy to understand.

Social environment is an important contributing factor to the style of the shoes we wear, and whilst it is true that the present social conditions have little to do with fashion, repeated similarities in our lives tend to produce a repeated fashion in another shape. Thus an industrial revolution in the techniques of industry in the nineteen-sixties can reproduce a feeling for the fashions of the first industrial revolution.

The importance of the great couture houses has always played a large part in influencing fashion, for they have been the root and cradle of fashion for a long time. Situated as they are, particularly in Paris, within an atmosphere more conductive to regarding fashion as an art, new ideas have a better chance of development. But a new revolution has been growing over the years and has now come to fruition; it is that of the young and their influence on design both as designers and as the consumer market.

In early centuries, it was such people as kings and queens, emperors, the philosophers and the courtesans of Rome who set the styles. Later it was royal favourites, mistresses, and great ladies whose clothes were copied, and so on up to the actresses of the eighteen-nineties, the film stars of the 'twenties and 'thirties, up to the pop stars of the nineteen-sixties and seventies. In all those days, except our own, fashion began at the top with the wealthy and upper classes and filtered down until, when it had reached the whole country, it was no longer fashion but merely clothes and shoes.

Now—but for how long is impossible to say—it is the young and uninhibited who start fashions on their way, and no longer the wealthy of any one class.

By a look at the change in other aspects of social design, architecture, interiors, furniture, the graphic arts, and more recently cars, one can see how fashion is part of an integral whole and not, as we tend to think, clothes alone. It is true that clothes and shoes reflect it in a manner that is most clearly appreciated because it concerns us all no matter how uninterested we think we are. Fashion begins its change firstly in music, though if one is removed from the so-called "scene" one will not be immediately aware of this.

An example illustrates this..pop music has recently moved gently and almost imperceptibly from rock-and-roll, through jerky jazz "shapes" to smoother, gentler, "mood" rhythms. This was echoed in clothes by the gradual change from the shock shapes introduced by the space age, via the extreme of mini-skirts, to the softer, more feminine, clothes of 1968.

But this transition and interpretation of fashion does not occur in clothes as quickly as the head-lines from Paris would have us believe. As already mentioned, it shows first in new music, which concerns a relatively small percentage of people, is then picked up and unconsciously interpreted in architecture, which is a transference from appreciation by the ear to that of the eye, concerning a larger percentage of the population. Then, because architecture, especially in homes and offices, demands a matching interior, it increases its influence to an even bigger proportion which includes most of us, and changes the things we live with. Cars and transport of all kinds add their demands at this point and govern the shapes and lengths of the clothes we wear, in order for us to move about in the way we do. This is probably an unconscious alteration, in the same way that carriage designers of the last century were compelled, perhaps without realizing why, to change the width of their doors to accommodate the crinoline. Finally, although the fashion designers will deny they are the last in this sociological cycle, the accumulation of all this creates a demand for clothes to match the world we live in and the kind of life we must lead within it.

To those who are not students of design this may be difficult to see in the things around them, and particularly where shoes are concerned. But one has only to take the parallel case of architecture and one easily sees in it the basic shapes of the shoes of the same period, no matter where one starts.

There are two outstanding examples, the Plantagenet and the Tudor, which are probably the periods most familiar to anyone interested in costume. James Laver has explained this in great detail, but one can simplify the matter considerably for an introduction. The Plantagenet years were the great period of church and cathedral building all over Europe. Everywhere, those soaring pointed steeples were to change church architecture from the square Norman shapes. They were echoed in the tall head-dresses worn by women, in France called a hennin and modestly accepted in England; men too, wearing the long liripipe sleeve and cap, wore clothes of similar shape. Both men and women wore shoes with long, slender, pointed toes which followed the same outline.

When this shape had gone too far and the fashionable toes had grown too long for comfort, fashion took another turn, this time in the opposite direction. Not as suddenly or as unpredictably as it would appear, toes became square and as broad as the square, spreading buildings of the Tudor architecture whose shape was echoed in clothes.

Thus it can be seen that it is the spirit of the age, the *Zeitgeist*, which makes clothes and shoes what they are, rather than the whims and fancies of designers, or women. Nor is this *Zeitgeist* confined to any one particular country, but it is found in all countries at the same time. That some countries rise above the rest and become fashion leaders is due more to social circumstance, industrial development and attitude toward design than to an inherited dictatorship. As one studies history one finds that no country retains the influence undisputed for ever, though some hold it longer than others, each one taking its turn for differing reasons.

All that is said of clothes fashion applies also to shoes. There are certain industrial limitations and developments which make the shoe industry rather less flexible and less open to transient influences than what is called the "rag trade." More and more, however, as women become nearer to being equals of men, their shoes become a much more important item of fashion than they ever were before. Design training, hitherto considered unnecessary, now offers equal opportunity for women as well as men. Part of this training includes the essential study of shoe history.

2

A Brief Outline of Shoe Terms

THIS SECTION is not meant to be in any way technical, as it is assumed that those who are seriously engaged in the shoe trade will know these terms in common usage, that students will have access to books specifically devoted to shoe manufacture, and that potential shoe designers will be on their way to learning them. It is meant for those who merely wear shoes, or who are newcomers to the retail trade, or who are interested in understanding, no matter how amateurishly, the words the craftsman uses.

The terms used for various parts of the shoe, and the equipment used to make them, are often used without any knowledge of their original meaning. These are indicated below where they are of any importance.

THE LAST (often still called "the wood"). The wood on which the shoe is made. More often than not, this is now a form of plastic, which is more durable. Its shape varies according to what is in fashion, but the shoe's toe shape or heel height cannot vary from that of the last on which it is first built. To change a last shape is a very expensive business. Each heel height has to have a different last, as does each size and each width. A last is made as near the average foot fitting as possible, and is hinged so that it can be pulled out of the shoe without damaging the shoe shape.

A shoe is generally composed of an upper, a sole and a heel. The upper is that part which covers the foot, cut in one piece with a seam at the back, or into two or three pieces according to the cut of the pattern and its economics. The upper has two main parts—

THE VAMP. That part of the upper which covers the front of the foot as far as the back of the joint of the big toe.

THE QUARTER. The part of the back of the upper which covers the heel; the back of the shoe, as far as the point where it meets the vamp. So called because it is a quarter of the whole.

Other parts of the upper are—

CAP. The toe cap can often be of a different material or colour from the rest of the shoe, or match it, according to fashion.

PUFF. The light reinforcing inside the upper which gives the toe its shape and support.

COUNTER. The overlaid piece at the back of the upper corresponding to the toe cap which can be of a different colour or material. The cap and counter are most noticeable in a "co-respondent" shoe.

STIFFENER. The inside stiffening of the upper, covering the heel and giving the back of the shoe support. Unlike the puff, it can seldom be dispensed with.

TOPLINE. The top edge of the upper. No matter what its shape or height it is called the topline.

THROAT. The front of the vamp.

LINING. A shoe is partly or wholly lined, or left unlined.

HEELS. These have different names which have been given them either for their shape, or after the person of fashion with whom they are associated.

LOUIS HEELS. Are easy to spot because the sole continues up under the arch and down the front of the heel. This name applies to any height or any shape in which this method of making is constant. The heel takes its name from Louis XIV, in whose reign they were first worn.

CUBAN HEEL. So called because the boots worn by the gauchos of South America had short straight heels to enable them to be worn with stirrups. Cuban, or knock-on heels, are distinguishable by the termination of the sole at the top of the heel which is completely covered or sprayed.

There are also leather heels which can be made of layers of real leather, called lifts; or stacked heels made in the same way but of synthetic materials. Leather heels can be simulated in many ways.

Heels have subdivisions of their own and have separate parts—

BREAST. The front of the heel under the arch.

TOP-PIECE. That part of the heel which comes in contact with the ground, corresponding to the sole. Called the "top" piece because, in making, the shoe is worked upside down, so that the bottom of the heel as it stands on the ground becomes the top.

SEAT. The concave part of the heel that fits to the shoe and into which the heel of the foot sits.

The sole is that piece of leather or other material which comes in contact with the ground.

INSOLE. Between the sole and the foot there is a piece of leather, or other material, on to which the upper is lasted. In making, it lies closest to the last. The layman should not confuse it with the sock.

SHANK. In modern shoemaking there is nearly always a piece of metal inserted between the sole and the insole, lying along the arch of the foot. This gives the foot support and the shoe strength.

WAIST. That part of the last and the shoe which corresponds to the instep and the arch of the foot.

FEATHER. That part of the last and the shoe where the upper's edge meets the sole. The inside and the outside of a shoe are fairly obvious, but it is not commonly known that they are not the same size and shape. The inside of the upper is higher than the outside because the foot needs more support on the inside. Neither is the left foot necessarily the same size as the right. Only in comparatively recent history has there been any difference between the left and the right shoe and this is most noticeable in the shape of the sole. On a normally arched foot only the outside touches the ground, leaving an indentation under the arch on the inside.

JOINT. The large joint where the big toe meets the rest of the foot.

In addition to these general terms which apply to all shoes, no matter what their quality and purpose, there are various names for the different basic types of shoes. These names often have historical origins and are so called because of their associations with the people who first made them fashionable.

TIE SHOE. This is probably the most basic of shoe shapes. It has several basic styles and each has a name. The most well known are—

OXFORD. It can easily be distinguished because the vamp is stitched on top of the quarters and facings which carry the eyelet holes and laces. Its name is historically associated with the students of Oxford University. It is a type of tie shoe and is worn by men and women alike.

DERBY. Again easily identified because its facings and quarters are overlaid and stitched on to the vamp; the reverse of the Oxford. Like the Oxford it generally has a tongue in classic styles, but this is not an essential. Worn by men and women. Associated with the Earl of Derby.

GHILLIE. This is a very old style whose shape goes back to the earliest periods in our history. It is characterized by the separate facings for each lace and eyelet, which can be looped or not according to the fashion. It takes its name from the ghillies who accompany a shoot.

There are many variations on these three themes, most of whose names are self-descriptive, invented as the occasion arose. For example, the U-Throated Tie; the Saddle Oxford; the Lamballe Tie, which was a shoe laced with a ribbon tied through a single eyelet and named after Princess de Lamballe (1749–1792), friend of Marie-Antoinette. Cap and counter styles speak for themselves, but are not necessarily confined to tie shoes. Neither is the term "brogues," which is a method of describing a pattern of stitching and punching on a fairly classic style of shoe.

Next is the *Court Shoe*, the plainest of all shoes, which bears the same name whatever its height of heel. So called because it was a plain shoe similar to this that was accepted dress at the courts of Europe. There are variations on this shape also—

D'ORSAY COURT. A vamp and quarter court with an open waist. Can be made on any heel height. Named after Count D'Orsay, who is said to have invented it.

SLING BACK COURT. A self-explanatory name of fairly recent origin. This shoe can have an open or closed toe, but has the common denominator of an open back.

GUSSET COURT SHOE. This is any step-in type of shoe with a high cut front made accessible by an elastic which can be inserted at the front or sides.

JESTER COURT. A shoe of any heel height with a peaked front. Fashionable in 1941, but originates from the jester shoe of the middle ages.

OPERA COURT. Another vamp and quarter court but with a closed waist. The upper is cut in three basic parts. The same cut, applied to a man's slipper, is a basic shape in masculine footwear.

The *Moccasin* was originally the soft deerskin shoe of the American Indian (see page 301), but now has many modern variants.

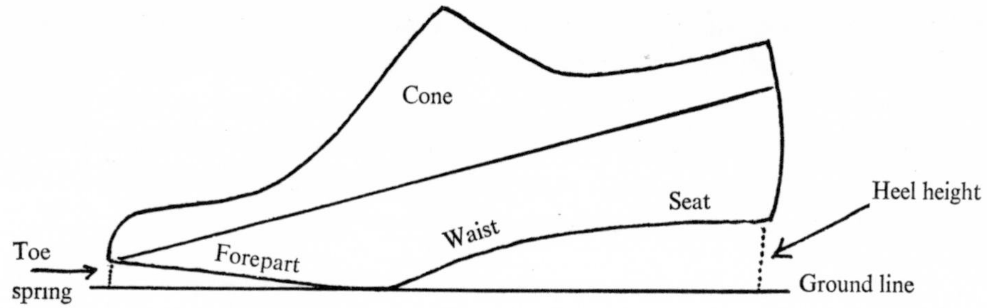

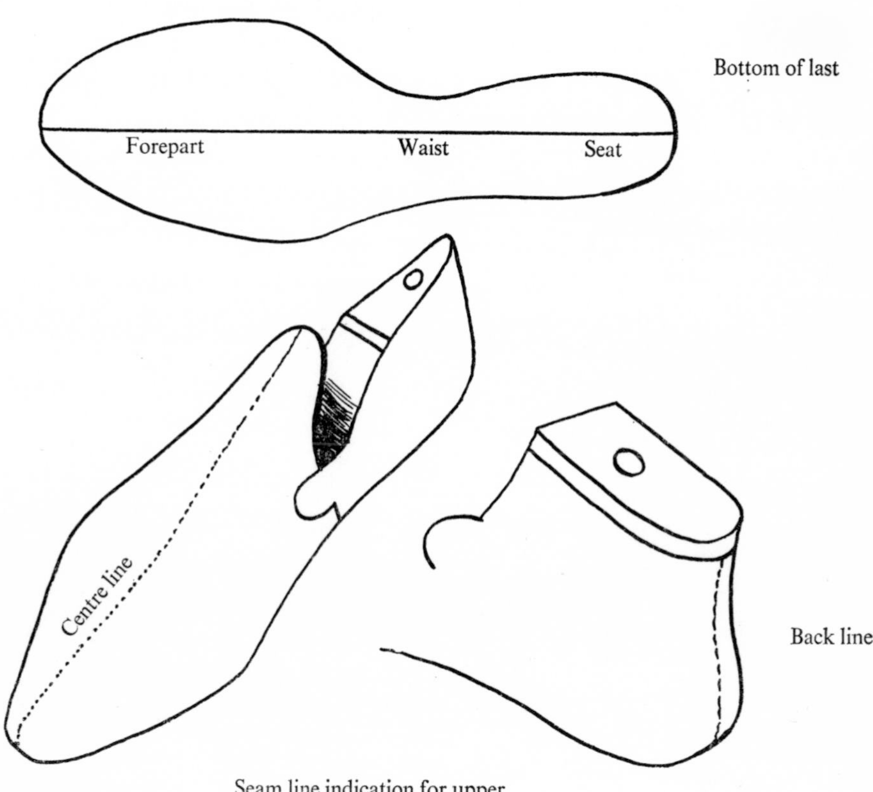

I. VARIOUS PARTS OF THE SHOE AND LAST

2. THE UPPER AND THE CONSTRUCTION OF THE SHOE

THE UPPER

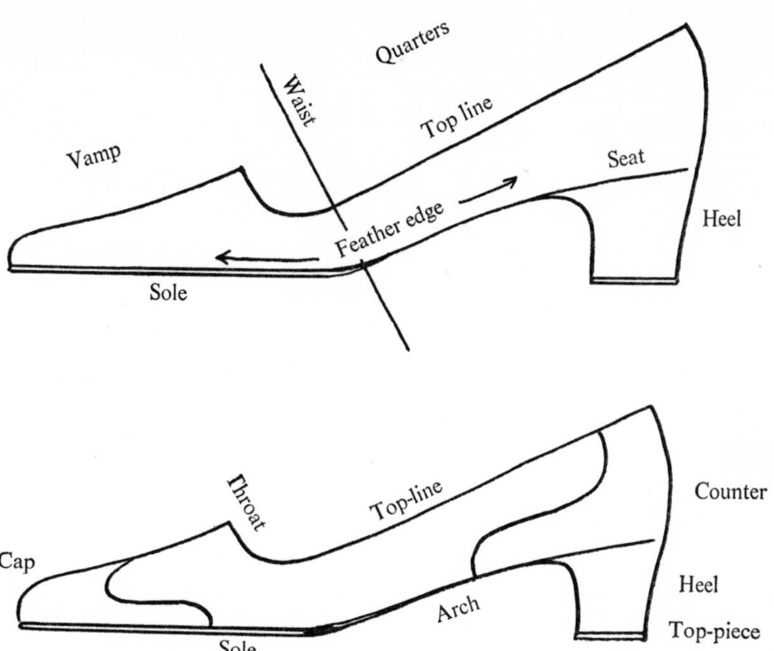

CONSTRUCTION

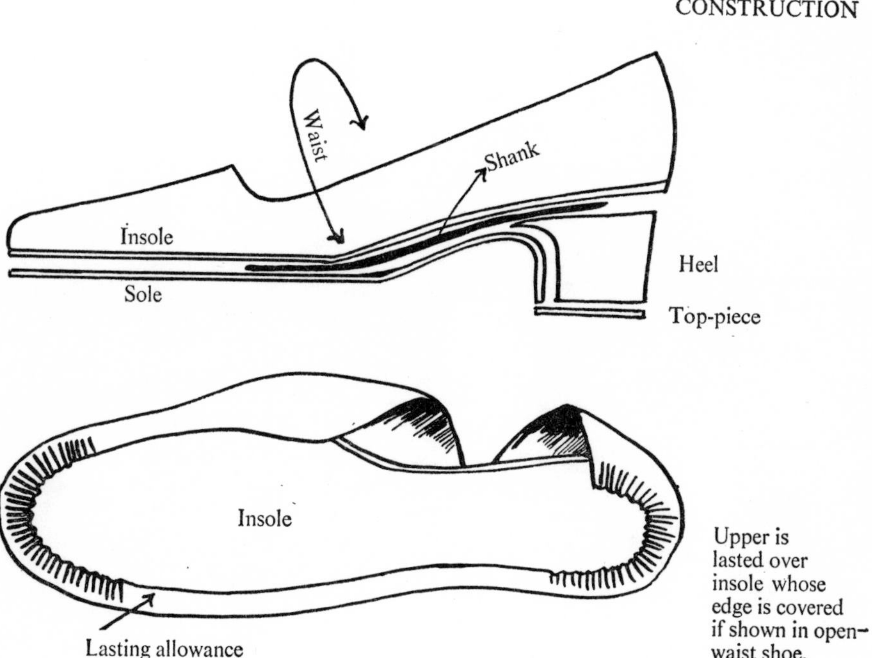

Upper is lasted over insole whose edge is covered if shown in open-waist shoe.

These are basic shapes only, which give a general indication of the various types of heels. There are many versions of each one, and a very high shape or a low one does not involve a change of the type name.

3. HEELS

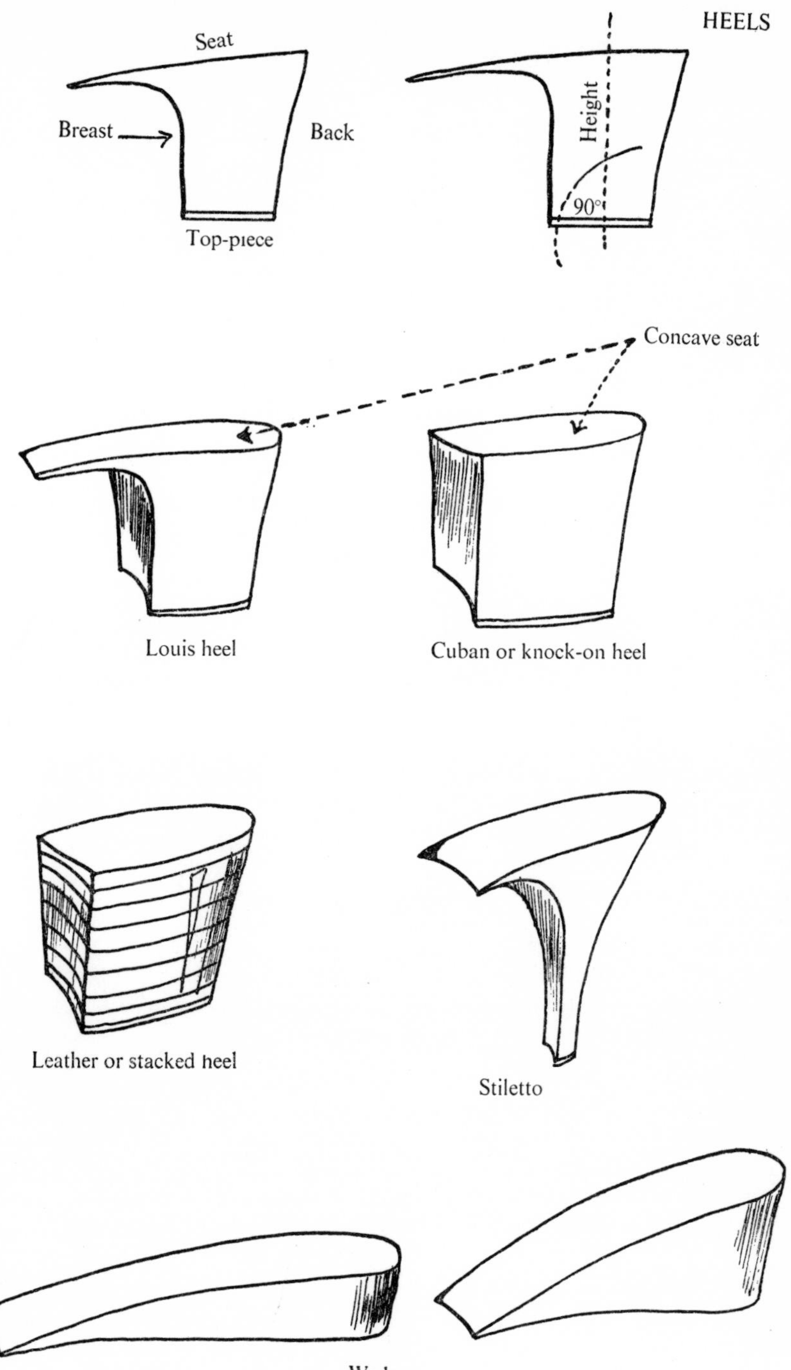

Louis heel

Cuban or knock-on heel

Leather or stacked heel

Stiletto

Wedges

4. MODERN HEEL SHAPES

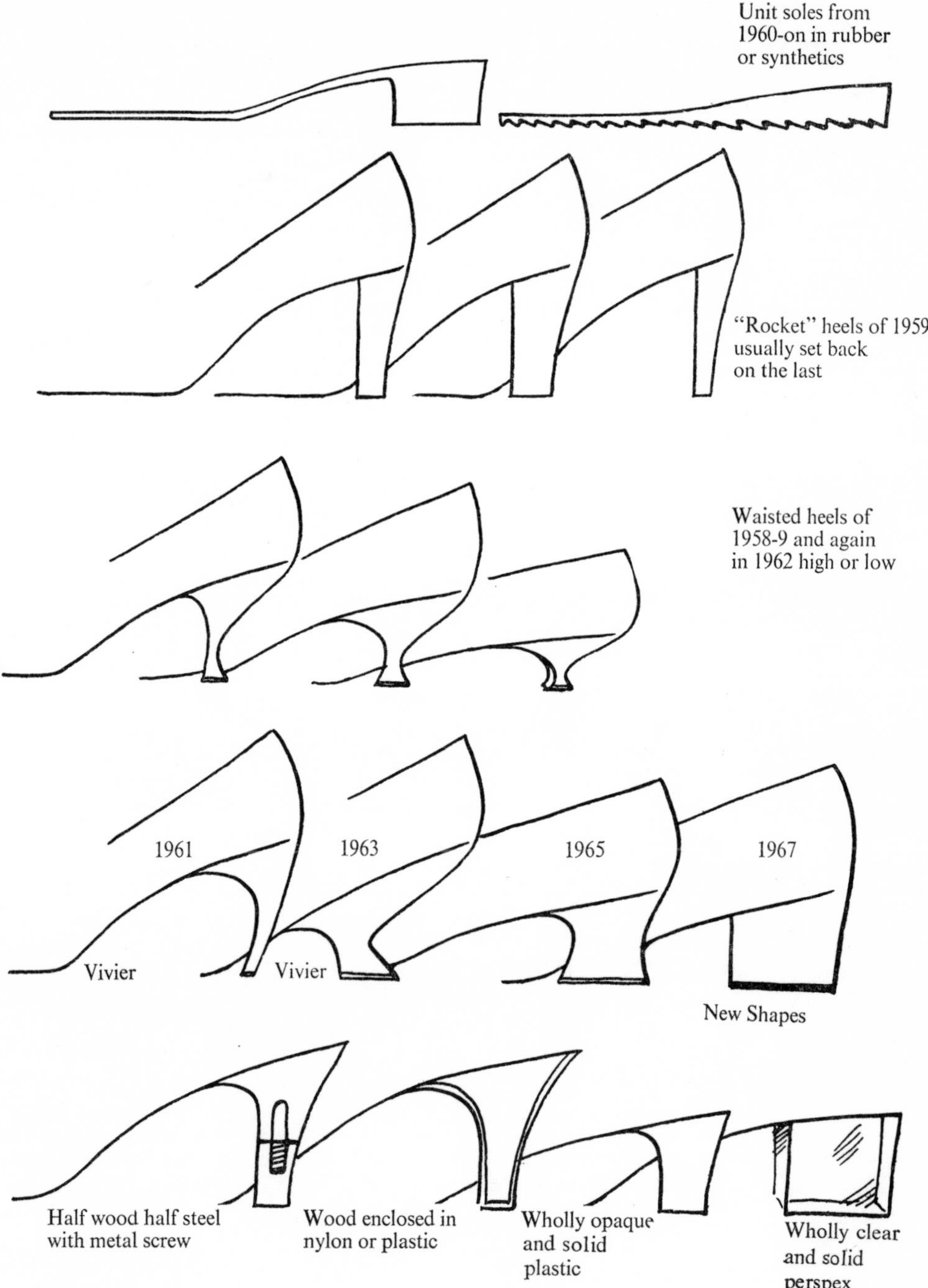
Unit soles from
1960-on in rubber
or synthetics
"Rocket" heels of 1959
usually set back
on the last
Waisted heels of
1958-9 and again
in 1962 high or low
1961
1963
1965
1967
Vivier
Vivier
New Shapes
Half wood half steel
with metal screw
Wood enclosed in
nylon or plastic
Wholly opaque
and solid
plastic
Wholly clear
and solid
perspex

5. SHOE TYPES AND TERMS

Tie shoes
Court shoes
Oxford
Plain closed court
Derby
Sling back
Ghillie
D'Orsay court
Gusset Court
Shoe
Opera

3

Pre-Roman Britain to 55 B.C.

For the purpose of shoe history it will be essential to group the periods of Palaeolithic, Neolithic and Celtic Britain together, although the archaeologist and the historian may disapprove. Insufficient evidence remains of the types of footwear worn by the various tribes in these periods and until more is known we must assume that Ancient Britons went barefoot or merely wrapped skins round their feet.

Shoes were not yet a matter of fashion though it can be taken for granted that there must have been slight regional differences in the manner of using the skins. Jewellery differed and there is no reason why clothing should not have differed also. The primary object of footwear was to keep out the wet and the cold, and since the flint scrapers, which might have dressed the hides have been found, we know they used animal skins for different purposes. Needles have also been discovered, and Palaeolithic man also used a form of awl, showing that he was an expert craftsman.

The Neolithic men were more civilized, and discovered how to put spinning and weaving to use; we can assume that the cloth his womenfolk wove was used to cover his feet as well as his body. Since he wove grass to use in his houses and as fencing, it may be that he also used it to strengthen the soles of his shoes.

Much has been found in the burial barrows from which comes most of our knowledge of this period, and though not much evidence of footwear has been discovered in Britain, burials from a parallel period of history in France and Germany lead us to suppose there must have been similarities in our own country. We are tempted to call these people primitive, which, in comparison with our own period of development they were; but set against their own background they were amazingly developed and cultured, considering how they lacked knowledge of the rest of the world. As necessity brought about change, the shapes of the foot-covering must also have changed, and as they learned to make use of the things around them they must have found that foot-coverings could be made simpler, more comfortable, easier to put on and pull off. Thus methods of lacing became more practical as they learned how to cut the strips of leather and with them pull the hides together over the foot. As the use of lacing grew, they must have realized that other shapes were more easily pulled together, or that holes in the skins would draw together an otherwise cumbersome piece of material. Laces were used also to bind coarse cloth or skins round the legs for warmth in winter or for protection against rocks and thorns. By the time the men of the Celtic Age had achieved their high level of civilization in pre-Roman Britain, clothing had become more than the primitive body-covering it once had been.

The Celts (c. 600 B.C.) brought the Iron Age which established itself first in the south. They imposed the Celtic culture on the rest of the people as far as they could, because they considered themselves the superior race. Politically divided into warring tribes, independently ruled by chiefs, they were all more or less at the same stage of cultural development by the time the Romans made their first landings in 55 B.C.

The Celtic civilization is the most developed of the early cultures in Britain, and provides us with more evidence on which to build. Much more has been found belonging to this period, telling us what kind of footwear the Celts wore, than to any earlier one. There is also a great deal of contemporary evidence in sculpture, both in these islands and, later, in the remains of sculptured records in Rome.

The shoe was now developing as an item of clothing in its own right and was no longer merely a foot-covering. The most familiar item known to most of us through our history books is the leg-covering called *Brigis* in Ireland, and by the Romans *Brages* or *Braccae*. From this our word "breeches" is derived. It consisted of linen trousers, overlapping or including cover for the foot, cross-gartered with linen or leather strips binding the linen to the legs. There are many different versions and it is mostly from Roman records that we learn what they looked like.

Women did most of the spinning, weaving and dyeing, and a great many of the tools and implements used in these trades have been found, proving their importance. Great skill and art were used in their production and fragments of cloth that have been found show that design and colour were used not only in jewellery but in the cloths the Celts used for clothing. Trade with other countries was developing fast so it is certain that outside influences were strong, and that fashion began to develop independently of utility. Trade in metals between Phoenicia and Britain was extensive and later the Greeks also established trade and brought with them enamels, amber, and pearls.

Many of the beautiful buckles and beads found in Celtic graves and hut settlements may have been used on shoes.

On their heads the Celts wore crudely laced caps of conical shape which followed roughly the same shape of the shoe as it was drawn up round the foot. Both were made of raw cowhide and thonged. Shoes similar to this were worn in the remote parts of Ireland and Scotland until comparatively recently, and there is a pair in excellent preservation, having been rescued from the peat, in the National Museum of Ireland in Dublin. Mr. Thornton of the Northampton College of Technology also has a pair which he made up himself, using a similar method of manufacture to that which the Briton must have used.

One of the shoes in Dublin is of cowhide drawn together by a cord over the foot, following the natural shape. The other has a leather thong fastened under the heel on the inside and then over the instep, drawing the leather into a purse-like shape. Those worn in Scotland had holes in them so that the water they took in when their wearers were crossing bogs could pass through. The shoes were extremely pliable.

ANCIENT BRITON

Animal skin wrapped round body, thonged together with strips of hide. Hair left on hide in winter, de-haired in summer. Spiked club carried as weapon; animal teeth as decoration. Hair and beard long.

1. Shoes and sandals of raw-hide, laced ghillie-fashion over the foot with strips of raw-hide lacings. With wide open toes, primitively wrapped round the foot, and laced up the back.

2. A similar shoe wrapped round the foot with the fur on the inside or outside according to season.

3. The ghillie style of lacing, the most practical method of fastening, and sometimes tied several times around the ankle. Lacing sometimes up each side. Toe-shape, when the toe is covered, is natural but crude.

4. Shoes, fur in or out, often laced with raw-hide thongs over bulky linen breeches. These breeches, called "braccae," are early forms of trousers.

5. The basic shape of most shoes at this period follows that of the foot; cut from a square of hide and roughly wrapped round the foot.

6. Flint tools, widely used in dressing the hides, were the only implements available.

7. Cowhide shoe pulled up into pleated vamp by the thongs which tie round the ankle. See Mr. Thornton's example at Northampton.

6. PRE-ROMAN (1)

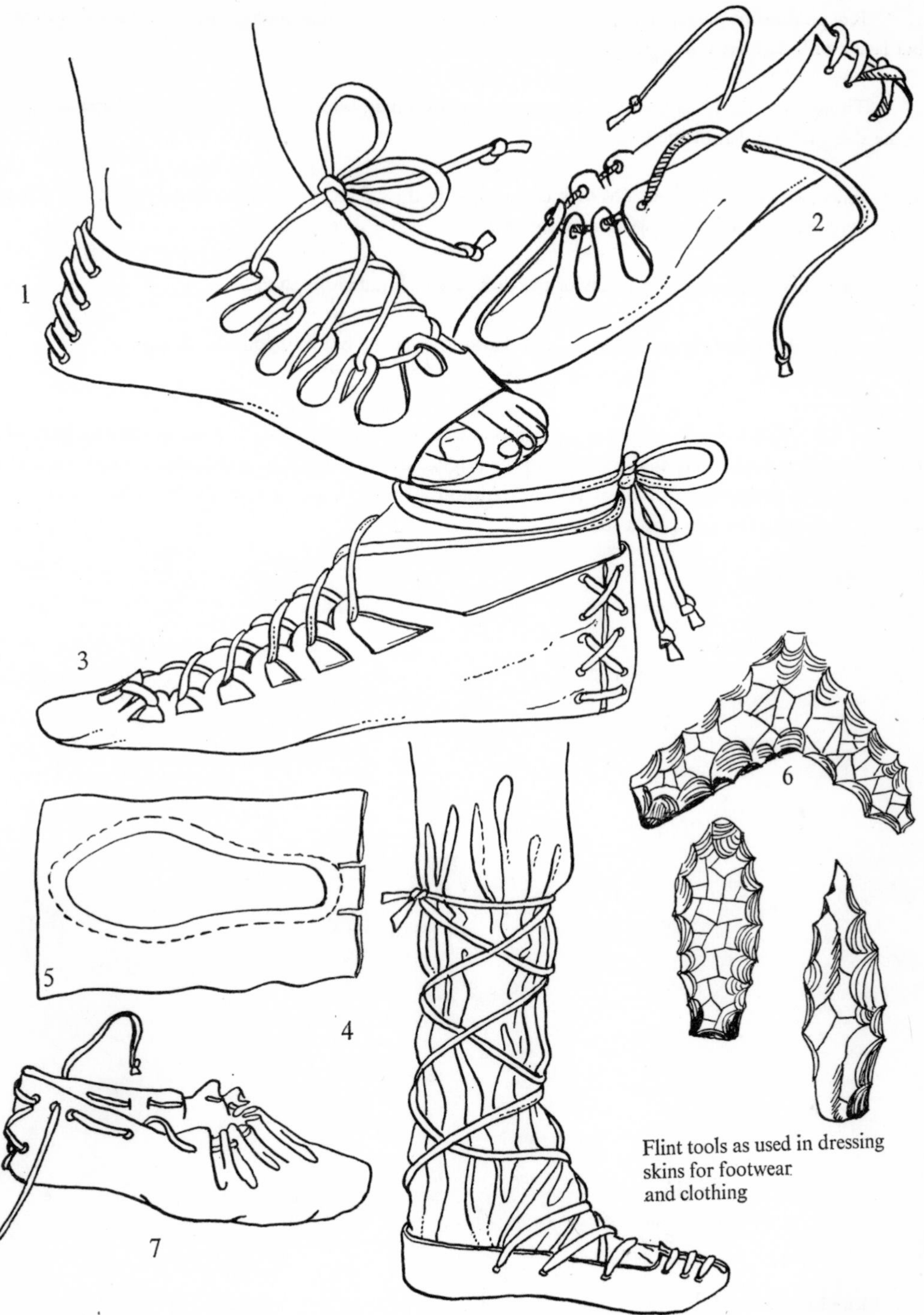

Flint tools as used in dressing skins for footwear and clothing

1. Rough fur shoe pulled up round the foot and laced with raw-hide thongs. Shoes not stitched together, but laced with de-haired thongs.

2. Thonging is the usual method of fastening, even on hats, which follow the natural shape of the head as the shoes follow that of the feet.

3. Linen, often used as a form of sock covering only the ankles. Soft leather boots folded into a draped shape over the foot and held together by thongs.

4. Linen braccae, worn over or under the thongs which fasten the shoes.

5. Ghillie shoes, cut flat and pulled round the foot, over the braccae, with the thongs.

Shoes of this type are closely related to the pampooties still worn on the Isle of Aran in Galway Bay, which can be bought today. There is an example of the original in the Northampton Museum, which must be the earliest shoe in preservation in Great Britain. Almost all were made of raw-hide on a moccasin type of construction, with front and back seams.

7. PRE-ROMAN (II)

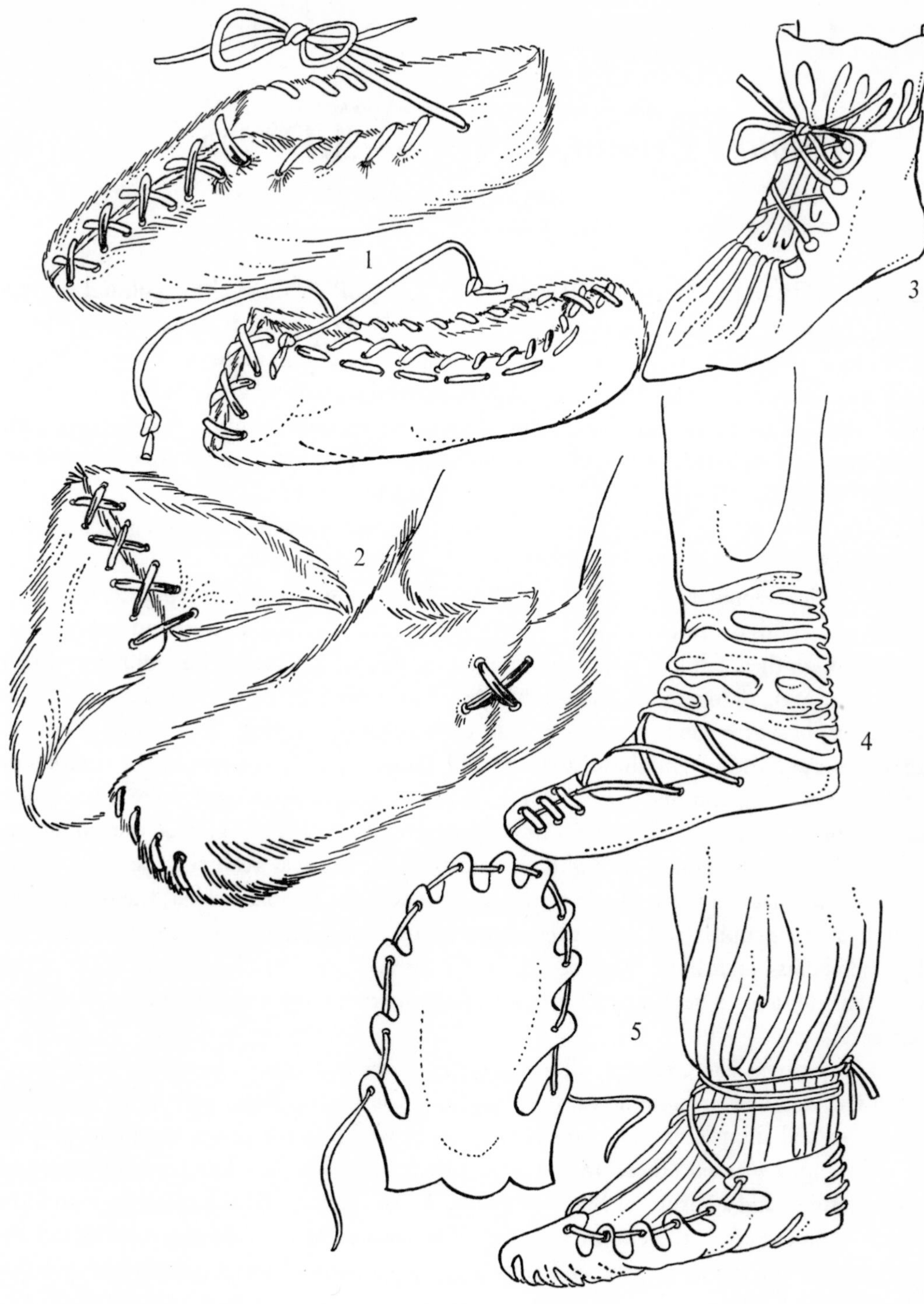
1
2
3
4
5

4

Roman Britain, 55 B.C.—A.D. 700

CAESAR'S TWO INVASIONS of Britain, in 55 and 54 B.C., made little cultural impact on this country. It was not until the conquest in A.D. 43 that the Romans brought their civilization with them and became the first major outside influence on Britain. Rome itself had derived much of its culture and fashion from conquered Greece and some of this was passed on to the Britons during the Roman occupation between A.D. 43 and 410. It is necessary, therefore, to divide Roman footwear into two classes, that which they brought with them to Britain, which remained as a received fashion, and that which the Romans themselves had taken from other countries and by which they themselves were influenced.

In a developing civilization the Britons were ready for the acceptance of shoes, which were both ornamental and functional. A great many have been found as evidence, and although these fall into many different types, there is a common denominator which links most of them together. They are very well preserved since most of them were made in leather, black for the lower and peasant classes and coloured for the wealthier classes, the officers of the army and the aristocrats. The Roman soldier had two sets of equipment one for marching, and one for parading. When he fought it was generally in bare feet, sacrificing protection for mobility. After the settling down which followed the Conquest, and in spite of the numerous fights on the borders, life was relatively peaceful. It is logical then, that it was the parade clothes and shoes of the Roman soldier, the first settler, that the Britons copied, and not the aggressive campaigning styles. The army was followed by merchants, craftsmen, and others, who formed part of the normal pattern of civilized life, and these brought domestic fashions to an otherwise previously military scene.

Many towns had a theatre, all had temples, baths and inns. The larger, more prosperous towns had an amphitheatre or stadium for chariot races and fights featuring gladiators and animals. Private houses were set in well-planned streets in parallel pattern at right angles to each other. In the large towns there was an administrative centre or stone Basilica, and a Forum or Market Square. So the Roman-British town came to look like its counterpart at the empire's centre. The owners of the land ran their estates by slave-labour for the most part, and thus there were marked social distinctions and the clothes worn indicated social standing. Tanners, cobblers and tailors provided leather goods, which were now common, and clothing, which had a similar style to that worn in the Mediterranean countries, with concessions to this climate.

There are many examples of Roman footwear to be seen in museums all over the country, and it is becoming almost commonplace for leather shoes to be found in a good state of preservation whenever a Roman site is excavated. It is, in general, the black leather shoes of the lower classes which are preserved, as much of the rich brocades, furs and other materials, worn by high officials, did not last. The brooches, clasps and buckles which fastened them did, however, and these we can also find in profusion in the local museums which contain the treasure found on a Roman-British settlement or villa.

Much of Roman footwear derives from Greek, and there is little difference between many of the sandal shapes originating in both countries. The *Cothurnus*, the first evidence of a platform or heel, comes exclusively from the Greek drama and, although its influences developed into other shapes this is where its importance lies. Consisting of a sandal with a thong between the toes, it had many styles of interlaced straps, and could be of any height above or below the ankle. It was the platform which set it apart. This was anything up to six inches in height, and was used to raise its wearer above other people surrounding him. In the drama, the main characters, or those representing gods, wore this elevating shoe so that there was no doubt that, in height at least, they were superior to mere mortals. The very opened-up sandal was also Greek in origin, consisting either of slots cut into leather and expanded into large openings or with criss-crossing straps; it exists in our modern age in a shape very little different from its Graeco-Roman originals.

It was the commanding officers of the Roman army who set fashions. For them, at home as well as in Britain, there were laws governing the types of shoes which might be worn by certain ranks; colour also was governed by rank, even among civilians. Purples and reds were reserved only for Emperors, and the coloured bands round a man's toga denoted his position in life. These colours were extended also to the shoes he wore.

All shoe types had names, and whilst there was much deviation from the basic shape, probably much more than in our own day, these names serve to differentiate one from another. The *Crepida*, for instance, was a flat sandal, generally with a filled-in back and a thong between the toes. It was composed of slit and expanded leather rather than cross straps, and had a leather flap, often decorated, called a lingula, covering its lacings or method of fastening.

The *Soccus* was a two-piece sandal composed of a flat sole with two side straps meeting between the first and second toes, and a white linen sock with divided toes to accommodate the toe-post in the sandal. This was worn by both men and women and from it comes our word "sock". (The same style can be found in modern Japan, the sock being called a "tabi" and the sandal a "geta.")

The *Caliga* was a widely open-toed shoe on a flat sole, made of canvas or leather which laced up the front and covered the ankle. It was generally worn by foot-soldiers and it varied in design according to rank. Its heavy sole was hobnailed with bronze or iron nails, which were the only item of equipment the soldier had to provide for himself, though some generous Emperors distributed them freely. The *Caliga* of the senior officer was not nailed and was reinforced with an extra strap to differentiate it from the rest. The Emperor Caligula (A.D. 37–41) was nicknamed Caliga not only as a play on words but because as a small boy in his father's camp he wore a pair of hobnailed shoes made especially for him.

Two sandals, made either of plaited straw or strips of leather, were the *Solea*, from which we get our word sole, and the *Baxea*. The former was a flat sole with side loops through which was slotted a long fastening strap. The latter was a slip-on style with straps between the toes. Another sandal was the *Crepida* worn mostly by the army, but also for civilian wear. It was on a flat sole and had a wide open toe. Big openings of many shapes were cut in its sides, leaving long laces to be tied over a lingula. There are too many versions of this to describe each one, but often those of high-ranking officers were decorated by the heads of small animals, or, if at home, the officer repeated the small head in ivory or precious metal to show he had been on campaign.

Women's shoes were very much the same as those of the men but they were lighter and more freedom was given them with choice of colour and material. They fastened their shoes with the same jewelled fibulas with which they fastened their clothes. Shoes were so valuable to the Roman that they were considered to be works of art and important enough to have the famous artists of the day employed in their creation. Poems were written about them, and lovers cherished them as dearly as a lock of the beloved's hair.

The root of the generic name for sandles or shoes, "calcei," survives in our language and in languages based on Latin, even today. Discalced friars are those going barefooted or wearing sandals, not shoes; *calzatura* is modern Italian, meaning boots or shoes; and *calzado* is modern Spanish for footwear.

Slaves went barefoot to ensure that they would not get far over rough country, and criminals wore heavy wooden shoes so that escape was difficult. Priests and philosophers, who considered themselves above fashion, children, and all the lower classes wore straw sandals resembling those of the Egyptians. Intellectuals also wore this kind of simple footwear, which was intended to indicate their humility.

Lin Yutang, in *The Importance of Living*, suggests that clothes and shoes indicate softness and that the necessity for them must have been first suggested by women. Certainly Greek women wore shoes that looked more like shoes than any worn in Rome or Britain at the time. They were often of soft kid and were highly decorated and embroidered with gold thread or jewels. They also had an early form of "mule," called a *Sandallion*, which had a high-cut front and no back, and their sandal straps were made of ribbons. They wore the *Pedilla*, which was a light sandal with a loop for the big toe and laced round the ankle. There was also an open boot taken from the Persians, called a *Persaiki*, which was made of soft material and had an ornamental brooch in its centre joining the two parts.

In Greece all classes went barefoot indoors but outdoors, except in the summer, they wore shoes and boots, whilst peasants wore a primitive sandal. For those who set fashions, sandals were gilded and their straps decorated. For riding they wore high boots laced below the knee and made of soft leather. The aristocracy wore pure white for clothes and shoes and the peasants wore greys and browns. Felt was used extensively in all classes.

Careless dressing was deplored by Greeks and Romans alike, and to tie the straps of sandals badly was considered very bad taste. It was also bad taste to show fear or pain, so that Spartan youths imitated the army in wearing red boots which were so coloured to conceal blood flowing from leg wounds.

Although sandal soles, made of leather or cork, were more often than not straights and not lefts or rights, a size stick was used to measure the size of the foot which was to wear them. A historian of the fifth century remarked that people, for vanity's sake, often wore shoes too small. Sandal soles were sometimes used as places of concealment for notes, which were inserted in specially made slots. Craftsmanship was of very high standard, as this would indicate, and cobblers had become very prosperous tradesmen. So much so, that Domitian, A.D. 31–96, ordered the removal of the cobblers' shops from the streets as too many of them were hanging their wares outside their shops..a Roman Oxford Street!

Tools were very much as ours are today, though in less refined form, and a certain Daedalus is reputed to have been the inventor of the awl that is still used in shoemaking.

The Greeks

The Greeks exercised a strange influence over the Romans, their conquerors, as they have done over many other men since. Romans sent their sons to the Greek university at Athens, copied the fashions of the Greeks, used their art and acknowledged the Greeks as their superiors in learning and philosophy and in the arts. They were willing to learn from the Greeks, recognizing that there were many things in which this country they had conquered could instruct them. So much that is Greek is now part of our own modern thinking that we cannot afford to ignore the influences they had, indirectly via the Romans, and later by their learning, on our own country.

Xenophon, writing on household management, comments on the symmetry of his countrymen's lives and the elegance of everything they did. "It is beautiful to see the footwear ranged in a row . . . garments sorted according to their use . . . cooking pots arranged with sense and symmetry." The footwear they made so exquisitely, whose designs are still evident in the sandals the ordinary person wears today, are not too trivial to be mentioned.

Only landowners could be aristocrats, but in later years some of the wealthy were admitted to this class. They were the descendants of those who had established estates when the earlier wars were over, so they were used to an outside country life and versed in the skills of the countryside. This is why we find such exquisite craftsmanship in everything they owned. We find scenes depicting these crafts on the terracotta vases and bowls with which we are familiar from museums and illustrations. To the Greek, art was of high importance and no scene of life too small to be immortalized by it. It is for this reason that we find poems about clothes and shoes, and that even their household utensils were beautiful. Their vases are famous the world over for their balance and perfection, and from them much knowledge of what the Greeks wore is to be gained. Men, women, animals and monsters were the subjects of carefully-planned designs which were masterpieces of composition. Figurines of amazing delicacy have been found in clay or bronze, surviving the centuries and telling us much of how their drapery was arranged and decorated. Even the more than life-sized statuary, which formed many of the columns supporting the architraves of their temples, provide perfect replicas of the classical clothes of their day.

In the Ashmolean Museum, Oxford, there is a black painted vase showing a shoemaker measuring his customer's foot for a pair of sandals. The foot is placed on the leather and the shoemaker is cutting round it with a knife very similar to our modern clicking knife.

ROMAN

Military

Leather or metal helmet. Leather jacket banded with bronze or iron and fastened at the front, supported at the shoulders by metal straps. Woollen tunic.

Senator

Woollen toga, usually white.

1. Many fastenings for clothes and shoes are in the elementary form of the fibula. They have an open shape, more often than not circular, through which the material is pushed and secured with a bar, and are made of metal, either plain or jewelled, or of bone or tortoishell. This is the shoe as worn by women, but there are other versions for men.

2. The strapped caliga of the foot soldier with a strap, either between the toes or over them, and buckled up the leg. The sole was sometimes spiked for campaigning and the quality of the spikes indicated the wearer's rank.

3. Leather sandal with raw-hide thongs. Joint of thong between the toes covered by a metal or leather decoration, often heart-shaped. Deep, built or covered platform, an adaptation from Greek footwear.

4. An army officer's boot in tooled leather with thonged fastenings through decorative studs. Soft leather tongue ruched under lacing. The top often decorated according to the personal choice of the wearer with the paws and head of a small animal. This head often modelled in precious metal, ivory and jewels for wearing at home.

5. A ghillie shoe copied from the countries the Romans conquered. Made in leather but often gilded.

6. A soccus (from which we get our word sock) or udone, made in soft leather or wool; over it was worn a padded leather sandal. Note the divided toes of the sock. This type of shoe is still found in the East, especially in the Japanese white cotton tabi, which is worn with a wooden geta (high platformed sandal). In place of a knot there is often a jewel or a metal decoration.

8. ROMAN (I)

Fibula
1
2
3
4
5
6
Soccus

1. Crepida made of leather, unstitched except for attaching to the sole. The heart-shaped tongue, one of many shapes, attached by slotting the tied thongs through just under the knot. This type of sandal always had a wide open toe. This is a simple form, there were many with extremely ornamental openings. An early example of fenestration—decoration via openings.

2. A Buskin with Greek origins. Covering the back of the foot and leg, intricately latticed up the front, the thongs slotting through loops in the back of the binding. Made of soft leather, often found in heavily-ornamented versions.

3. A Greek Cothurnus, adapted from the drama, for ordinary wear in Greece and Rome among the patricians. In its original form, the depth of the cork platform indicated the importance of the character played.

4. An officer's campagus (campaign boot) from the Roman army. Heavily tooled and gilded according to his rank, its laces anchor a long leather tongue to protect the front of his foot. Real animal head, or one carved in ivory.

5. The ordinary soldier's Caliga, made of leather gartering buckled round his foot and leg. Buckles often hidden on the inside. There are many forms that this gartering can take.

Greek and Roman footwear is often indistinguishable since the conquering Romans had adapted a great many of Greece's fashions and customs. Origins can often be traced, however, by remembering that the peaceful articles came from Greece, like the Cothurnus of the drama, while the military ones came from Rome.

The Lunula (tongue) was found in many kinds of footwear, mostly among the military, but on domestic sandals also; women also wore it. It was of different shapes and often decorated.

9. ROMAN (II)

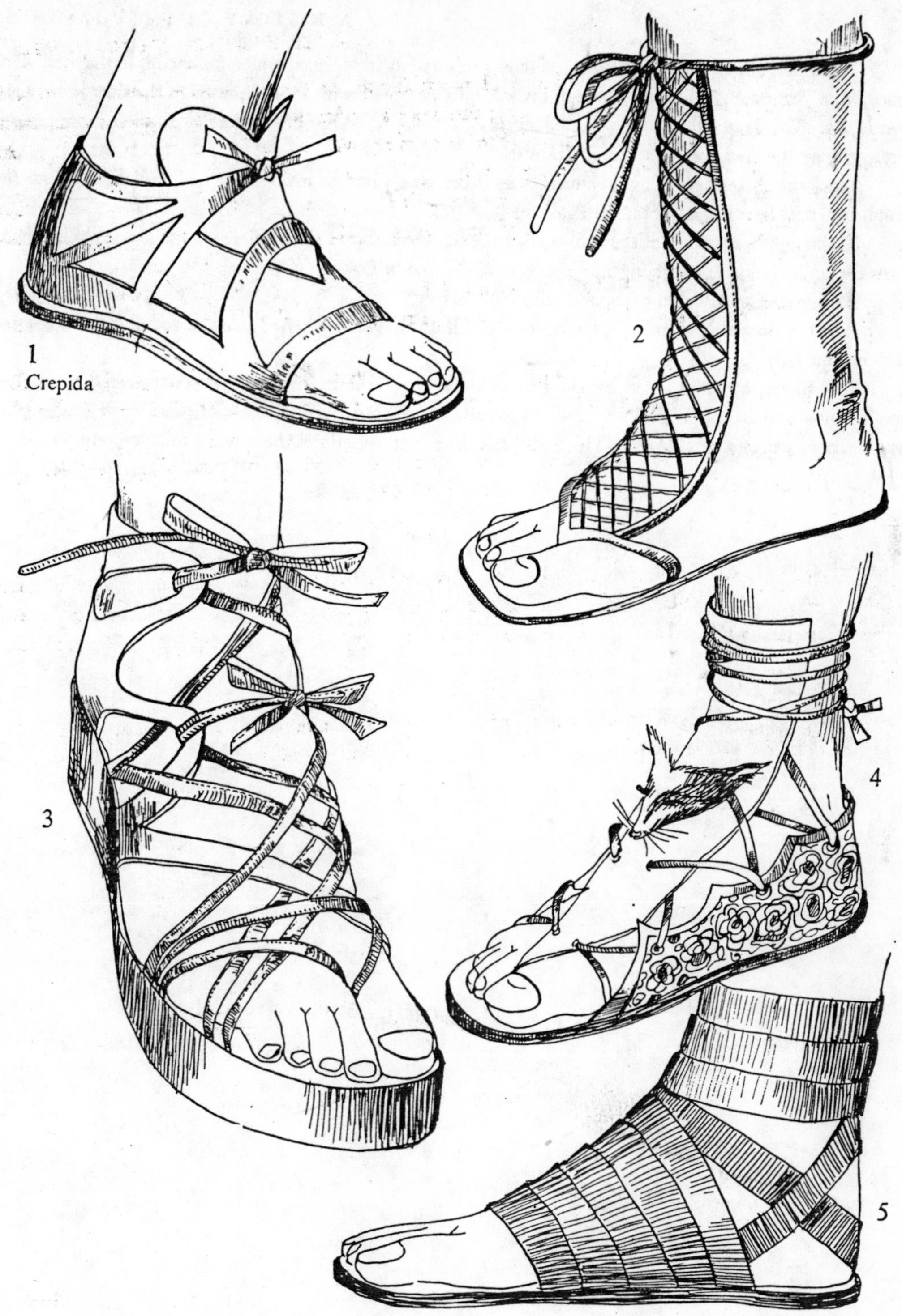
1
Crepida
2
3
4
5

1. The Solea, a basic sandal consisting of only a sole and its strappings, which fastened it to the foot. Our word "sole" has its origins here. Made of thick leather or straw, with loops inserted at the sides in between two layers. The strap either of flat plaited straw or raw-hide. Many hot countries, in their more peasant areas, still use this form of sandal made from straw.

2. Thick black leather, heavily punched in decorative patterns makes this country shoe. Note the simplicity of its fastenings. Found at Saalburg (A.D. 34).

3. This is another version of the leather shoe above, which shows close affinity to the crude ghillies made from fur or cattle-hide in Britain. 2nd century. Exhumed in London (Guildhall Museum).

4. An ornamented Buskin decorated with embroidery.

5. Another Buskin as worn by soldiers. Made of leather, it has a stitched sole and rolled collar decorated with ermine tails.

6. The Baxea, a sandal worn by children and the lower classes, or those who considered themselves humble intellectuals such as philosophers and priests. Made from woven straw of palm or vegetable fibre with a straw base of several layers. This is its basic shape but sometimes there was a toe-covering.

10. ROMAN (III)

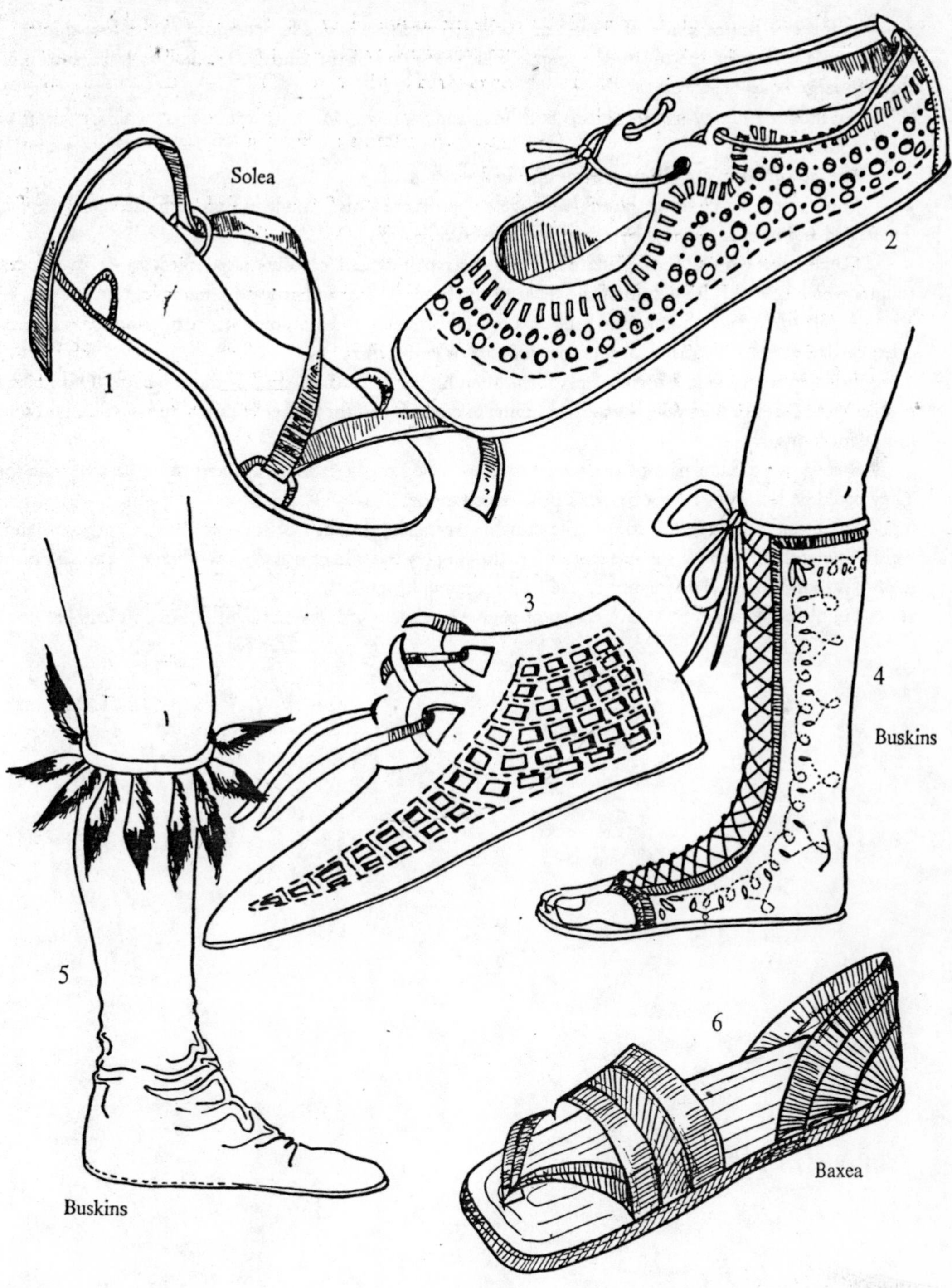
Solea
1
2
3
4
Buskins
5
Buskins
6
Baxea

1. A form of puttee made of canvas or leather strapping was the leg-covering of the foot-soldier. In this example it covered the top of the lingula which was part of the sandal. The leather lacing was pulled through large holes or eyelets.

2. An indoor mule was common to both men and women. Made of soft leather, wool or felt, it was built on to a flat sole.

3. Simple sandals were also worn by men and women alike.

4. Some soft shoes covered the ankle yet were open at the waist. Made in two parts the vamp was often fenestrated and held to the top by a jewelled brooch or button.

5. Sandals were often formed of complicated strappings and cut-outs laced through or over a high tongue which covered the whole of the front of the foot. These sandals were often coloured.

6. A soft fold-over tab concealed the method of fastening and strapping of many sandals. These tabs often carried personal forms of decoration, jewelry or embroidery.

7. Built-up soles made a form of platform often higher at the heel than in the forepart. This building of soles was a form of heel which was to continue in many forms for many centuries, and is still found today in peasant footwear.

8. Puttees were often part of the sandal itself, attached to the front straps and those between the toes. They could be laced up the back over a protective tongue.

9. Some soldiers wore the straps criss-crossed over a simple form of toe-less shoe. Campaign sandals were made with or without spikes according to the country the soldier was in, and whether he was a cavalryman or a foot-soldier. The quality of the nails indicated his rank.

10. Simple boots worn by many classes of people in various colours, made of felt or soft leather.

11. ROMAN (IV)

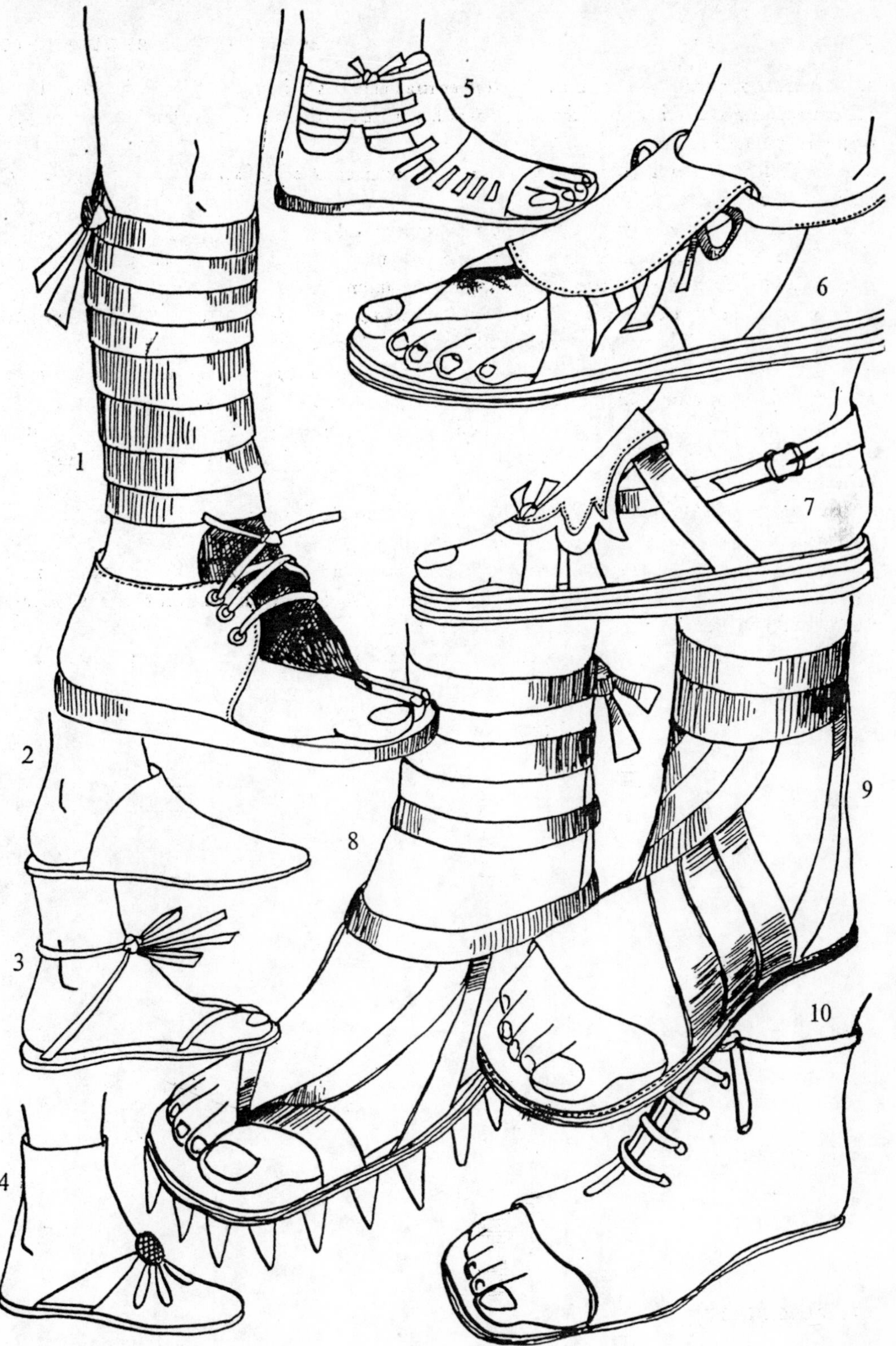
1
2
3
4
5
6
7
8
9
10

5

Post-Roman Britain, A.D. 700—A.D. 1066

THIS PERIOD marks a change in both Britain's history and its clothes; the Roman rule ended and the Anglo-Saxon period began. Although many of the old customs, the manner of dressing and much of the way of life remained, the Saxon invaders brought with them a new civilization which was to be the foundation on which the England we know now was to be built. They discarded the Roman way of life as unsuitable to an agricultural country, and destroyed the established Christianity, but were themselves converted in the sixth century. It is from many of the books of gospels they translated and illuminated that we draw our knowledge of what they wore. There is some physical evidence in the shoes which have been discovered in settlements in various parts of the country, but a close study of manuscripts will reveal much that fills in the gaps.

They were farmers and warriors but they were also craftsmen, and although their standards of development were not up to those of the Romans there is much to be admired in their work. Manufacture was domestic, but spinners, weavers, carpenters, smiths and shoemakers were to be found universally. Trade had diminished and was not to improve until the arrival of the Danes, who established interchange of commerce with Ireland, Scandinavia, Germany and France.

There was marked class distinction, which is revealed in the finds discovered in the burial grounds of the Saxon period. Ordinary people used poorly-made pottery in contrast to that used by the wealthy warriors and the upper classes. The warrior classes used ornament on everything, embellished their utensils and implements with precious stones, and richly decorated all they used. The peasant classes had rough bowls, coarsely woven cloth, brooches and other ornaments of bone and bronze. Much of this remains, and a great deal is to be learned from it. They extolled their crafts and their artists in song, which reflected their passions for jewellery and design and for the beautiful metals. They believed that their smiths and craftsmen were descended from gods, so it is no wonder that everything they used reflected their high artistic ability. That they were carefully studied crafts is shown very clearly in their graceful designs, whether on sword hilts or in gospel manuscripts.

The monasteries turned out much of this marvellous work, as they employed the craftsmen who worked in enamelling, chasing and silver plating, though craftsmen of all kinds were to be found in every village community. The women were as artistically developed as the men and theirs was the responsibility for making the clothing and embroidering in coloured threads. They cared for the home and its domesticities, and they also herded the cattle, tended the sheep whose wool they spun into thread, dyed and wove into heavy cloth. They even tanned the hides into leather for the craftsmen to make into shoes.

Clothing was simple. For a warrior nation it had to be, and it also had to be serviceable. When the Saxons settled to their later peaceful life, these two factors remained important. For outdoors working men wore skin and leather garments and for indoors a woolen shirt or tunic which was of mid-thigh length over long woollen trousers and thick stockings. These trousers were cut fairly full and were cross-gartered, as had been those of their predecessors. At other times they wore fur or leather tunics, often decorated if the warrior was wealthy, and flung over them heavy cloaks fastened by very ornamental buckles. Many of these buckles have been discovered and reveal the high quality of their skill. Fur played a great part in their dressing, but it was much more tailored and well-cut than fur had been before. It was made into caps and gloves and, with the hair turned in, made into shoes. They fastened their leather belts with richly ornamented buckles, similar shapes of which were often found on their shoes.

Women wore woollen clothing, some of which was beautifully ornamented and decorated with rich embroidery using real gold and precious stones as well as many-coloured threads. Their dress was in the form of a long loose tunic which reached their feet and over it another, or a coat of knee-length with wide sleeves. The over-tunic's hem and sleeves were embroidered with a deep band of floral or animal decoration. Much of the interlaced strap designs found in manuscripts were also applied to clothing in the form of embroidery. They seem to have been very vain about their clothes, for even in battle they were lavishly dressed in bronze, gold and silver. Men and women wore bracelets and necklaces, brooches and rings. It is due to the finding of these things that we know so much about their high level of artistic achievement and culture.

Women did the weaving and often achieved intricate diamond and other designs. One assumes that since they did all the sewing they also made the shoes.

It is very difficult to be sufficiently accurate about anything of this period. There are so many conflicting ideas, any of which are possibly correct, as to how the Saxons lived and dressed. There are few English peat bogs in which garments might have been preserved, as in Germany or in Ireland, and the only pieces of cloth preserved in the heathen graves in England are fragments. It is said that they were of various qualities, varying from the texture of a modern flannel shirt to that of Harris tweed.

The best reference is the study of the Franks casket in the British Museum. Costume is portrayed on this whalebone box of Northumbrian origin; it is late, 650–750, but is the nearest we can get to a portrayal of costume in these early times. It shows us that shoes for the most part completely covered the foot and followed its natural shape. The foot appeared to be wide, accentuated by the fact that there were no heels so that all shoes were flat to the ground.

The leather used was mostly cow-hide and the shoes were made of it in both its dressed and its undressed state. Although they covered the foot, the shoes were low in shape and not yet boots; sometimes the cross-gartering started from their tops and bound the woollen trousers over them. Soles were made of leather and the Roman use of an iron last was still continued. But for ordinary people shoes often had plaited straw soles or soles made of wood. Black leather was the most universally used and, as this is preserved relatively easily most surviving shoes are made of it.

The men's tunics had hems to just above the knee, like kilts, sleeved jackets and cloaks attached to the shoulder. There were clumsy puttees wound round the legs, whilst in other cases the legs were bare or covered with loose hose. Close-fitting breeches, cross-gartered, were a feature of Anglo-Saxon men's wear. One of the best examples of clothing is the exhibit in the museum at Kiel. This is a man's body preserved in the peat which was discovered at Damendorf in Schleswig, with his clothes preserved with him; a large cloak, his shoes, and his puttees wrapped up in his trousers. Bronze workboxes were found in women's graves of the period, containing bronze needles, tweezers and knives. These graves also preserved the gay dress of the Saxon woman, into which a great deal of labour must have been put. Jewellery has been found in large quantities, and it had few if any equals elsewhere in Europe. The warrior class had gold-embroidered tunics, such as those remains found in the chieftain's tomb at Taplow. He had gold buckles and his drinking horn was also embellished with gold.

In a sense fashion changed then more than nowadays, because it varied from district to district, as is evidenced by the study of the jewellery found in the graves discovered in different parts of the country.

Workmen and poorer people went barefoot; priests wore simple sandals but bishops wore a more ornate form and ecclesiastical footwear was often decorated in liturgical colours. Noblemen wore long stockings to the knee which had ornamental tops and were cross-gartered with embroidered and gilded laces. In footwear it is generally men's footwear that are depicted, since women's feet were seldom seen under their ground-length dresses. There was a highly-developed sense of colour.

The Bishop of Seville, Isidorus, about A.D. 600, attempted to write a complete review of knowledge and productive techniques as they had now come to be understood. In this is contained a page on the art of making shoes, and this is to be seen in a tenth-century copy at the Bally Shoe Museum at Schönenwerd, Switzerland.

To a certain extent overlapping with this period came the replacement of the fallen

Roman Empire by the Byzantine Empire which was ruled by Constantine, after whom Constantinople (Istanbul) was called. This was the greatest influence on European art up to around A.D. 1100 and it cannot, therefore, be ignored since it must have exercised a corresponding influence on clothes and shoes. Clothes were long and straight, as it was considered sinful to reveal any of the human figure beneath them. Shoes of this influence were less broad than those of the Anglo-Saxons, since a slight point was developing and this tended to minimize the width.

Embroidery, coloured inlays under intricately cut-out vamps, jewels and appliquéd patterns made shoemaking a very highly skilled craft indeed, and many versions of the soft flat shoes that illustrate this are to be found in stained-glass windows and brass rubbings. Ankle boots with rolled collars, made of wool or leather, were the general masculine attire of those who were not of the church. Although the basic shape was plain it varied widely as regards both colour and applied decoration. Cut-outs showing coloured stockings underneath, coloured lacings, buckles and brooches were all found on the shoes of this period. The turned-back collar is the most typical fashion familiar to most people, but even this varied from the plain self collar of the lower classes to the gold-thread-embroidered version of the rich. Edges were gimped and slashed, the collar lined to show contrast, and stitching and jewellery distinguished the plainest version from that of those who could afford to show their rank. Toes were extending slightly but as yet were not stuffed or padded.

Shoes with wooden soles were worn by higher ranks also, such as those worn by Bernard, King of Italy and the grandson of Charlemagne. When his sepulchre was opened, many years after his death, his shoes were still intact, with wooden soles and red leather uppers laced with thongs all preserved. They were straights, rights and lefts not yet being used.

It was not only the ecclesiastics whose shoes reflected the rich decoration of the age; nuns also dressed as though they were fine ladies. Indeed, the fine lady who became a nun carried her bright-coloured clothes into the convent and wore a violet underdress and a scarlet tunic with wide sleeves and hood, both faced with silk. Her shoes were of ornamental red leather and she wore necklaces, gold bracelets and rings of precious jewels. The Council of A.D. 747 complained of monks who cross-gartered their legs and of nuns who wore bright clothes, which proves that the bright clothes of the Saxons were more than a passing fashion.

This was the Golden Age of the Saxons, but it was soon to be disrupted by the Viking settlements. Their small-scale invasions had been an annoyance for some time. But as soon as the Vikings decided seriously to colonize Britain their influence on these islands became evident in the decorations of the things they used and which the Britons accepted for common usage also. Much of the best Viking art is to be found in Ireland, as they occupied that country for two centuries. Here they were differentiated and known as the Finn-Gael and the Dubh-Gael (the "white strangers" who were the Norsemen and the "dark strangers" who were the Danes). In the Viking burial ship that was found at Sutton Hoo, Suffolk, there were the remains of textiles, a leather bag, small silver shoe buckles and three pairs of leather slippers.

VIKING

Metal helmet with animal horns. Woollen tunic under leather corselet scaled in metal or horn. Cross-gartered leg-covering. Animal skin or woollen mantle fastened at neck.

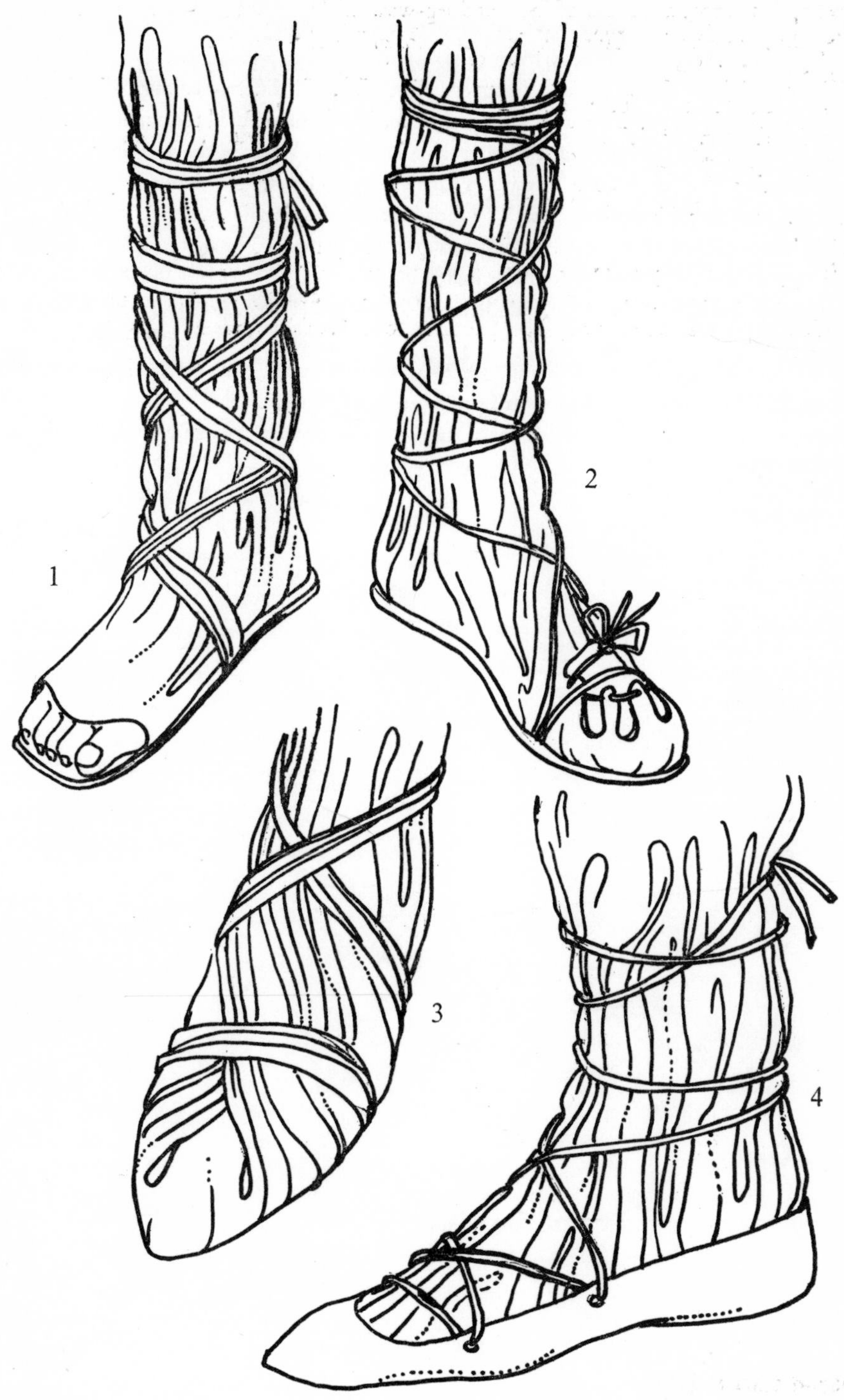
1
2
3
4

1. Simple boots in soft leather or wool worn over woollen tights. The inside slightly higher cut to protect the leg when riding was the only form of transport. A short pointed toe.

2. Soft boot with loose-fitting leg and turnover collar, often of a different colour. The foot covered by a separate shoe of simple shape, often with a short peak matching the pointed toe; made of raw-hide. The whole worn over bare legs by the lower classes, over coloured stockings by the wealthier.

3. Loose breeches of wool or linen, in colours for the upper classes, in white or beige or brown for the peasantry, worn over a simple leather shoe. The foot bare. A simple sole externally stitched.

4. A plain buttoned shoe often found in the paintings of the period, covering the ankles. Lightly rounded toe. Crude buttons and unstitched buttonholes increasing in use.

5. Shoes tied or buckled at the ankle. Made in coloured leather according to rank. The toe still short but slightly pointed.

6. This is the most usual shoe shape for the period, typical of many, plain or decorated according to the wearer's position. Worn over coloured stockings and with a light sole.

7. Another common shoe shape of the early Anglo-Saxon period. In one colour, or with a contrast colour for the collar.

13. POST-ROMAN (II)

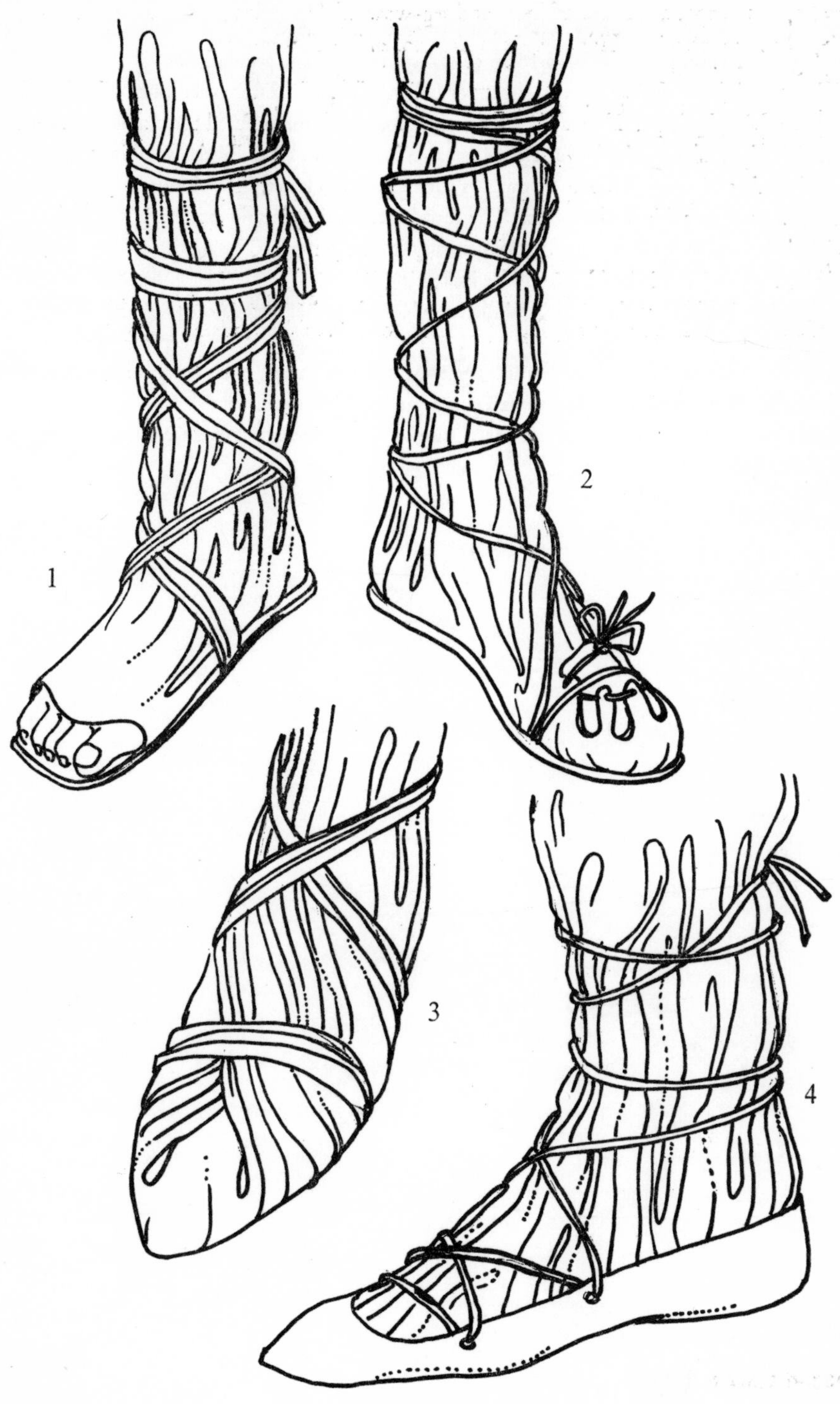
1
2
3
4

1. Simple boots in soft leather or wool worn over woollen tights. The inside slightly higher cut to protect the leg when riding was the only form of transport. A short pointed toe.

2. Soft boot with loose-fitting leg and turnover collar, often of a different colour. The foot covered by a separate shoe of simple shape, often with a short peak matching the pointed toe; made of raw-hide. The whole worn over bare legs by the lower classes, over coloured stockings by the wealthier.

3. Loose breeches of wool or linen, in colours for the upper classes, in white or beige or brown for the peasantry, worn over a simple leather shoe. The foot bare. A simple sole externally stitched.

4. A plain buttoned shoe often found in the paintings of the period, covering the ankles. Lightly rounded toe. Crude buttons and unstitched buttonholes increasing in use.

5. Shoes tied or buckled at the ankle. Made in coloured leather according to rank. The toe still short but slightly pointed.

6. This is the most usual shoe shape for the period, typical of many, plain or decorated according to the wearer's position. Worn over coloured stockings and with a light sole.

7. Another common shoe shape of the early Anglo-Saxon period. In one colour, or with a contrast colour for the collar.

13. POST-ROMAN (II)

Considerable Danish influences are found in this period

1. The short boot grew in popularity. Covering the ankle its length was growing. In leather, laced at the ankle, the collar often turned back to show another colour.

2. Buttons, a growing type of fastening. This boot fastened to a contrast stocking.

3. This shoe, with both types of fastening. Tied by a thong through loops, an extension of the ghillie style. A T-bar buttoned to the vamp. In raw-hide leather.

4. Contrast collars with matching buttons on a coloured shoe. The toes gradually growing longer.

5. Toes varied in length as can be seen in this sketch and in Nos. 4, 7, 8 and 9. Differently-shaped collars, some shoes showing fenestration in the upper. This kind of opening occurs over several centuries, but the actual word was not used until the Norman invasion.

6. Stockings themselves grew longer in the foot and padded; sometimes had a sole cut to the same shape, laced to the stockings by the cross-gartering method. Cross-gartering itself, however, is growing less.

7–8. These show that the variations in collars were legion and opportunity for the wearer's self-expression was enormous. Some were stitched in colour or metal thread, others were quilted and jewelled, edges were crenellated and pointed.

9. Some shoes bound round the top so that the binding formed long laces. These laces tied in the decreasing cross-gartered style.

10. Collars on slip-on styles as well as laced shoes. Some toes long but lightly rounded.

14. POST-ROMAN (III)

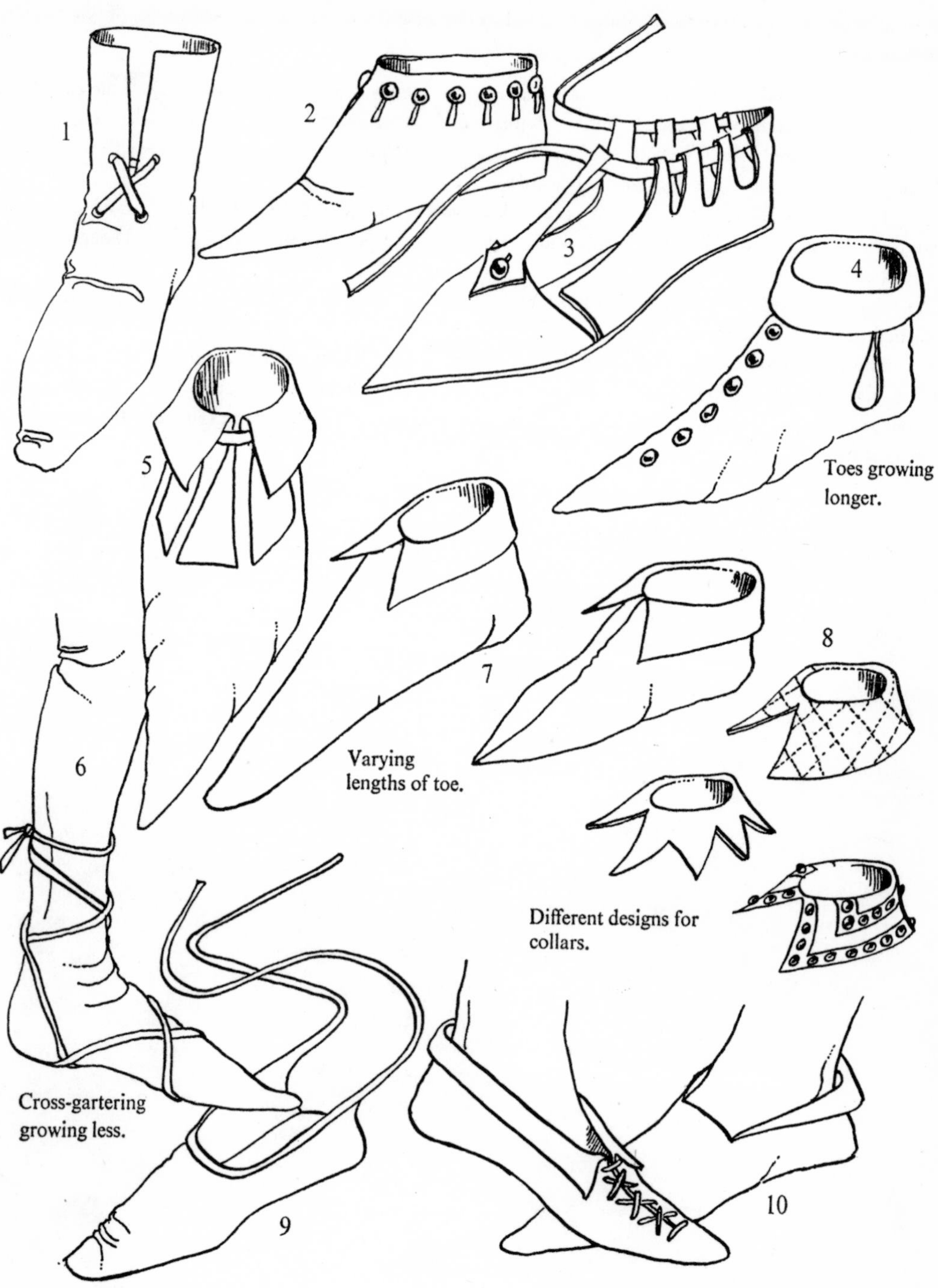
1
2
3
4
Toes growing longer.
5
7
8
Varying lengths of toe.
6
Different designs for collars.
Cross-gartering growing less.
9
10

Cross-gartering took a more sophisticated turn in this period and we find various forms of it, of which these are only a few.

1. The simple raw-hide or linen cross-gartering over loosely gathered linen breeches. Still continued but the cut-outs on the shoes became more ornamental. The whole, however, was still rather shapeless.

2. Acquiring more shape because of closer fit, this kind of "puttee" wrapping was shaped to the leg and the foot, but still bound over loose-fitting trousers.

3. Trousers became closer-fitting except at the knee where they were bound closely with thongs wrapped round the leg and attached to the leather shoe. Black still the popular and useful colour, though natural undyed colours common.

4. Bandage forms of binding wide tapes around the leg made it more shapely; sometimes they were attached to the shoe, sometimes free.

5. The development from cross-gartering to thonging over hooks to fasten leggings was not long in taking place. These leggings, plain or ornamental, covered the gap between shoe and knee effectively. In the upper classes decorated with jewels and embroidery. The ends of the thongs tucked under the ornamental garters at top and ankle.

15. POST-ROMAN (IV)

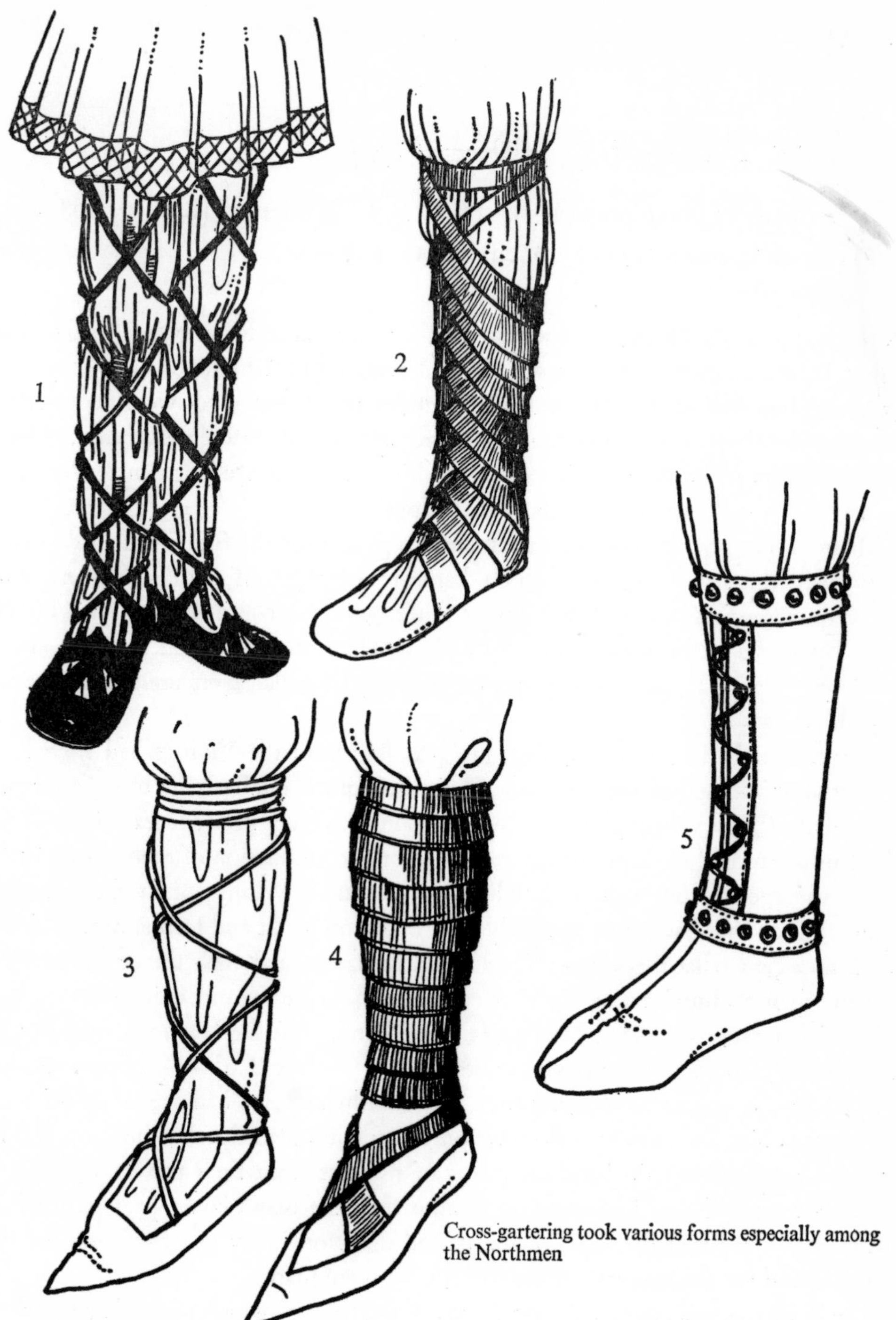

Cross-gartering took various forms especially among the Northmen

6

The Normans, 1066—1154

William I (The Conqueror), 1066–1087 William II (Rufus), 1087–1100
Henry I, 1100–1135 Stephen, 1135–1154

FOR the period of the Norman Conquest and the years that followed when Britain was a Norman kingdom, there is much more physical evidence of the kind of shoes they wore. There is a great deal of pictorial and documentary proof that shoes were beginning to look more like shoes, were more functional and were worn almost universally. One of the main sources is the Bayeux Tapestry, to which Master Wace's *Roman de Rou* serves as an accompanying text and describes what happened.

Many of our laws and customs date from this period and the first French (or Norman as they were then) influences on fashion came into being. After the Conquest, when trade was resumed again, there was much traffic with the continent and with the rich eastern countries, which made commerce with travelling merchants much easier. Homespuns were replaced by richer and finer fabrics, many of which were used in the shoes of the wealthy.

The Saxons had been a slow-thinking people whom the Vikings had stirred into more active thinking, but the Normans, with their quick intelligence, brought about a reassessment of values throughout the whole country. They brought learning and new craftsmanships to add to those already extant and the combination of them all seemed to produce the greatest outburst of building and artistic development in the history of Britain. The Saxons had given relatively little attention to art and to literature and were content to accept what there was. They were not concerned with the development of their Church or of church art. They were content to be left alone and, as long as they were, showed little interest in what other people were doing. But the Normans were not like this and it was partly because of this contrast that they won the Battle of Hastings. William the Conqueror is one of the greatest men in world history; he had the art of attracting other men to him and was able to draw on their abilities to develop his empire. The Norman Crusaders brought back the riches of the east from their travels, opening the way to wider and bigger influences on fashion than the island could provide for itself. Thus we now find that the shoes of the period draw on many other cultures for their decoration and for the materials from which they were made.

The Normans had adopted the feudalism of the French, which made class distinction in clothes even more evident. Their Norse origins made them pirates at heart, which brought the treasures of their conquests to the use of all they conquered. They quickly learned the art of advanced building, so that the most wonderful cathedrals in Europe are mostly of Norman origin. All this knowledge they passed on to Britain and made it a truly civilized country.

Norman architecture and clothes go together, as they do in most other periods, and if we look first at the square towers and steeples of Norman churches we shall see their parallel in the short conical head-dress worn by the knights and soldiers of the period. Legs were covered with thick stockings, made of wool or linen. These were bound and cross-gartered, as were the trousers with feet, called *Chausses*. The garters were leather thongs which, among the knights, were often decorated. This was a fashion which had had a long life and which continued until knitting was invented, with which to make closer-fitting stockings. Toe shapes had not yet fully developed into points, except that formed by the natural shape of the foot and, like the Norman character, were rather blunt. They were, however, of more elegant shape than those worn by the Saxons.

Boots were now no longer low but were cut above the ankle. The collar was banded with coloured strips or turned over to show contrasting colour, but this was now well above the ankle and sometimes almost to mid-calf. These were worn later with tighter-fitting hose, often of another colour. The variants on this theme were enormous and many are to be found in contemporary illustrations and brasses.

During this period the Moors of Spain supplied Europe with beautiful soft leathers, made particularly in red, called Cordoba leather. It was called so not especially because it came from Cordoba but because the Caliph and the grand lords of his court, which was at Cordoba, wore shoes made of it. Cordoba was the capital of Moorish Spain. From this word derives many of the terms used in shoemaking, because England also used the name from the leather supplied to them and called it *Cordewan*. From this word the shoemaker was called a *Cordwainer*, a term used even in today's English. In France the same word was corrupted to *Cordonnier*. There, the tanners found they could make leather in the Moorish manner and just as beautiful, so that they became cordonniers and, in turn, this word came to mean shoemaker also.

Occasionally we find evidence of shoes made for the left and the right foot but, in general, they were still *Straights* and only wear changed the shape into a pair. Evidence of the short point growing longer is found in the Cotton MS., for it began to come into general use about the time of William Rufus. The clergy were forbidden to wear them but little notice can have been taken of this ban as points continued to grow. Some toes were stuffed with hair or wool or even moss, and twisted into a ram's-horn shape. Whilst still not yet very long, the stuffed point now began to be made into various shapes, some quite grotesque, others fanciful like the *Pigace* toe. There are examples of these fashions in museums, as several shoes have been preserved. In the London Museum there is a particularly good one, of somewhat later period, which was found in and preserved by the Thames mud. William of Malmesbury, the chronicler, says the toe of these turned downwards when used for riding to keep the foot from slipping out of the stirrup. Planché, in his *History of British Costume* (1874), says peaked-toed shoes were called "Ocrea rostrata" (beaked greaves) and the clergy could not wear them, though other fashionable clothes were allowed.

There is a complete change in colour for shoes of this period, in contrast to the previous one, in that they are rarely made in black. Henry II wore green shoes banded with gold. The half-boots of Richard I were striped with gold, and ornamented shoes in general became worn by the nobility. A pattern of circles is mentioned as decoration for shoes in the time of John and the Bayeux Tapestry shows that many other colours were commonplace: red, blue, green, and purple. Though some writers say that yellow was worn only by Jews this is not definitely proved.

It is incidental, but interesting, to note that Duke William of Normandy was the bastard grandson of a tanner of Falaise. Robert the Devil's mistress was Herleva, daughter of the tanner, and was later married off to the Viscount Conteville. It is also of interest to note that both William the Bastard and his half-brother Robert Count of Mortain both stayed in Bermondsey, later to be the leather centre of London.

NORMAN

Woman

Head-dress similar to Saxon. Kirtle worn under long gown banded to emphasize slit at front.

Man

Head shaved at neck. Inner and outer tunics similar to Saxon, with embroidered neck and sleeve-bands. Woollen leg-coverings (chausses), cross-gartered.

1. The still fashionable ankle-boot, by now one of the most popular styles of the period, is seen in illustrations for many years. Sometimes with fore-and-aft points and a border of colour, often embroidered or jewelled.

2 and 3. Open versions of the same ankle-boot, with a high back and low sides. 2 has close-fitting but fly-away wings and a seamed peaked front, while 3 has a buckled strap fitting above the ankle.

4. The toe, still short and pointed, sometimes showed a tendency to turn up, needing to be strongly padded to keep it firm.

5. A popular style showing an early T-bar with buckle and strap over low cut-away sides attached to a high winged back.

6. The height of the boot was not standardized and many different lengths were in favour. Some rose up to the knee and were laced and collared. Lacing was either on the inside or the outside, seldom up the back. When the lacing was on the inside many shoes appeared, on paintings, to have no fastenings.

7 and 9. Decoration was often in the form of real jewels round a collar, or in cruciform shape on the vamp.

8. A simple peasant shoe, made of plain leather with raw-hide lacings on inside or outside. Thick layered sole. Toes uncovered.

10. Loose-fitting ankle-straps with buttons fasten all types of shoes. Made from various materials, plain or embroidered according to rank.

Legs were covered in coloured hose to match or contrast with shoes, or were left bare.

16. NORMAN (I)

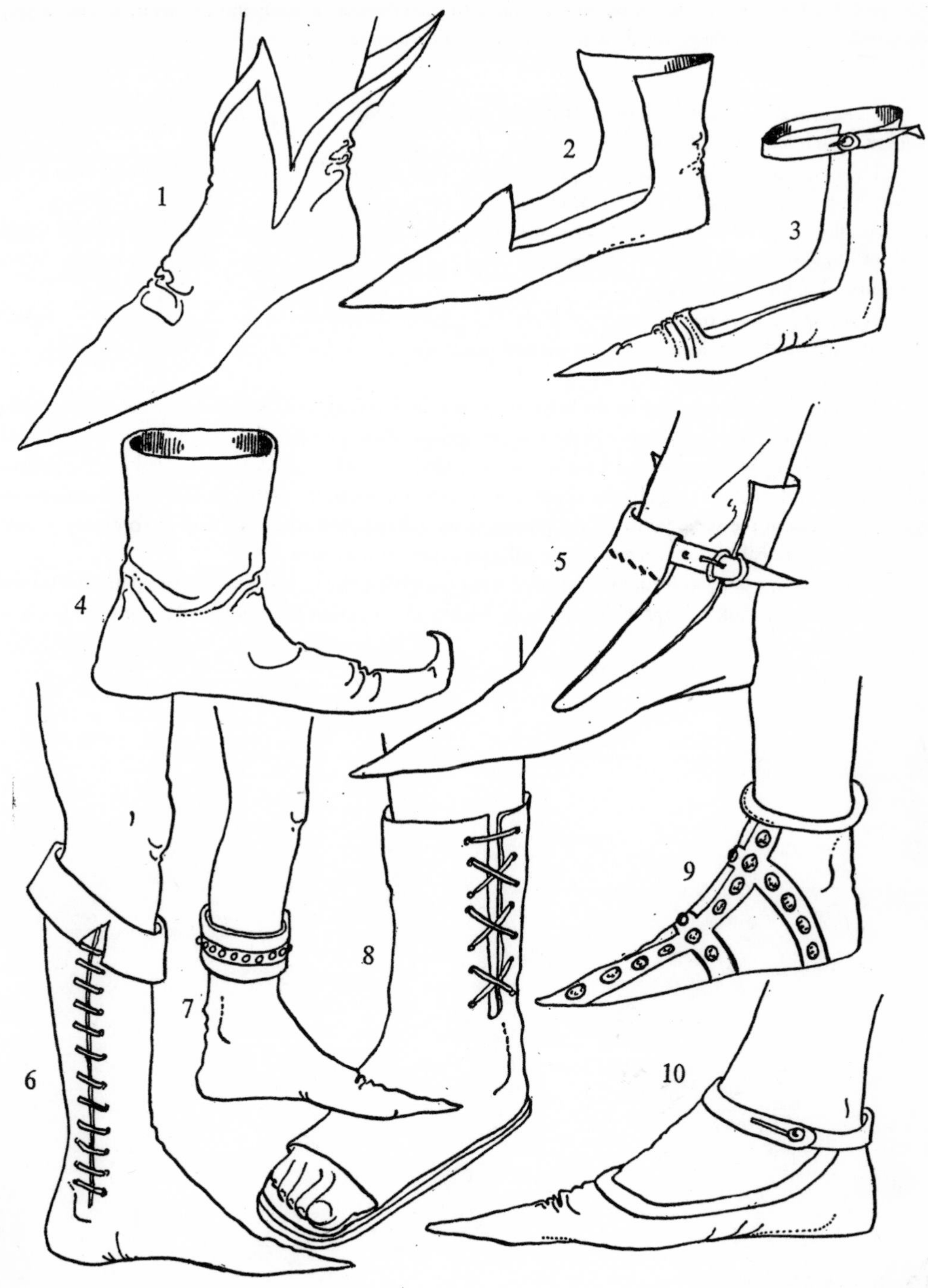
1
2
3
4
5
6
7
8
9
10

The use of the Cross as decoration was not confined to ecclesiastical clothing and footwear, but developed into a universal stylized form of enhancement by colour or with jewels.

1. Ecclesiastical footwear made of embroidered and bejewelled wool. Note how the pattern follows that found in church interior and vestment decoration.

2. The cross used as decoration in a priest's shoe. This style of shoe, often translated into colours for those worn by the upper class, also formed the pattern for armour.

3. Another piece of ecclesiastical footwear showing detailed embroidery on the lightly pointed vamp, with gold binding at the topline. Diminishing cross-gartering now exchanged for simple lacing. Worn over white or coloured stockings.

4. This sketch shows the underside of many shoes, particularly those of the simple style of 2. Folded over a thicker insole, the leather cut and stitched under the sole in this manner. Often the underside lent itself to decoration as well.

5. An ankle-boot, developing its shape from the previous period, now jewelled and decorated for the Norman aristocracy. Prelates wore only the colours of their office, purples, reds, rich blues, white and gold.

6. Originally a papal slipper in soft white leather, gilded and embroidered, copied in colours for prelates and worn in a wider colour range by the upper class. It must be remembered that though there was a similarity of style between the shoes worn by the princes of the Church, the aristocracy and the ordinary people, it was colour and quality that separated their different types of footwear.

7. Fenestration, a popular form of Norman decoration, giving rise to wide interpretation in cut-outs and coloured underlays. Ankle-straps with buttons, or buckles the common form of fastening for these low-cut, high-backed shoes.

17. NORMAN (II)

1
2
4
3
6
5
7

1. The ankle-boot remained unchanged in basic shape but was now acquiring decoration in the form of coloured linings which showed in flared collars, and an ornamental jewel on the front to cover the top of the seam. This being a period of romance, hearts and flowers were a common decoration for men's footwear. Worn over stockings of different colour from the shoe.

2. Embroidered stockings or hose, revealing the shape of the leg, often worn with a light sole so that they needed no shoe. Or, with them, the foot was covered with a light soft shoe such as in sketch 1. Flowers and heraldic motifs used as decorations and the stylized form of the cross.

3. A simple shoe, worn by the common people, made in black or brown raw-hide or natural untanned leathers. If in colours or in softer leathers and sometimes decorated, the footwear of the upper class. This shoe invariably made with round toe, flat sole and no heel lift.

4. The closer-fitting trousers or tights are often footless. The lower classes often barefoot, but other classes wore shoes over coloured hose.

5. Some boots covering the knee had a rolled top of a different colour and worn over breeches. Or, pulled over loose fitting hose. Worn under the knee, a plain or decorated garter.

6. A riding stocking used for hunting, sometimes worn without a boot, but with a reinforced sole and a leather patch at the heel.

7. The light soft ankle-boot continued in this form of simplicity.

8. A boot of mid-calf height, often worn with a jewelled garter at the ankle.

18. NORMAN (III)

1
2
3
4
5
6
7
8

1. An embroidered shoe, simple in shape but lavish in decoration. Often made of tooled leather and decorated with real gold leaf. Similar shapes repeated in armour designs.
2. Simply-cut leather ankle-boot slit at side to do away with lacing.
3. High-backed shoe with edges bound in contrast colour and piped centre seam. Some shoes are showing quite substantial soles at this period.
4. The turned-up pointed toe became extravagant and the Scorpion toe, or the ram's-horn, made their appearance.
5. Even the more modest point became thinner and twisted slightly to the side.
6. The twisted toe point lent itself to all sorts of fanciful ideas and the Fishtailed shoe was one. Known as "pigaces" as a group, these toes were stuffed with moss, hay or wool to keep them firm.
7. A tall-backed shoe, bound and laced in colour and with a modest point, worn by Henry of Anjou, who it was said, had a deformed foot which pointed toes concealed.

At this period, toes, hats, and sleeves all follow the same theme. The liripipe toe was the same shape as the liripipe sleeve and the long hanging point of the headgear had the same name.

19. NORMAN (IV)

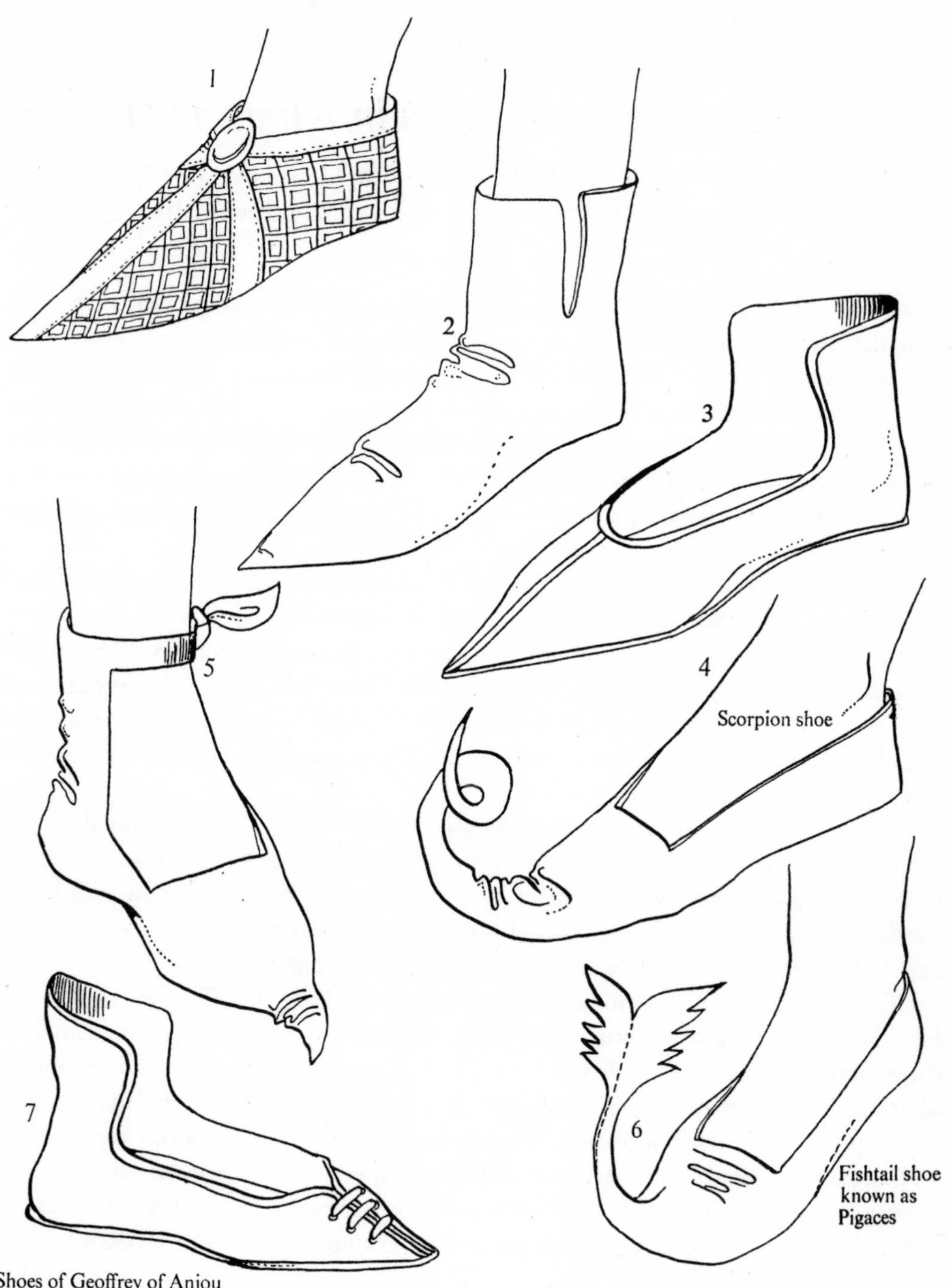
1
2
3
5
4
Scorpion shoe
7
6
Fishtail shoe
known as
Pigaces
Shoes of Geoffrey of Anjou

7

The Plantagenet or Angevin Kings, 1154—1399

Henry II, 1154–1189 Richard I, 1189–1199 John, 1199–1216 Henry III, 1216–1272 Edward I, 1272–1307 Edward II, 1307–1327 Edward III, 1327–1377 Richard II, 1377–1399

THESE ARE the fantastic years, the years of extravagance, colour, and decoration; the years when the pointed toe reached its famous and excessive extremes. Ordinances were established for the Guild of Cordwainers in 1272. It was the century in which the church of St. Crispin and Crispianus was built at Soissons in France to commemorate the death of the saints in A.D. 287. Their day, 25 October, is celebrated by shoemen in Britain each year in Bermondsey at St. Crispin's Church. These two young men are the patron saints of the shoe trade since they supported themselves by shoemaking whilst preaching to the people.

The pointed toe is said to have originated in an attempt to conceal Henry of Anjou's deformed toe, but this like many other stories of origins may or may not be strictly accurate. Some toe shapes had grown into a double twist which gave them the name of *Cornatus*, or twisted ram's horn toe. There is no hard clear line where fashions begin and end, hence it is not possible to draw the frontier of fashion between this Henry and the next, though there are few years between them. The pointed toe, in its varying length, links them all.

It must have been still unusual to find shoes made in lefts and rights for there is a note in Gough's *Sepulchral Monuments* that quotes the discoverer of the shoes found in a tomb as saying that they were "pointed at the toe, narrow and made to fit each foot." But there seems to be no definite period when this was uniformly so, until quite a late date, and some Greeks and Romans had boots made rights and lefts.

The cross motif as decoration features strongly in shoes as well as on clothes, for since the time of William Rufus many of the knights had been engaged on Crusades. Those who took part were entitled to wear a cross of red cloth sewn into the front of their white tunics, which they wore over armour. But one sees the cross repeated in decorative banded patterns of colour or jewels on many shoes other than those which were part of the foot-covering of armour. Armour itself becomes even more important during these years and takes on a fashionable shape of its own. In most cases the foot-covering had to be the same shape as the shoe, though shoes were not necessarily worn beneath it. The cross motif was used on armour also.

The *Solleret*, the armoured shoe, followed the fashion of a long pointed toe, curving downward to prevent the foot slipping through the stirrup. Hinged and riveted together, it consisted of layers of plates over the foot and a leg-covering which laced down the back of the calf. The foot part had a metal loop corresponding to a similar loop on the plate which covered the knee. Some say these were jointed by a chain but it is more likely that they were used to adjust the fit.

During John's reign colour was important and shoes were cut from fabric, silk, and leather, dyed in a variety of rich shades which matched or contrasted with clothes. They were jewelled, gilded, and embroidered for the nobility, but the poorer classes mostly wore plain boots of the same shapes but in buff, brown or black.

Building had now reached magnificent proportions. It was the perpendicular period of design and it was during this reign that the ever-present parallel between architecture and clothes was at its clearest. Tall pointed steeples were echoed in the French fashion for women of the tall pointed hennin head-dress. Long slender cuffs to sleeves, called the "liripipe," were matched by long tails to caps and hoods and the pointed toe was growing longer. All underline the corresponding urge to build wonderful cathedrals with soaring slender steeples. But there was opposition to new fashions then, just as there is now. In 1215, in Paris of all places, there was a law passed that the professors of the university were not to wear the "liripipe toe." But again, the dandies of the period must have ignored the ban, because the toe appeared everywhere and grew longer and there is much pictorial proof of its acceptance.

Shoes and small boots were still laced and now the fastenings were on the inner side of the foot, seemingly for no other reason than fashion. Women's shoes were also laced, but their toes were not so pointed as were the shoes of men, probably because they would have got in the way of the still ground-length hem. Good examples of costume can frequently be found in the statuary in old churches, and a typical shoe of this period for women can be seen worn by Lora, wife of Robert Marmion, in West Tanfield church, Yorkshire. It is interesting to see how the half-long points of her shoes point outwards and are still positioned over the big toe.

Tight woollen trousers or hose played a great part in influencing the shape of shoes, for they were very figure-clinging, and the shoe had to follow suit and fit the foot closely. The hose were of matching colours or, often, parti-coloured, one leg in one colour, the other in another. Sometimes one was striped or checked and the other plain. There was no limit to what the individualist of the day could devise in order to outdo his fellow dandies. Great importance was attached to clothes, as is clear from the frequency with which they are described and commented on in contemporary literature. Both Chaucer and Piers Plowman mention shoes in this connection.

Richly decorated garters were very important, some being worn just above or below the knee, others at the ankle. When riding or hunting an extra stocking, in the form of a soft high boot, was worn to the knee, and over that a short ankle boot. Some continued a more decorative use of the cross garter to fasten these extra boots closer to the leg and these were also lavishly jewelled.

It is interesting to see from illustrations how the ordinary people were not slow in putting fashion to their own use. The shoes they wore were of similar shape but with a more modified and subdued form of decoration. Though they were not in the bright peacock hues of the dandy, being in black, brown or white, they were felt to be just as important.

Velvet, imported from Italy, was a favourite material for clothes and shoes. Furs were used for bordering edges and linings, ermine being the royal preference. English and foreign furs were used a great deal, and sables, fox and squirrel were very fashionable.

Applied design was simple, mostly in the form of geometrics or plant form. Many shoes were embroidered all over in gold or coloured threads, and leather knotted together was used as a simple form of button.

Knitting pins had come from the Orient and from the Moors, and a form of modern knitting is now found to have been used for both clothes and shoes. Naturally it was still all hand-done, as were all other forms of shoemaking and dressmaking.

In the reign of Henry III people were realizing the value, no matter how trivial and transient, of exclusiveness. Many of the wealthy wanted clothes and shoes which no-one else had and would cast them off as soon as they saw something similar. This accounts for the impossibility of illustrating all the changes of fashion which occurred. One has only to look at pictures and manuscripts of the period to find that although many of the basic shapes are repeated the variants on each are inumerable.

Although the point was growing longer, in this reign and in the reign of Edward I shoes themselves became more basic in outline, as if it was realized even then that when there is one dominant excess of design there is room for little else. There had been a good deal of political strife and the final conquest of Wales and the continued battles with Scotland could have been another reason, since wars tend to quieten fashion.

It was during these years that the *Poulaine* and the *Cracowe*, the longest points of all, are said to have originated in Poland though there is little evidence in Polish literature or in seals of the period to confirm it. Nothing has been found of the shoe with the point which had to be fastened to the knee with a chain and ornamental garter to hold it up and prevent its owner from tripping. But it appears so often in paintings that we have to assume that its existence was a fact. It serves to stress another phenomenon of fashion, however, and may be worth preserving for this fact alone.

It is noticed repeatedly throughout history that when a fashion becomes ridiculous and uncomfortable it has topped its peak of importance and is due for a decline. This means, to those aware of these trends, that a new shape is about to appear. We have only to look at shoes of the Plantagenet period to find the archetypal illustration of this fact and for this alone this period is worth studying. When the toe reached its extravagant length a new fashion was not far away, and although the Plantagenets did not know it we do and can learn from their inability to see the future.

Edward III's laws restricted those who wanted to climb the social ladder by adopting the clothes of those socially above them. For instance, the laws forbade jewellery to be worn by the wives of gentlemen under the rank of knight. Those who were wives of esquires owning £200 in land, might edge their clothes with miniver but not with ermine. Later, shoes were included in these sumptuary laws and the long pointed toe was forbidden to those with an income of less than £40 a year, with which a man was relatively rich. A prince could wear his toe-points as long as he liked, but six inches was allowed for a commoner, twelve inches for the gentleman and twenty-four inches or more for the nobleman. Some wore a small bell on the tip of the point, or on the garter at the knee, and it is sometimes said that this is the origin of the nursery rhyme "Ride a cock-horse to Banbury Cross," which dates from this period..the cross at Banbury being one of the Eleanor Crosses marking the resting-places of the funeral cortège of Queen Eleanor, Edward I's queen.

Towards the end of the Plantagenet period points diminished considerably and were now only 6 inches longer than the foot. They were still stuffed with hair or wool or moss and the sides of the half-boots were held up with whalebone.

Richard II was the last of the Plantagenets. The French alliance was ended, English had become the universal language, the wool trade was bringing wealth through its exports, and the standard of living was greatly improved. Wool and leather were within the reach of all and fashion, once only for the few, was now for everyone.

This was the late Gothic period, which covered approximately the years from 1350 to 1480, and was another great period where architecture and fashion ran parallel. The builders had such feeling for vertical lines that, probably unconsciously, people extended their costume by tall head-dresses and long shoes, repeating the same Gothic lines. But it was also the period of stained glass, and cathedrals, churches, and other buildings possessed the beautiful windows which give us many clues about contemporary costume. One style of shoe had an intricately-cut vamp in a circular pattern through which the bright colours of an underlay showed through. This was the Rose Window shoe, whose colourful decoration was taken from the Rose Window of St. Stephen's chapel, Westminster. This had a much shorter point and was often cut with a bar and buckle, although there were many other alternatives.

The wooden pattens, which lifted the foot from the ground and protected the shoe from the dirt of ill-made roads, had taken the same extravagant shapes as the shoes they were worn with. There were as many shapes for these as for shoes and some were highly decorative, painted or covered with leather. Until now they had been strictly utilitarian but now they became works of art in their own right and were high fashion, worn by men and women alike. As they grew higher they paved the way to experiments with heels. There is an excellent example of the simple form in Jan Van Eyck's painting of Arnolfini's wedding, in the National Gallery, London.

The finest guide to fourteenth-century England is, of course, Geoffrey Chaucer's *Canterbury Tales*, in which there are many descriptions of clothes and shoes then in fashion. The great medieval scholar, Edith Rickert, illustrates this period in her *Chaucer's World* with many contemporary pictures and much documentary material.

PLANTAGENET

Woman

Butterfly head-dress hiding all the hair. Floating gauze veil supported by wire frame. High-waisted gown, fur-trimmed, long tight sleeves.

Man

Roundlet head-dress; rolled brim with draped crown and trailing streamer. Wide-sleeved gown (houppelande) with high rolled collar; folded into regular pleats under the belt; fur-trimmed; worn over long-sleeved tunic. Leg-hose with cod-piece. Long toes stuffed and tied back to leg.

1. Ornamented and heavily embroidered stockings commonplace among the fashionable gentry, who repeated patterns on to their armour. Often the decoration different for each leg.
2. This simple leather shoe is preserved in the London Museum. It is made of black leather and has raw-hide side lacing.
3. A simpler form of chain mail without metal plates. The spur is held to the foot by leather straps.
4. The cross motif used on armour and on hose, especially for Crusaders.
5. The traditional and most frequently seen medieval footwear with a fore-and-aft peak.
6. Another version of the solleret, the shoe portion of leg armour, showing how the plates were layered one on top of the other and riveted. The metal greaves laced down the back and the knee covered with similar overlapping plates. A metal loop on the foot attached by a chain to that on the knee to support the weight of the foot after it had been slipped through the stirrup.
7. Further detail of overlapping armour plates on the foot showing how the toe shape followed the fashion. A plaque of metal for extra protection to the foot.
8. Triangular embroidery, a favourite motif in Plantagenet design, following the general shape of other objects such as simple hats for the women, the liripipe sleeve, church steeples and tournament lances and their triangular hand protection.

20. PLANTAGENET (I)

1
2
3
4
5
6
7
8
Solleret

Pointed toes, at the beginning of this period, were modest, but increased to extravagance at the end. It must always be borne in mind that the ordinary people, though adapting many of the current fashions, were never extreme in the clothes, and that the exaggerations in shapes belonged only to the wealthy classes.

1. Even ecclesiastical footwear shows a class consciousness in decoration and colour. This is the shoe of a high prelate; ordinary priests wore a plain shoe as in 2.

3. Shoes with decorative cut-outs showing coloured silks underneath, or coloured stockings. Pointed toe matches peaked front.
4. Embroidered shoe with moderate toe and buttoned strap.
5. A fenestrated shoe in Rose Window pattern, in leather.
6. Chain mail is an important part of armour, also knitted into long hose worn under metal which has a toe of long fashionable shape. Spurs, part of the decoration as well as being functional.
7. Lacing, developed from cross-gartering, now becomes a usual means of fastening shoes.
8. High backs, and coloured binding for all classes.

21. PLANTAGENET (II)

1
2
3
4
5
6
7
8

1. Slip-on shoe from Spain, versions of which worn in England. With wide cutouts to show the coloured stocking underneath, these are the forerunners of the Tudor slashed shoes. Heavy coloured stitching adds further decoration.

2. Wooden patten with leather strap stitched and punched and attached with nails.

3. Mule with thick leather side and pointed toe. Peaked front, laced vamp and tongue sits high on the foot.

4. Pattens acquire the same pointed shape as the shoe in order to support the toe. Their wooden or cork shapes covered, painted, or left natural.

5. Armour follows the same shapes as in shoes, riveted together in the same decorative manner as the straps which hold pattens to the foot. The soleret, an armoured shoe composed of overlapping layers of metal.

6. Sometimes the hose under armour or inside the shoe attached to a patten, is cut away at the front and heel. For the peasantry worn without shoes.

7. Embroidered hose worn inside armour by the aristocracy, or without shoes at home. Real gold thread often used for this decoration.

8. The long pointed toe called a Poulaine. Its toe often attached to the jester front by a chain and tassels or by ornamental cord.

22. PLANTAGENET (III)

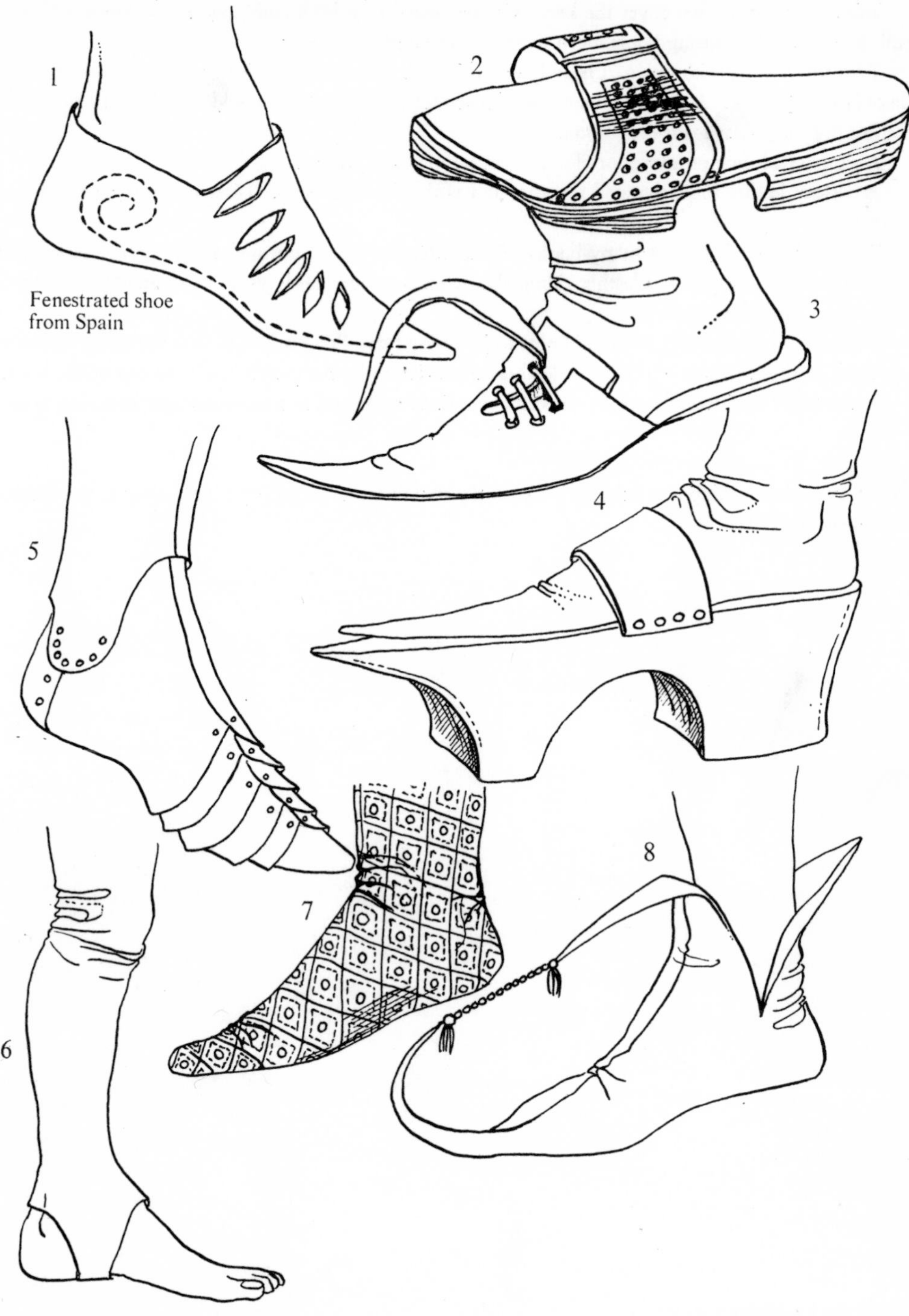
1
2
3
4
5
6
7
8
Fenestrated shoe
from Spain

1. Tall riding boots often cover the knee with decorated turn-back cuff; two inside loops with which to pull them on. Close-fitting boots worn over hose of a different colour.

2. Two-toned hose, with one part heavily embroidered, often accompanied by very ornamental garters made of lace and jewels. A detail of the parti-coloured leg fashion, which would show a plain leg and hose to accompany this extravagant decoration.

3. A simple tied shoe of leather or cloth, worn by men and women.

4. A cut-out leather shoe, thonged together and with a buckled strap. These cut-outs reveal underlaid silk panels.

5. This shoe, though seen in many books of costume, has been confirmed as a theatrical shoe and not true to the period. Intended as a leather riding shoe with a wooden heel, but it is too early for heels which did not appear until the late Tudors.

6. The method of attaching hose and boots to jerkin by tying "points," or laces at the sides. Often very ornamental, or simply made of ribbon or leather strips, tied to leather panels inside the top of the boot.

7. A one-piece Carbartine worn by peasants over linen socks and in turn worn over ill-fitting hose.

The contrast in the clothing and fashions between the various ranks of society is very clear in the difference of ornamentation.

23. PLANTAGENET (IV)

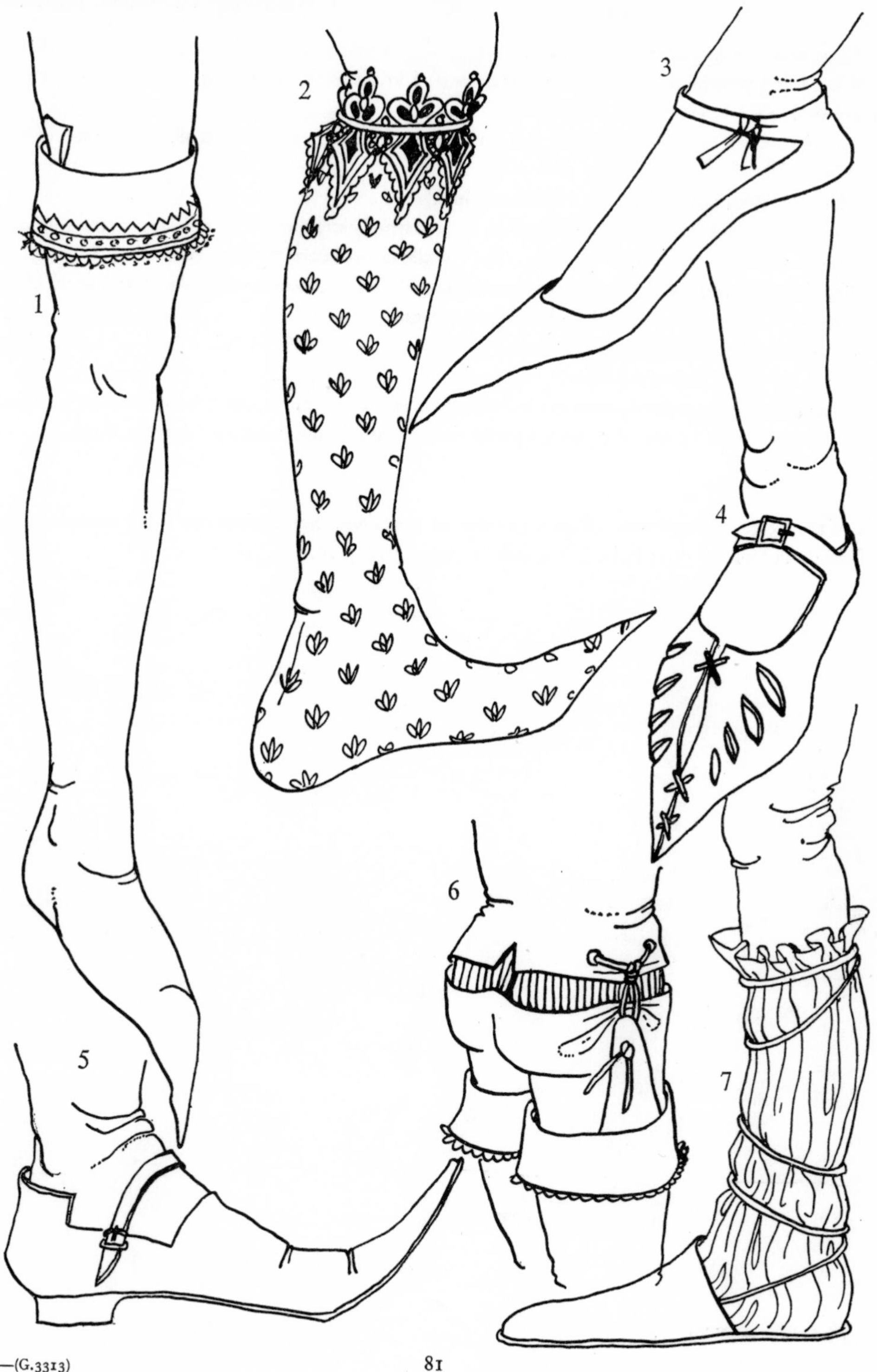
1
2
3
4
5
6
7

1. Some wear the unpadded pointed toe.

2. Tooled and patterned leather, as well as imported brocades from the east, used in shoemaking. A decorated shoe, plain hose and vice versa.

3. The cross motif is often so stylized that its clarity is lost, as in this shoe which makes use of bound panels.

4. The same bound panels used in a buttoned shoe.

5. Though not made in lefts and rights, shoes are not strictly straights. The toes turn to the outside and become more pronouncedly shaped by wear. For a while inward-turning toes also used.

6. The elongated pointed hose, sometimes embroidered up the sides over the ankle, thus introducing the earliest clocks. These often use real jewels in the decoration.

7. Lacing now becoming decorative as well as functional, and often set into a contrast coloured panel. At times the toe is thin and string-like.

8. This is a flat sandal type of patten made from wood or cork or straw, and laced to the foot with leather thongs. Its toe long, to support the padded toe of fashion, had an upturned tip for protection.

Points of the longest variety were called Cracowes or Poulaines. Some historians think these were called after fashions in Cracow or in Poland, but there is little proof.

24. PLANTAGENET (V)

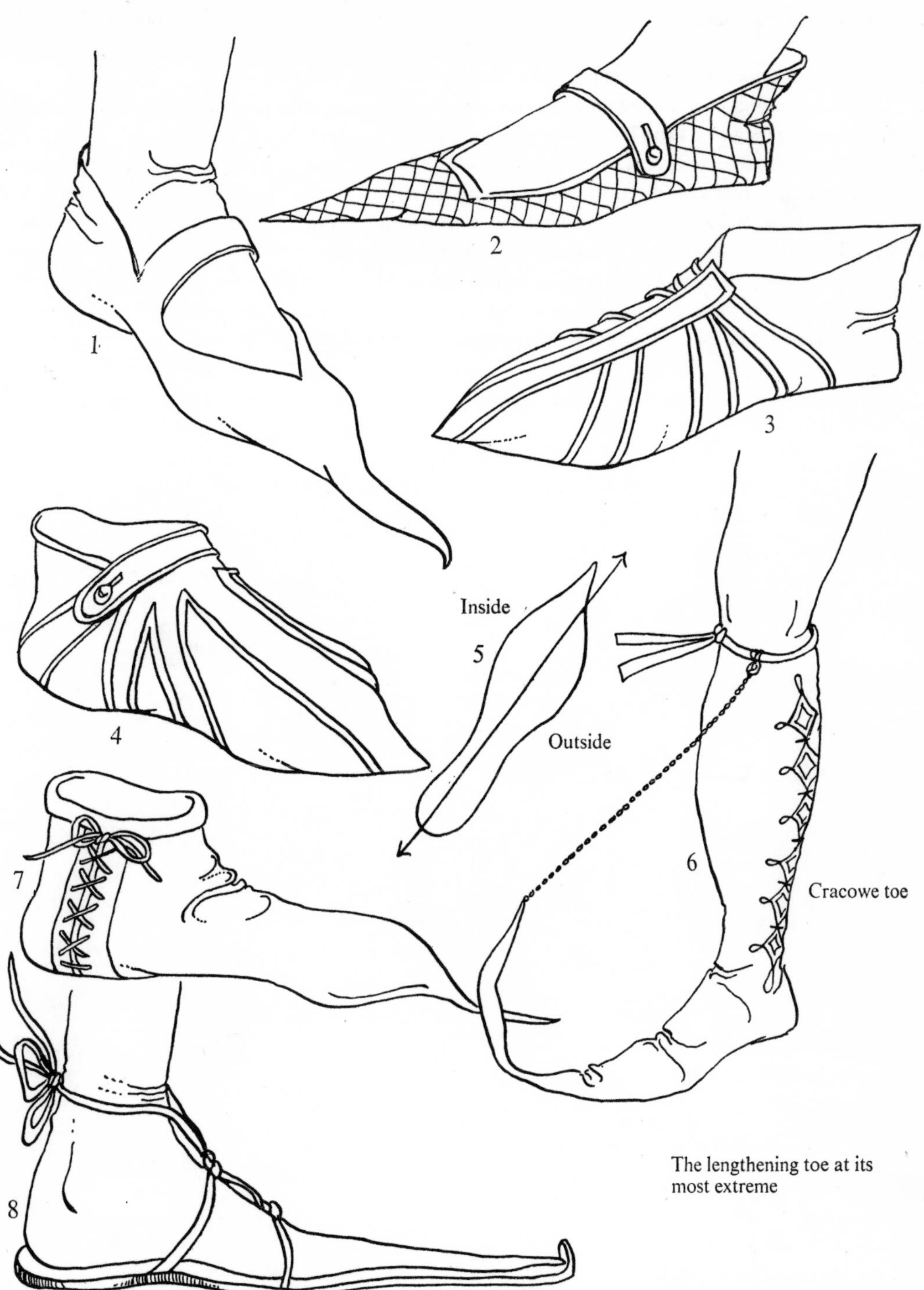

The lengthening toe at its most extreme

1. A loose-fitting ankle-boot in soft leather or cloth, made either plain or embroidered according to rank.
2. Riding boot with turned-down contrast collar and lacing on the inside.
3. Ankle-boot with double buttoning worn over loose-fitting breeches of another colour. The vamp has an ornamental inset panel and button decoration.
4. Coloured binding, as on many shoes, an important feature. Cross quilting or coloured stitching, often in gold thread, on many shoes. Button fastening.
5. Fur-lined leather boot with button fastening worn by the wealthy to match the fur linings of their cloaks. Rank indicated the type of fur which could be worn.
6. A close-fitting ankle-boot with jewelled panels and collar. The pointed toe not worn by everyone.
7. A stylized cross motif in a two-coloured shoe.
8. An ankle-boot in coloured leathers with contrast binding and jewelled decoration.

25. PLANTAGENET (VI)

1
2
3
4
5
6
7
8

It is easy to remember the peak period of the pointed toe. One might stress the *peak* period without making a pun, as being part of the three "p"s of the Plantagenets pointed toes, pattens and poulaines.

1. Horses being the only form of transport, and used by everybody, great attention paid to riding boots, worn by both men and women. Some of plain leather with a turn-back cuff, others in colours, some in cloth with leather reinforcements. Their toes were of the fashionable shape and spurs were strapped on with leather.
2. The basic form of patten used by all, decorated or plain, held to the foot by strips of leather. There are many versions.
3. A patten with an ornamental instep bar, the whole being carved from one piece of wood.
4. The simple leather shoe of the peasant, laced with leather thongs.
5. Another ankle-boot with a half collar turned back to show contrast. Its patten consists of a block of wood held by leather straps.
6. A close-fitting boot on a single-bar patten.
7. Sometimes a small jewel or bell stitched to the tip of an extreme point. From a development of this form of decoration the traditional cap and bells of the jester is adapted. When the jester used it for his costume it passed out of fashionable use. This shows a wooden patten with a nail- or jewel-studded leather strap for decoration.
8. Another one-piece patten carved from a single piece of wood and worn over a very decorated shoe in two colours of leather, silk or felt.

26. PLANTAGENET (VII)

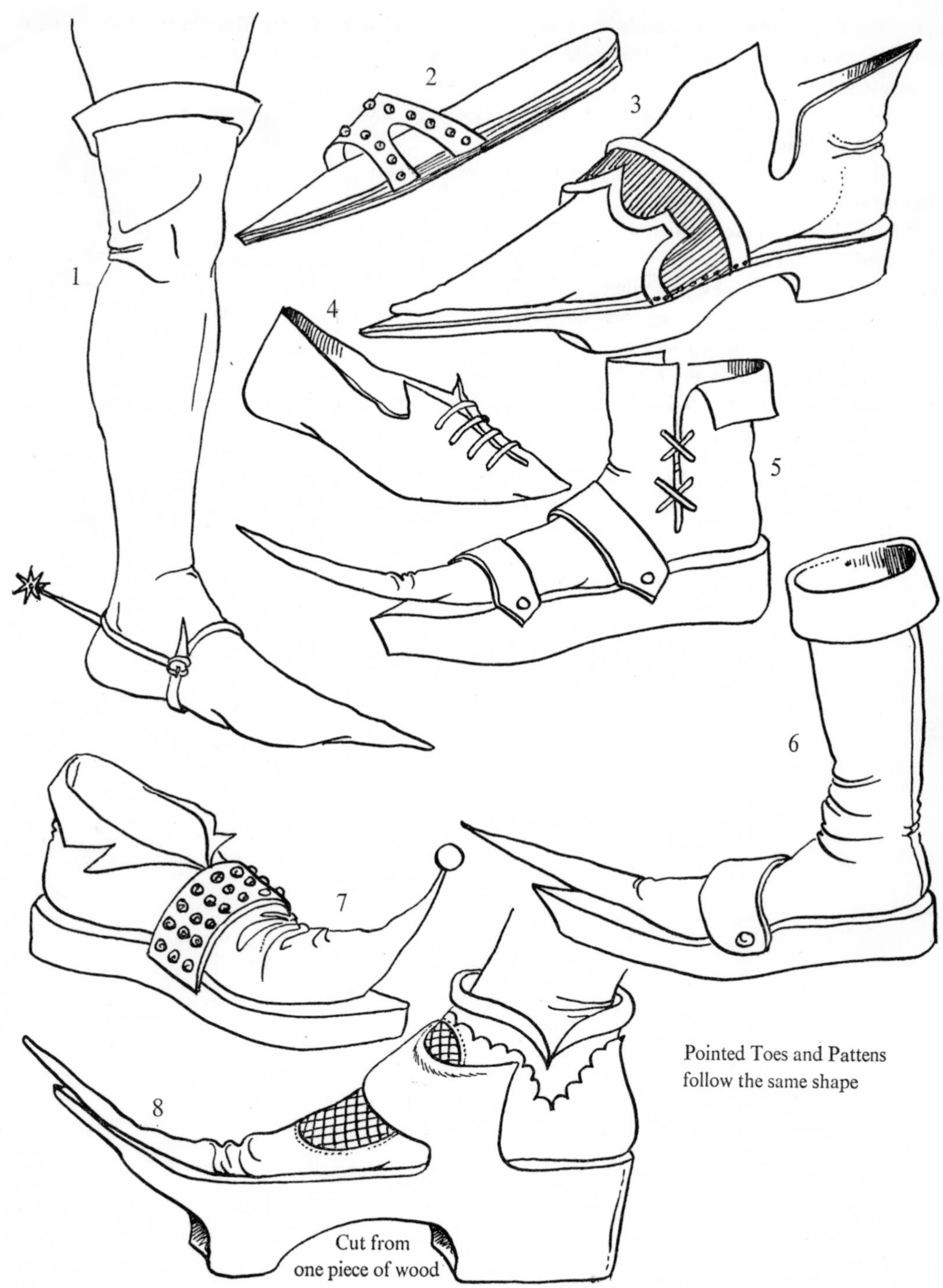

Pointed Toes and Pattens follow the same shape

1/2. The Rose Window Shoe named after the round stained-glass window in Westminster Abbey. There is another in the Sainte-Chapelle, Paris, and there are other examples. Cut-out, or fenestrated, in a decorative pattern, the vamp shows coloured stockings through the openings; or coloured silks show through the cut-outs. Buttons and bars the usual manner of its fastening. These shoes were also called "carved shoes" because of the knife cuts.

3. Embroidered and strapped shoe worn over a coloured stocking. Stylized cross still used as decoration. This form also used on armour.

4. Soft, long-toed shoe, with low back, of embroidered fabric. Leather sole stitched to the upper. Often found on statues of the period.

5. The pointed toe now extending considerably and, although padded with moss or wool, needing a chain attachment to the leg by an ornamental garter. Fenestration lightens the look of the ankle-boot.

6. The stocking has an extended toe in common with shoes, which is attached to a buckled garter-strap by a chain. Worn only by the dandies of the upper class.

7. The more conventional shoe has a longer toe. A more restrained version worn by women. Attached sole pointed to match toe.

Although these shoes are for the most part illustrated as plain, there were heavily ornamented versions of the same shape, and embroidery and jewellery played a great part in shoe decoration. Colours and materials were lavishly used and personal taste could be indulged in many different ways.

27. PLANTAGENET (VIII)

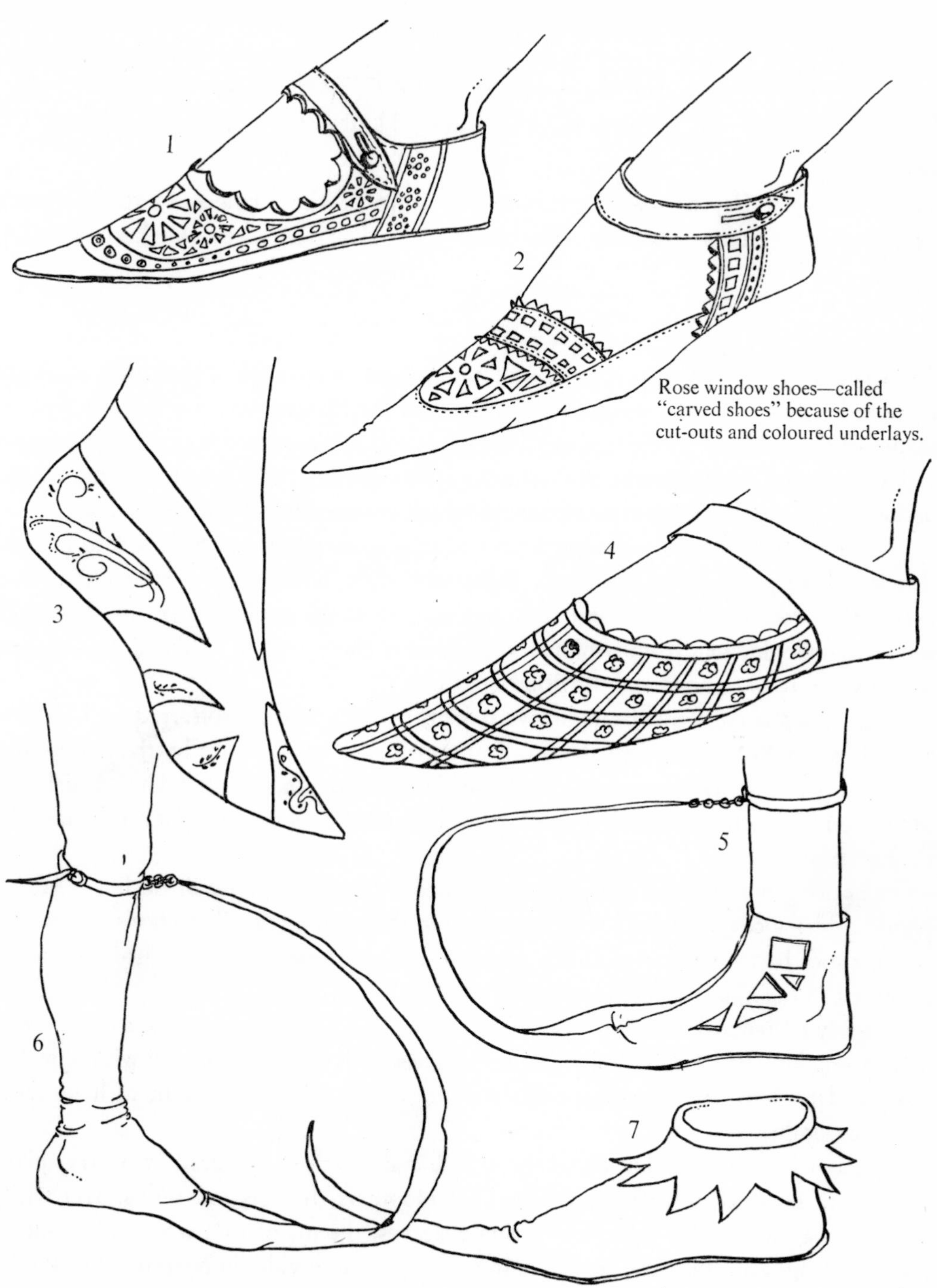

Rose window shoes—called "carved shoes" because of the cut-outs and coloured underlays.

8

Lancaster and York, 1399—1485

Lancaster: Henry IV (Usurper), 1399–1413 Henry V, 1413–1422 Henry VI, 1422–1461

York: Edward IV, 1461–1483 Edward V (one of the Princes of the Tower), 1483—reigned two months, Richard III (Usurper, the Wicked Uncle), 1483–1485

ALTHOUGH A FAIRLY LONG period of time, these years mark a transition stage for fashion, between the long slender vertical lines of the Plantagenets and the low squarer shapes of the Tudors. There is always such a period between two major fashion shapes and though the time shortens as communications quicken it is worth looking at this period because it involves a type of fashion which occurs often in different guises.

There is never a sudden change from one style to its opposite, rather it is so gradual that it is hardly noticed at the time. Eighty-six years, however, is a longer transition period than could occur now and, although fashion at the beginning of that period of time was quite different from fashion at the end of it, there is no rigid line of demarcation to show where one ended and the other began.

The Wars of the Roses brought two colours strongly into fashion. . red for Lancaster and white for York. We find them occurring often as motifs worn by their respective factions. The rose itself becomes a frequent decoration, either via heraldry, which was often used to quarter a tunic or a shoe, or in the embroidery women put on the linen of their menfolk.

The long pointed toe, having been limited by law, was now in decline. After a period of defiance (paralleled by the resistance to the banning of stiletto heels in our own time), shoes became more modestly pointed and the long shape that had had to be anchored to the knee became obsolete.

Henry IV reigned but a few years only and was succeeded by his eldest son Henry V. This young king had a great deal of border troubles with Wales to contend with, but they did not deter him from dressing well. Paintings of the time show him to have worn exquisite clothes.

Shoemaking became known as the gentle craft and was lyricized in poetry, plays, and songs. Long, tight stockings attached to "bloomers" had become tights, over which was worn a short belted tunic with liripipe sleeves. Points of toes were still about six inches in length but the forepart of the shoe was growing wider in contrast. Duckbilled shoes, which had a wide padded forepart and a slight central point, were beginning to be seen. Some shoes were not real shoes at all, but long tights with extended toes and with reinforcing under the sole for strength and protection. The red and yellow parti-coloured costume, which had been very fashionable, became the wear for jesters at the court and so passed from modish wear. So did the small bells on the tips of the pointed gelots.

In the mid-fourteen-hundreds the Byzantine Empire came to an end with the fall of Constantinople to the Turks. Learned men fled before the invaders and spread their knowledge to the cities of Europe, thus opening the way to the period of new learning known as the Renaissance.

Primary colours were used for clothing, fashion still being strongly influenced by heraldry, making dress as conspicuous and as visible as possible, and a means of displaying rank and occupation. Shoes were as strongly coloured as clothes. The lighting in houses and other buildings was so bad that bright colours in clothing were probably a necessity.

Henry VI, King of France and England, married Margaret of Anjou, who was as strong as her husband was weak. She founded Queen's College, Cambridge, although women were not to be admitted to the university until hundreds of years later. Women's clothes were as decorative as men's and the same use of heraldic devices applied equally to the costumes of both sexes, but women's shoes were still modest and unobtrusive because of their long concealing skirts. They did, however, wear wooden pattens, decorated and pointed.

Thigh boots of soft leather buckled under the knee with a jewelled clasp were very popular with the wealthy classes. These boots were called *Boteurs*. They were lined with a contrasting colour which showed when the top was turned down.

In 1439 Henry VI granted a charter to the Guild of Cordwainers, for whom there had been ordinances from about 1272. It is interesting to note here the Cordwainers' objections to the Cobblers who sold old shoes. When the Cobblers repaired the old shoes they used new leather, and this was a matter of great concern to the Cordwainers.

Brocade was imported from the East and was used extensively for clothes. When Edward IV became the Yorkist king, the white rose was used as a decorative motif on his clothes and on his shoes. The embroidery of the time was exquisite. The wars with Scotland had no great effect on fashion, although armour became more decorative. The hingeing on the foot-coverings of armour is always worth close attention because of the intricate details which made it work. In spite of its great weight, armour was an effective protection, although the wearer was vulnerable if the opponent could find the weak spots between the hinges or where plates overlapped.

Leather was used for armour as well as metal and was one of the earliest forms of protection all over the world. The Romans used it in the form of square pieces cut into overlapping plates and linked together with metal loops, so did the Genoese of 1435, and some of it is found amongst English armour in various periods. The "cuirass" (from the French *cuir*) was a protective leather covering for the upper part of the body. In our own time, in the mid-sixties, Paco Rabanne and other French couturiers used leather pieces linked together on a "chain-mail" jersey base, making it into attractive casual wear for the young. In recent years shoe designers have also used panels of silver leather stitched or riveted on to shoes which had a look the medieval knight would have instantly recognized.

John Rous's *Life of the Earl of Warwick*, gives a great deal of information about this period. He was chaplain and historian to the Warwicks.

This period of Lancastrian and Yorkist England, which covered almost the whole of the fifteenth century, was essentially one of contrasts. It was marked by incessant battles, political disagreement, industrial unrest which hampered the latent possibilities in Britain's position as an exporter, and commercial stagnation. Not only was fashion in a transitional stage between one high peak of interest and the next, so was the country as a whole. This points again to another parallel the student of fashion can utilize for himself in forecasting things to come. When one high peak of commercial and political importance is passing or past, the next one seems slow to develop. Fashion reflects this faithfully. We see a parallel with clothes, a waiting for some other new trend to develop and a waning of the previous extravagances. Similar periods can be marked in eras other than our own, but of course in the fifteenth and other early centuries, communications being slower, the time-lag was longer. This was the time when thought, activity, learning of all kinds, art, architecture, music, were becoming revitalized and were soon to turn into the period we call Modern in historical terms.

The Hundred Year's War with France had led Henry V to revive the romantic Age of Chivalry and it was this that had given rise to the kindling of interest in heraldry and its application to art and design. This was one of the times when false genealogies were created and romantic poems about knights and fair ladies were written, much of which writings have given rise to a great deal of historical controversy ever since. So it is not surprising that fashion also has its defenders and romanticizers as well as its denigrators. There is, however, a significant amount of physical evidence for this period, as most museums will testify, and those which specialize in costume and footwear are able to offer the student plenty of examples. But it was this long war which led to the "War of the Cousins," usually known as the "Wars of the Roses," which destroyed the power of the nobles, weakened feudalism, and increased the strength of those Middle Classes who were going to exert their influence from now on.

Although this was the period which led the way to the despotic monarchs, it must not be regarded as totally a Dark Age. It established England as English, set Englishmen on the throne and paved the way to much commercial enterprise. Cities grew in size and manufacture in importance, and English learning became able to rank with that of Europe. It was during this time that the King's Law became Common Law, traditional liberties were established, the national Parliament and its democracy was founded, and the English language came triumphantly to be our common tongue. It was in these years that Caxton started his printing press near Westminster Abbey and published his first book in 1474, bringing learning, reading, and general information within the reach of all. Though it would be small-minded to decry the illuminated manuscripts of the monks and scribes, common sense tells us that printing speeded up communications in a way impossible to the handwritten word.

Gunpowder had been discovered, thus freeing the aspenwood, the use of which was once strictly limited to the making of bows and arrows, to be made into pattens. Another law about pointed toes was passed, forbidding them to be made longer than two inches, but since the rounded toe was now growing in importance this law had no special significance. Men below the rank of yeoman were not allowed to wear padding in their clothes. This was significant as pointing to the fact that whilst hitherto not a great deal of noticeable padding had been worn except in the long pointed toe it was now increasing in clothes, marking a new turn of shape and direction. The vertical lines were slowly beginning to give way to their contrasting opposites, the horizontal.

Apart from the genuine shoes of the period, there is a great deal of information to be found in the illuminated psalters of the period in the Bodleian Library, Oxford, and in the British Museum. As learning grew, illuminated books of all kinds became more common, and these were used as fashion plates and embroidery manuals by the women, as well as for the use for which the monk-artists intended them. The demand for books grew greater as Caxton's press supplemented the work of the scribes.

Pattens were the original heels, and though there have been versions of them throughout history and in other countries, this was the period when pattens began to give rise to experiments with real heels. They were not to show as such, however, until the advent of the Tudors.

1. A metal patten consisting of a circular base supporting a wooden sole. These bases have various forms as did the upper attached to the sole. The uppers of thick leather, have eyelets or are knotted with an attachment of softer leather. Later, other materials used as well as lavish embroidery and decoration. Uppers sandalized or with closed toes. (1650–1730.)
2. A low-heeled wooden patten carved from hard wood and held to the foot by a broad strap of leather and brass nails. Later, both strap and nails become ornamental.
3. The original sabot as worn by the peasants of Europe and Britain carved from wood, and with iron nails or a metal rim for protection. Their use in the peasants' revolt for the destruction of the crops, gave rise to the word "sabotage."
4. Wooden soles worn by everyone, high and low. Those of the Duke of Burgundy of black wood attached to black woollen hose. It is difficult to see how these were attached, as the painting gives no visible explanation.
5. This simple sandal worn by monks throughout the century, very similar to the patten of fashion, except for its rough simplicity. Held to the foot by leather and nails.

Most pattens were worn separately over shoes or coloured hose, but later some were permanently attached to a shoe specially attached to the wooden sole.

28. PATTENS

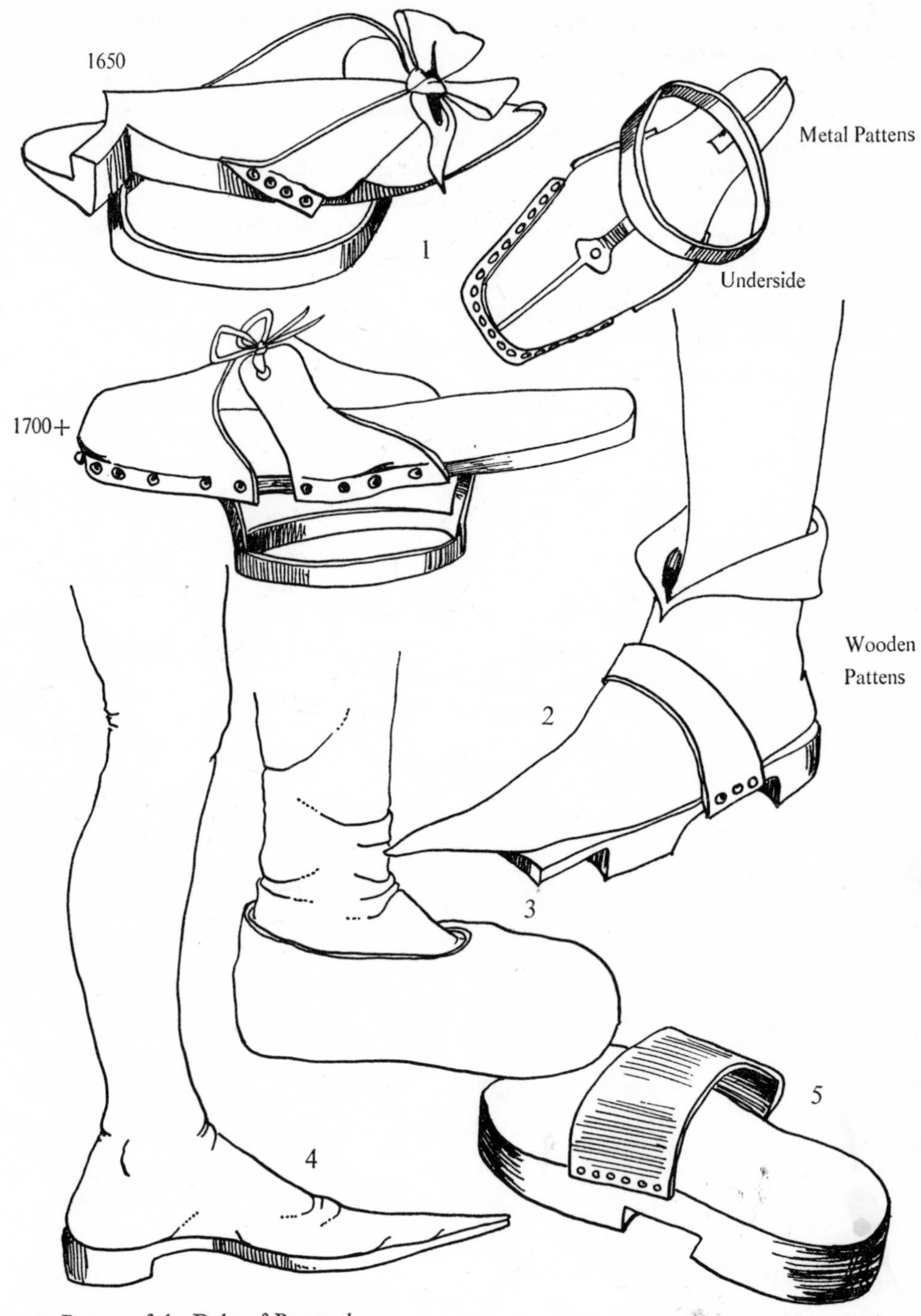

Pattens of the Duke of Burgundy.

1. This was the time of pattern, and legs were not excluded. A pair of hose often had one leg patterned, one plain. Striped legs were frequently seen.

2. Hose were often of two colours—one colour at the front another at the back. Or legs might be of two different colours. Embroidery was often worked in detail on one leg whilst the other was left plain.

3. Crenellated patterns on clothes were also fashionable. Hose were often richly gartered under the knee.

4. Short ankle-boots were sometimes cut in two colours, contrasted with hose.

5. One's crest or arms might be displayed on one's footgear.

6. Deep-collared boots hugged the ankle and were often cut into heraldic shapes at the edges.

7. A short ankle-boot such as this could be attached directly to a wooden sole and worn over coloured hose.

29. LANCASTER AND YORK (1)

1
2
3
4
5
6
7

1. Heavy black leather shoe with high-cut front and buckled fastening. Attached sole stitched with coarse black thread. Thin point extending about 4 inches beyond the foot.

2. High boot covering the ankle and closely laced with leather thong. Short point 1 inch longer than the toe. Stitched sole slightly thickened at heel with a lift. Found on the Lich site at Worcester; now in Worcester Museum.

3. Thick black leather shoe also found on the Lich site at Worcester. The opening is cut off-side and stitched with coarse black thread, as is the sole.

4. Not all shoes were narrow and long; some, from the later part of the period were already beginning to widen as shown in this 15th-century sole from Walworth Road Museum (found in London).

5. High-cut front cut in one with the ankle strap. Thick black leather with rough button fastening.

6. Triple-arched wooden patten attached to the shoe by black leather straps which fastened with a jewelled clasp. Illustration from a painting by Jan van Eyck.

7. Simple pull-on shoe with soft short toe. Collar of jewelled or patterned woven ribbon.

30. LANCASTER AND YORK (II)

1
2
3
4
5
6
7

9

The Tudors (I): 1485—1558

Henry VII, 1485–1509 Henry VIII, 1509–1547 Edward VI, 1547–1553 Mary I, 1553–1558

WITH THE TUDOR reigns came the long-expected change in fashion and the beginning of the period known as "modern" to historians. Even if we were unaware of what happened in these reigns we might make a near guess by looking at the clothes, since fashion reflects social changes. Whilst clothes were less decorated and toes were less extravagantly pointed, there was still a great deal of colour. Shoemaking as an industry was growing and, now that the Guilds had set certain standards for their craftsmen, quality and workmanship were very high. The general shape of the forepart was widening like the shape of the clothes. This was paralleled in architecture, which had a different shape from that of previous reigns. Buildings were long, low, and squarish. Many were black and white and it is interesting to find this style was analogous to the fashion for black and white in clothes, inspired by the Spanish court, which dressed in black velvet and white linen. Although the magpie architecture is mostly found in the Midlands there are other examples of it in many parts of the country.

Spain was exercising an increasing influence on fashion in Europe and later, when she was exploiting South America and adding to her Empire, new colours, jewels, and materials became available to her people. At the end of the fifteenth century, however, when Columbus discovered America, a new aspect of clothes and shoes and their making became important. This was a period of discovery and increased material wealth, which was reflected very clearly in developing fashions. One has only to look at the paintings of Holbein to get a good idea of how fashion had changed. This was the period of the Merchant Adventurers, the pioneers of modern commerce who traded with Flanders, the Baltic, and the Mediterranean, taking with them cloth from the east and north of England and wool from the west country. It was the period too of the great sailors.. Sebastian Cabot who sailed from Bristol and Vasco da Gama who sailed from the Tagus toward India. All this involved a fruitful exchange of ideas with the rest of the world.

Weaving had developed considerably during the fifteenth century. Mostly carried on by the women, because families were nearly self-supporting, they made their own sheets, blankets, and the cloth for their clothes, using the spindle, which preceded the sixteenth-century spinning wheel. Some of this material was used for indoor shoes and the linings of outdoor shoes.

Tapestry was also made and used for wall-coverings, bed-hangings, carpets (when rushes were not used), purses, bags and shoes, as well as for clothes. These tapestries were first made at Arras, in France and were called after that town. (Wall-coverings from Arras are mentioned in *Hamlet*). Many of the popular entertainments are depicted in these hangings and a great deal is to be learned from them about the clothes of the period. It must be borne in mind, however, that on the tapestries these were simplified and often romanticized.

Shoes were made of thick cloth, wool felt, soft leathers or, for the peasants, thick hide leathers, which were generally black. The thick cloth shoes were not waterproof and pattens were essential wear with them. Buttons, lacings, and hooks and eyes were used on dresses and buttons and hooks were used on shoes also. Lacings had eyelet holes which were sometimes merely punched in the leather, sometimes, when the shoes were of higher quality, stitched round in a buttonhole stitch.

Rebellions and border battles, in the previous years, had not altered the look of shoe fashion except for developing the durability of soldiers' shoes and boots, which became more serviceable.

Henry Tudor, Earl of Richmond, became the first Tudor king of England after a long experience of poverty. He was a wise man who knew the value of money and he was not prepared to risk his throne and country by waging wars abroad. When he died he had secured England's position by the wise marriage of his children, Arthur into the Spanish royal family and his daughter to James of Scotland; by these unions he hoped to cement the peace with these countries.

The length of men's clothes, which had alternated between the two extremes of shortness and length, now became temporarily fixed, the fifteenth-century period of transition being over. The hems of men's coats and tunics and the length of their bloomer-like breeches was around mid-thigh. Women's skirts were still ground-length, though their shoes began to be more interesting from now on: their feet began to be noticed and were even mentioned in poetry. This is the beginning of the extravagant and exaggerated shape with which we are all familiar as being the most typical feature of the Tudor costume.

Here is another fashion pointer to note: there are three stages to all styles, each of which must be borne in mind in relation to the others. The first stage is when a fashion is worn by those who initiate changes, when it is slowly gaining a hold. The second stage is when everyone wears it and it can be truly called the fashion. The third stage is when it reaches ridiculousness and is on the wane. It is just before the start of this third stage that the intelligent and intuitive designer starts the next move. It is as important with the Tudor as with any other period, to be aware whether a fashion is slow because it is on the increase or is slow because it is on the decline.

There were still hanging sleeves but these were now fastened back. Ruffles made of lawn or lace were beginning to appear; we see these mostly worn at the wrist, by men and women alike. We also see sleeves slashed from elbow to wrist to show puffs of lawn.

The French court had become very important and its fashions exercised a strong influence in England, owing to the exchange of courtesies between Henry VIII and Francis which reached their peak on the Field of the Cloth of Gold. From that time gold as a fashion was highly valued; the king had a complete suit made of it. It is interesting to note that much of the money gained from the spoliation of the monasteries was spent on clothes for the king.

Shoes were now getting very much broader and the slashings on sleeves were repeated on their vamps, to show puffs of lawn or lace. The toe was padded at the sides with moss or hair, as the point had been, and was now almost as wide as it had been long. The *Duckbilled* toe, square with rounded corners and a central point, became increasingly splayed. Even after the point had been dropped the padded squareness continued to increase and in the reign of Henry VIII an order was issued limiting its width to a maximum of six inches. Shoes covered the foot to the ankle and were fastened with laces or buckled straps, some buckles being very ornamental. In 1515 a lower cut was reverted to and in museums we can see many of the backless mule type. Some of these were mere toe-caps, slashed and puffed with a contrast colour. Edges were pinked in different designs and vamps were often cut out in geometric designs. Jewels were often sewn on to add to the ornate decoration.

Around 1509 *Startups* were a popular high-fitting country shoe which took the form of a kind of legging. As soon as these shoes were worn by those of lower station, aping their betters, these shoes were discarded by the fashionable and the word "Startups" gave rise to "upstart." Boots and buskins had also been discarded except for riding or by soldiers. They were loose-fitting, reached to the knee, and were slit for a short way at the top of the back seam to aid the knee's bending. Their tops, as in the past, turned over to show a gaily-coloured lining. Some boots were tight-fitting and well-shaped, laced by points (laces with metal ends) to the belt or breeches at the side. They were very decorative and were often slashed at the knee to show contrasting silks or taffetas. Materials for these were mostly leather. Buskins were made of a softer Spanish leather or of velvet, and were lined with real fur or coney.

Pattens developed into a kind of overshoe at this period, although the original types still continued to be worn. They had a wooden sole with an open leather vamp and latchets for tying, or a wooden sole of one piece without a fastening, consisting of a toe-piece into which the shoe fitted; alternatively it was a larger version of an existing shoe which fitted almost completely over other footwear. Contemporary accounts all vary in description and there are many versions. Pattens, though still worn to protect a delicate shoe from mud, ceased to be fashionable footwear in the second half of the previous century, but continued to be worn as a necessity. The wood used was aspen, being light, and the sole was often carved to leave transverse bars under the heel and instep, much in the same manner as those found in Japan called *Geta* and made of bamboo. It will be remembered that the Romans and Greeks had a similar style. A few leather pattens were also worn.

Cockers were leather leggings, or high-laced boots, worn around 1514 by the countrymen, huntsmen and fishermen to protect the legs.

Boot-hose were items of clothing worn at this time and we shall see them develop as the years advance. At first they were inelegant stockings of a practical nature made to wear over the new silk stockings to protect them against the rub of the boot. In later years they became ornamental, were made of a finer material and were embroidered and edged with lace. They had bound or stitched tops and were sometimes fastened with decorative points to the breeches. Points were, in a way, the origin of our suspenders and garters. Stubbes, in his *Anatomy of Abuses*, has a great deal to say about them.

Stockings were largely tailored and cut to fit from material cut on the cross, as knitting was not yet sufficiently developed to be used extensively. By 1600 this kind of stocking was almost entirely replaced by knitted hose. A stocking frame came into being in 1589 and this affected the stocking trade considerably. The new kind of stocking improved the look of the leg and the shoe, since it gave a trim line to the ankle. Above the ankle bone these stockings were decorated with embroidered clocks which were very beautifully designed. There is a wide and interesting collection of stockings with clocks at the Assembly Rooms in Bath. Silk, of course, was for the wealthier classes and wool for the poorer. Sometimes people wore two pairs for warmth.

Socks and garters were also worn by both sexes. These garters developed from ornamental bands of ribbon, taffeta or sarsanet, sometimes trimmed with diamonds and gold lace, and with fringed ends. Ladies wore cross-gartered ribbons as garters.

Women's stockings were also growing in importance. They were long, tailored to fit and gartered at the knee by a knotted strip of material. Sometimes this strip was developed into a buckled band of material which lent itself to embroidery. Pattens were common for women, especially perhaps because their shoes were frequently made in more delicate materials. Otherwise their shoes looked very much like those of the men, but they did not wear boots.

Soles were still flat as there were no raised heels before 1600, though a low wedge made a tentative appearance. Some of the ultra-fashionable had possibly experimented with a high wedge by 1598, but there is no definite proof of this. Cork was used to thicken the soles and felt was used for tennis shoes.

Light shoes for both sexes were made of the skins of deer, goat, sheep. White leather was common, especially for women. After 1560 gimped slashes, without an underlay, decorated the vamps. Uppers were cut in three pieces and seamed at the sides and back. A few were cut in two pieces with no back seam, but these do not appear to have fitted very well. Until 1570 expensive shoes were cut in one piece, but most will be seen to have other seams. Soles were always separately made and were added by stitching to the finished shoe.

Leather jerkins were important for outdoor wear both for civilians and soldiery, having begun as military garments but been adapted in many ways for civilian use. They were known as "buff" jerkins as they were made of buff or spruce, which was ox leather dressed with oil and given a velvet surface. Buff eventually came to mean the colour of this leather and not the leather itself. These jerkins were cut in narrow panels, from waist to chest, laced and fastened like other jerkins. They were very practical as they were both warm and waterproof. A jerkin of this kind is described in the Inventory of Sir Thomas Bonham, in 1551. Jerkins were also often made in Spanish leathers, and later in materials which were plain or embroidered.

TUDOR

Man

Stiff-crowned copatain head-dress trimmed with small plume. Embroidered shirt (only worn by nobility) and stomacher. Doublet belted at waist and pleated. Sleeveless jerkin. Breeches-hose over leg-hose. Prominent decorated cod-piece.

Woman

Gable head-dress with black veil. Square-necked gown showing lace of chemise. Wide fur-banded sleeves narrowing to the shoulder. Fitted bodice. Skirt divided at front to show undergown.

1. The patten, made of wood in its simplest form, follows the shape of the shoe's toe. Held on by its thick leather strap and nails.
2. Rounded and cut from one block of wood. Worn by men and women alike.
3. Slashed mules sometimes made of velvet or brocade or coloured leathers.
4. Alternatively made of a low shoe shape and held on by a satin or velvet ribbon.
5. A black leather shoe with an extreme square toe, banded with coloured leather and showing puffed satin through the slashes.
6. Three women's shoes showing versions of the slashing form of decoration. Worn over bare legs or hose, for the upper classes, with a contrast lining rolled over the top.
7. Peasant shoe in plaited straw.

31. TUDOR (I)

Rush shoes
of the peasants

1. Bar-shoes with very square toes fashionable for both men and women. Fastened with a button with high-cut or low vamps and a strong sole. Plain, black, worn by the peasant classes; slashed with coloured satin puffs, worn with varying toe-widths by the upper classes.
2. Toes often parti-coloured and deeply padded.
3. Black and white striped socks form the leg of a black leather shoe slashed at the toe and puffed with white satin. The sock and shoe in one piece.
4. Slip-on shoe, the general shape for men and women though with many alternatives.
5. Peasant shoe, crude and clumsy and cut from thick leather; worn over bare legs or ill-fitting white stockings with bars or lace for fastenings.
6. A high boot in soft leather or felt with toes of the fashionable shape, tied under the knee. The top pulled up over the knee or folded down. For the upper classes the boot's top revealed a contrast lining when turned down.

32. TUDOR (II)

1
2
3
4
5
6

1. Man's black hide shoe with coloured satin pulled through the slashes. The toe has a slight point and there are at least two thicknesses of leather for the sole.
2. Crenellated shoe with coloured satin pulled through vertical slashes. Worn over coloured hose.
3. Peak-fronted leather shoe with coloured satin slashes.
4. The toe often as wide as 5½ inches. Made from thick black or brown hide, yellow or white satin puffed through the slashes, the colours of the Spanish influence.
5. Fashionable mules held on with satin ribbons attached to a double thickness sole. Most toes were padded at this stage with moss or wool. When they reached 6 inches they were limited to that by law.
6. Mules worn over coloured hose and decorated with satin loops.
7. Boots still an important item for men since riding was still the main form of transport. Tight, with soft tops they come to just under the knee.
8. Loose-fitting, square-toed boots just covering the ankle.
9. "Cow-mouth" toe. Square-toed shoe with padded "ears" at corners.

33. TUDOR (III)

1
2
3
4
5
5½″
6
7
8
9

1. Duckbilled shoe in soft leather or felt with wing-cut top and wide toe.
2. Duckbilled shoe of different widths but they are the linking fashion between the extreme point and the extreme square. Both square and pointed at the same time. This one has a low back and a high-cut zig-zag cut front.
3. Same shoe cut from wool or felt, in plain colours for the lower classes and in colours for the rest. Fits very loosely.
4. Ankle-boot, often with a stand-away cuff.
5. Ribbon decoration in various forms often just as loops on an otherwise plain shoe.
6. Many eccentricities of shape at this period showing the confusion between the two opposing fashions of the early period. Toes well padded to keep their shape, with wool or moss or hair.

34. TUDOR (IV)

Wide Tudor toes reached their maximum in this period

10

The Tudors (II): The Elizabethans

Queen Elizabeth, 1558–1603

THIS IS THE PERIOD regarded as the Golden Age of our history; it was also a period of adventure, discovery and upheaval. Queen Elizabeth's reign of forty-five years saw many changes in fashion. There are many plays which clearly indicate the clothes of these years, and there are numerous paintings and other records to which we may refer. The clothes of the wealthy were made of extravagantly rich fabrics, and money was spent freely on jewellery, embroidery, and ornament.

The general shape of fashion remained similar to that of the period before, that of King Henry VIII. The width remained and was augmented by panniers and enormous ruffs, and this width was echoed in the square winged houses of the Tudor style.

Nevertheless the Elizabethan age was a turning point in fashion, which, influenced by changes in people's way of life, began to take on a look that is recognizable as the basis of many of our styles. It was a period of prosperity which allowed many developments that had been impossible before, and this in turn brought many material benefits within reach of more people. Apart from religious controversy, the country was at peace, although not peacefully attuned to all her neighbours, and life was more settled than it had been.

A settled time brings stability all round and is reflected in the clothes which are worn. At this time, apart from decoration and rich jewellery there was not a great deal of difference in the clothes of different ranks.

Carriages were coming much more into use, though as yet they were uncomfortable and without springs. Litters were another form of transport and were the precursors of the sedan chair; the occupant of the litter was carried in a curtained chair, supported by four servants. Pillion riding on the back of a horse was the most usual form of transport for women, though many were horsewomen in their own right.

Transport being easier and much safer, people were able to get about more and shoes were now much more strongly reinforced under the foot. There are many examples in museums which have two and three thicknesses of leather for protection. Pattens were still worn by many.

Shoemakers had open shops, as did other merchants, and apprentices making fashionable shoes were to be seen in every town. Experiments with heels were made and it is in

Elizabeth's reign that the first ones made an appearance. Cork soles called *pisnets* and *pantoffles* were also worn. These had a heel about an inch and a half high and their wearers had great difficulties in managing them. So unaccustomed to heels were they that they found these new "heels" were uncomfortable and their calves often swelled and their legs became painful and had to be bandaged. Every possible colour was used in these shoes as sumptuary laws had ceased to be effective. The most fashionable colours were russet, saffron, black, white, red, green, watchet, blue, yellow and pink.

Hose were tighter and better-fitting and were made in as many colours as the shoes and clothes. They were made from jernsey, worsted, crewell, yarn, thread, and, of course, the fashionable silk. During the early part of her reign Queen Elizabeth was presented with a pair of silk stockings and after wearing them she decided she would not wear hose of any other thread. Such stockings could cost about five pounds a pair (a vast sum in those days).

Light-coloured leather shoes in contemporary portraits show the development of the front, which gained height, until very soon it became a tongue. The Queen wore high-tongued shoes that were often made in white silk to match the rest of her white clothes, a colour she favoured as symbolic of her Virgin Queen status.

Shoes from Spain influenced those of the rest of Europe, with the exception of the Moorish shoes which were still a popular Spanish fashion; these had turned-up toes and were lavishly adorned with Byzantine embroidery. Embroidery, however, had an important place in English shoe fashions, and brocades were much favoured for ladies' shoes. The Reformation had put an end to ecclesiastical embroidery in church hangings and altar cloths; many of these had been taken down from churches, and if not destroyed were used to make clothes and domestic hangings. So the artistic minds that had created them turned to other forms of expression and used their talents on gloves, clothes, shoes, purses, and wall hangings, and on many other articles to be seen in museums. The Hardwick portrait of Elizabeth at Hardwick Hall, in the possession of the Duke of Devonshire, shows this embroidery at its best and most luxuriant, down to the slashed and decorated shoes.

There are many chroniclers of this period who mention shoes in their correct setting, and it is interesting to compare the writings of Stubbes, Coryat and Morryson with contemporary portraits by people like Antonio Moro (1512–76), El Greco (1554–1614), and Rubens (1577–1640), a Fleming whose country was part of the Spanish dominions. There is so much evidence of Spanish influence in clothes and colour that the Spanish painters are valuable as recorders of fashion. At home, Nicholas Hilliard's portraits of the period are also useful, since he lived from 1547–1619 and so covered the whole of the Elizabethan period. His famous painting of Sir Christopher Hatton in the Victoria and Albert Museum is typical. Sir Christopher wears the emblem of the Garter over one high soft boot which is pinked and cut. His feet are thrust into pantoffles, slippers with cork platforms, which cover the instep and were worn over boots by many people on the bad roads of the time.

Stubbes says of the Tudor period: "... they wear corked shoes, pisnets and fine pantouffles, which lift them up a finger or two off the ground, some are of white leather, some of black, some of red, some of grene, razed, caruet, cut and stitched all over with silk, and laid on with gold, silver, and such like ..."

Shakespeare's Hamlet refers to chopines, when he says the players were "nearer to heaven by the height of a chopine." And Ben Jonson, in his play *Everyman out of his Humour*, says they "tread on Corked stilts at pris'nor's pace."

ELIZABETHAN

Pearl and jewel hair decoration. High whisk of lace round neck. Dress richly quilted, embroidered with pearls and jewels; padded shoulder-wings or epaulets; square neckline. Stiff stomacher down front of bodice. Skirt held out from waist by drum-shaped farthingale. Waist encircled by box-pleated waist ruff.

1. Leather shoe with diamond cut-outs which show colour of stocking underneath. Tied tab and bow. Thick sole leather runs through to top of heel.

2. Tall cuffed and slashed boot with protective leather guard round back of heel. Even on riding boots the toe is slashed to pull contrast material through.

3. Cork-covered chopine or platform, has a slashed and cut-out leather mule attached. Generally called a pantoffle when the shoe consisted only of a vamp. Worn over coloured hose, by women. Note the square back.

4. The position for correctly placing the heels had not yet been discovered, and though still in their early stages, in this reign, heels were attached in many ways. Slashing still continued, and the toe was narrowing.

5. Riding boots also with heels and rosette decorations. They often covered the knee, but could be turned back.

6. The stylizing of the cross motif, still a feature of ecclesiastical footwear. A crude version of a platform and sole made its appearance.

7. A single-bar shoe in cow-hide, as worn by country people, men and women. It had a rough form of buckle fastening.

35. ELIZABETHAN (I)

1
2
3
4
5
6
7

1. Red painted heel made from layers of leather suits this high-cut square-toed shoe. Although in fairly heavy leather it was decorated with a silk rosette.

2. A mule with a leather sole and red leather heel. A ribbon and an underlaid cut-out forms the decoration.

3. Shoe with high-cut sides and laced with a colourful knot of silk ribbon spreading quite wide and indicating a coming trend.

4. A square toe of this shape now almost universal, and the most universal form of decoration was still the ribbon rosette, which was getting larger.

5. There are still leather shoes with large cut-outs, but not all with puffs of colour under them, some being left empty to show the coloured hose.

6. Still a certain number of pointed toes about, in spite of the wide squares which were typical of the period, but these no longer fashionable. Dandies begin to wear heels, but still some shoes are flat to the ground.

7. Linen stocking laced at ankle and seamed at back.

36. ELIZABETHAN (II)

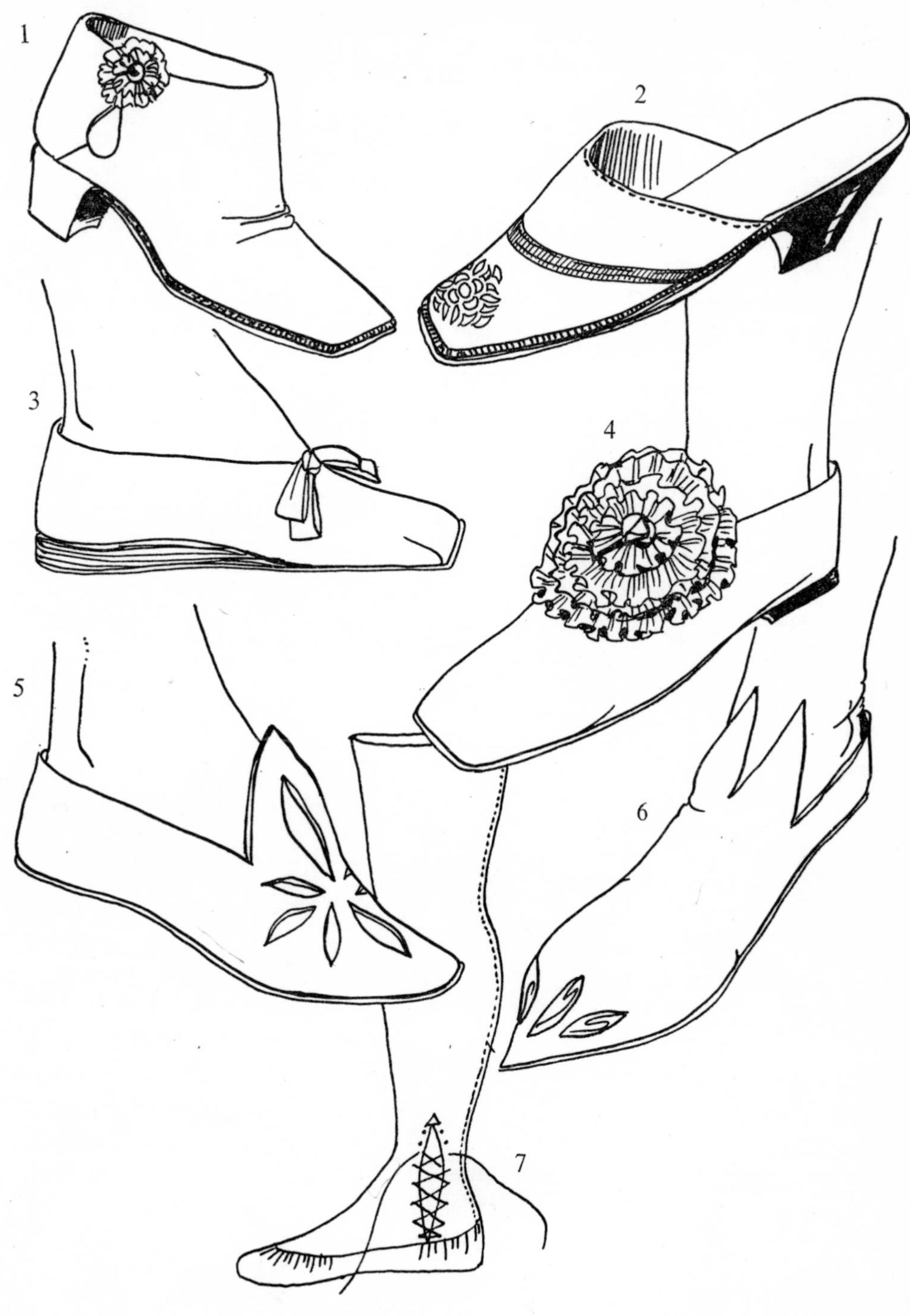
1
2
3
4
5
6
7

11

The Stuarts, 1603—1649

James I (VI of Scotland), 1603–1625 Charles I, 1625–1649

JAMES WAS A POOR MAN with a rich inheritance, and not an Englishman. Scotland and England were not united until later in his reign. Because of the continual border battles and James's parsimony, costume was more sober than in the previous reigns and fashion and colour had become much quieter. Nevertheless, a new style had begun to evolve and what we call the "Stuart" period (although it includes the Cromwellian influences) began to take shape. Men wore bombasted breeches as they had done in Elizabeth's reign, but they were not quite so exaggeratedly wide. (Our word "bombastic" comes from this material bombast, which was used to make clothes stand out.)

At the beginning of this period many changes took place and James had to adapt himself to fashions of which he did not approve. Breeches showed the main change of shape. At first wide at the top and tapering to the knee, they were decorated with lace, striped with velvet ribbon and embroidery, and padded for protection. It is said that James had so many enemies that he had to conform to the fashions in order to wear padded protection beneath his clothes, where it could not be seen. If it had been visible it would have made him even more unpopular than did his accession.

All laws concerning dress were repealed because they were ineffectual and inefficient. In spite of his disapproval of luxury and of money spent on fashion, James conformed and his era became as luxurious and decorative as the earlier reigns had been, but in a different way. It is yet another example of fashion having to reach its extremes before it can change. The Tudors had reached the ultimate in squareness, in both padded breeches for men and farthingales for women, and in the wide and high ruff for both sexes. Thus we find the years of James's reign becoming the transitional period between the Tudors and the extremes of decoration in which the Cavaliers indulged before Cromwell brought fashion to an abrupt halt.

The shape of breeches, diverting attention from the hips to the knees, focused attention on legs and shoes. Although not effeminate, men's clothes became softer and they had a closer affinity to women's. Both men and women wore lace ruffs at the beginning of the reign, and these were to develop into the wide and familiar lace collars. The lace wrist ruffles increased in size and became deep cuffs of linen, edged frothily with beautiful lace. Knots of ribbon decorated every part of the costume, especially the shoulders, the waist, the wrists, and the garters. Some garters were a form of drawstring, hung with tassels and made of gold braid, which pulled in the puff of the breeches at the knee.

Instead of being vertical like the Plantagenets, or square and horizontal like the Tudors, the Stuart exaggeration of fashion was gentle and downward. The only thing that was upward was the cut of the "*Bucket*" boot, which encased the foot and leg in a wide funnel shape. In time the tops of these boots echoed the lace of the collars and cuffs and were ornamented with knots of ribbon.

In the National Gallery and the National Portrait Gallery in London there are many portraits which illustrate these boots, and there are many actual examples in country houses and museums to testify to their magnificance. Authorities assert that the very wide boot of Charles I, decorated with lace and ribbons, did not exist exactly as the painters illustrate it, but this must remain a matter of opinion as much of the other illustrated costume is relatively accurate.

The development of these boots is interesting to note. A portrait of Robert Devereux, Earl of Essex, by Hollar, shows deep tops cut of the same stiff leather as the rest of the boot. The tops are lined with beige or white linen, which shows slightly at the top in a fine edge. They must have had some sort of stiffening inside to keep them rigid as the boots themselves softened into folds at the ankle. Stirrup leathers fastened a large leather plaque over the front of the instep of the boot: this was a fashion we find in boots up to the Georgian period. The toes were deep and square and the sole heavily welted; the heel, now well established and generally accepted, was broad, thick, and rather clumsy in shape.

This continued to be a basic shape for boots throughout the period, but the changes in fashion were marked by the gradual increase in size of the bucket top and its lace linings and other ornaments. Whilst the toe shape remained without a great deal of alteration, the width and size of the leather stirrup plaque had interesting variations. The heel, whilst remaining more or less the same thickness, grew higher as time progressed and at times was pushed right under the arch.

Stays were used in clothes to keep their shape, for both men and women, so it is not surprising to find them in boots when the cuff grew larger and too heavy for the sides to support them unaided. White was a favourite colour and many men were clothed from head to foot in white velvet. When this was the mode even white leather was used for the sword belt. A typical outfit for a gentleman of the period added white silk embroidered stockings pulled over white hose and rolled at the knee and shoes with white rosettes. Colour was introduced into such a costume only by the red heels which were now coming into favour.

This fancy for white led to the use of a great deal of white lace inside the boot tops, which often contained secret pockets. In these tops a man could conceal his letters, a perfume pad, his gloves, and a pistol if need be.

Two books of the period—Dekker's *Gul's Horn-booke* (1609) and Henry Fitzgeffery's *Notes from Black Fryers* (1617)—take a satirical look at the fashions of the day and both mock the extravagances of the times.

Low-topped shoes were growing fashionable now and were beginning to look more recognizably like our own. There was still considerable indecision about the placing of heels and they varied from the very flat to about two inches in height, with much allowance for the wearer's taste. It had not yet been decided which was the correct place to attach them for comfort and, although we find many examples of heels placed under the arch in what seems a most uncomfortable position, we can also find examples of heels set well back.

This whole period was one of experiments with shoes, as can be seen from a study of the paintings and drawings in art galleries. There is a common basic shape but, as in our own time, it has many variants of detail. The one feature common to most shoes, however, is the decoration called a shoe-rose. This also varied in size, depth and width, and colour, and though it began modestly enough it was to achieve enormous proportions. In fact, it is listed in many inventories of household and personal accounts as costing as much as, if not more than, the shoes themselves. Made of looped ribbon, lace or looped leather, it was in a colour to match or contrast with that of the shoe. Shoe roses matched the garters, which at this time were in the form of a sash, tied in a bow with lace-trimmed ends, at the side of the leg. *Friar Bacon's Prophesie* (1604) says: "When roses in the gardains grow, not in ribons on a shoe . . . and ribon-roses take such place, that garden roses want their grace," a lament that fashion had overtaken nature.

Some slashing remained during the early years of the period, but this was much more subdued and on the whole the vamps of shoes were plain, cut high, and with tall tabs to support the big shoe-roses.

There was not a great deal of marked difference between men's and women's shoes. It seemed that women's feet, at last beginning to show from the Elizabethan period onwards, were making up for lost time. On them were worn rosettes, knots of ribbon, lace, and leather. There were women's shoes with high pleated vamps, some made of ribbon, with curved red heels stitched at the front and base, and there were also riding boots and mules.

This is a period of which the fashions are amply recorded by the marble effigies in churches of the time. The detail in them is well worth the student's attention, for, although simplified, it is contemporary evidence of who wore what, and when.

The price of shoes is interesting, but it must be remembered, of course, that the relative value of the pound was much more than it appears in these notes from various household accounts. The Wardrobe Accounts of Prince Henry, dated 1608, lists a pair of laced shoes at 3s. 6d. At Saffron Walden, in Essex, a list of shoes in a diary is noted as "2 pairs of shoes, 6s. 6d; 1 pair of shoes 3s. od; 1 pair of boots and shoes £1." This is dated for 1630 by a foreign gentleman who lived in England for two years, mixing in the highest social circles. In Dillon's revision of Fairholt's *Costume in England* he notes that a pair of boots at this time cost 11 shillings, and adds that this is about the same relative cost as when his book was printed in 1885.

An interesting account, often related in costume books, is that of Count Gondomar, the Spanish Ambassador, who said that the citizens of London seemed always ready to go somewhere, as they were always booted and spurred. It was generally assumed at this period that a man must be a gentleman if he wore boots and spurs at all times. But a caustic comment of the time adds that many wore boots because they wished to appear to own horses when they did not.

Leather was considerably softer at the beginning of the Stuart years, as is evidenced by the wrinkles at the ankle, which were much prized. Boots were even padded and quilted to give this appearance. But, as the more austere years of Cromwell approached, leather increased in toughness and boots became heavier.

There were four phases of Stuart fashion in the seventeenth century, all of which, though variants on a similar theme, were different from each other. The first was that of James I which, until the end of his reign, was a bulky fashion. During the reign of Charles I a slimmer elegance prevailed, because of the downward trend of clothes. The Puritans and Cavaliers were an amalgam of these two lines of fashion. The Restoration of the Stuarts brought fashions from France with the return of Charles II in 1660.

STUART

Man

Royalist Cavalier. Shoulder-length hair; Van Dyck beard. Short-waisted doublet over tubular breeches. Panels of fancy ribbon and braiding as decoration. Van Dyck collar at neck. Linen boot-hose.

Woman

Hair longer with ringlets at side and high coiled chignon; curled fringe. Low- or high-necked gown with large lace collar. Fairly high waist trimmed with tabs. Lace cuffs on shorter sleeves. Mirror tied to waist.

1. Leather shoe, usually black, with high tongue, tied with a silk ribbon. Leather sole extends full length of shoe and forms a wedge; sometimes red-covered.
2. White brocade boudoir slipper with lace-fall and rosette.
3. There is almost the same basic shape to men's and women's shoes alike. With or without rosettes and "windmill" tailored ties. Men's shoes of leather, women's of silk or brocade and bound with silk. Heels, whatever their shape, are under-set.
4. Heels about 2 inches high, covered in leather, under-set.
5. Women's high-cut shoe, coloured brocade, with lace-fall collar.
6. Floral brocade, bound with silk, with tailored bow.
7. Leather shoe, with or without the added decoration of a rosette or bow. Large leather-covered heel with through sole.

37. STUART (I)

1
2
3
4
5
6
7

1. Brocade shoe with self pattern over-embroidered with cord on the vamp and with criss-cross gold thread at the instep. High, thick heel with minute stitching at breast, continuing into the sole.

2. Ribbed silk shoe bound with silk. Narrow square toe extends beyond the sole.

3. Leather shoe with narrow square toe. Intricate floral cut-outs show colours of stocking beneath. Silk ties over tall narrow tongue. Stitched heel cover on high under-set heel. Cut-outs sometimes replaced by heavy embroidery.

4. Gold braiding on olive-green velvet.

5. French silk slipper with neat silk rosette, worn with cork-soled pantoffle. Not a fashion developed in England to any extent, but sometimes found among the footwear of the French court in London.

6. Embroidered stockings, an important leg-wear fashion, held with garter under the knee. Long, narrow, rounded or square-toed shoe with deeply-open sides. Very large coloured silk rosette.

38. STUART (II)

1
2
3
4
5
6

1. The frilly "bastard" boot had various widths. Out of date by the 1660s and worn only by the officers of the cavalry and other horsemen. Stirrup-guards of quatrefoil shape and attached by leather "rivets."
2. Embroidered or cut-out leather shoes, deeply cut at the sides but high under the ankle, sport rosettes and lace of great extravagance.
3. Buff leather boot with triple lace frill. The square toe is as square as the stirrup-leather, which is attached to the straps by leather knots.
4. Under the boot, loose-fitting silk stockings worn, protected by a linen boot-stocking, and decorated with a large silk rosette.
5. Woman's shoe of brocade, plain or ornamented with a soft knot of ribbons. The heel is under-set and is continued under the instep and sole as a continuous piece of leather.
6. Double-soled shoe in striped silk with thick sole of covered wood or cork. Women's shoes are also decorated with extravagant rosettes.

39. STUART (III)

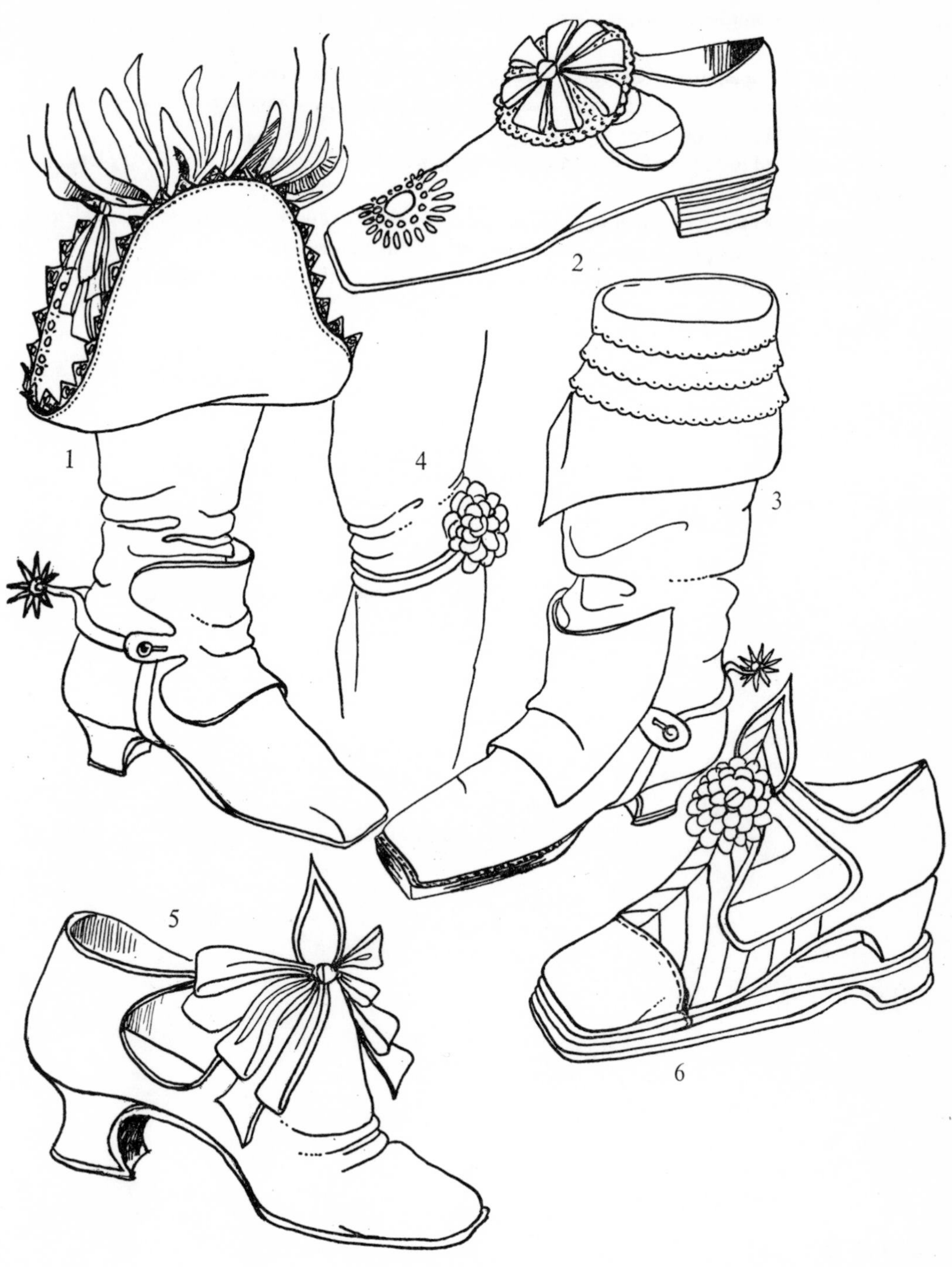
1
2
3
4
5
6

1. Square-toed leather shoe bound with silk. The ribbon tie, also of silk, is wide and stiff.

2. Rosettes, large and decorative, made of silk and sometimes jewelled. Red heels, becoming higher, fashionable.

3. Plaques of all shapes, mainly as a stirrup-guard, cover the front of the boot or shoe. This boot, with deep cuff, worn over a loose-fitting linen stocking, known as boot hose, with a lace collar or French fall. Even boots could add a pair of leather pattens.

4. Toes, longer and still square but with a deep doming over the toe. Vamp and tongue very long, and the tailored bow set high.

5. The bucket-boot top, a common sight and of various shapes, worn over full breeches. Stirrup-leather guards, sometimes boldly square and following the outline of the deep toe shape.

6. Thick black leather with red leather-covered heels and worn by the aristocracy from 1660.

40. STUART (IV)

1
2
3
4
5
6
Wide spreading
windmill bow

12

Chopines

EVER SINCE MAN has concerned himself with fashion, he has sought to add to his height, by means of his shoes or his head-dress, and often both together. From the earliest times and in many countries there have been several versions of what we now call the platform sole. The Greeks gave added height to the chief actors of their dramas and gave them a visible importance by means of the Cothurnus, and the Emperors of China emphasized their power with the aid of deeply-layered soles. Some eastern shoes were balanced on a single pillar of painted wood, which was attached in the centre of the sole under the arch. These shoes are indicative of another reason for the continued use of platforms and why they are found in different forms and heights across the ages.

In the East women's activity and freedom were restricted by high stilts which had the same effect as the bound "lily foot" of China. There were no utilitarian reasons for these high platforms, because the women who wore them were not required to go out on the wet and muddy road. They restricted a woman in her walking, which in fact was impossible without the assistance of a servant, or even two, and this itself served as a status symbol; they rendered her stance unstable and therefore added to the men's feeling of superiority.

For more practical purposes, however, thick soles were always a necessity until proper pavements made it possible to walk without having to go through mud and wet. Fashion often develops from a necessity and soon makes an essential into an attractive accessory. The platforms, the stilts, the layered soles became decorative and ornamental, and the wooden pattens which had become commonplace in England were influenced by the extravagant fashion for chopines which came from Venice.

These were indeed a status symbol since the tottering walk they created was impossible without the support of servants, and this by itself indicated that they were worn only by the upper and wealthy classes. They did not reach great heights in England, though there are excellent examples in various museums of these beautiful "shoes." Some were covered in white kid or silk, and were delicately tooled or embroidered. Some were even painted by the eminent painters of the day with scenes depicting the wearer's interests. The chopine itself was the forerunner of the heel, as was the patten-and was the ancestor of the "platform" shoe made famous in the 1940s when it reached its jewelled extreme in that worn by Carmen Miranda which was six inches or more in depth.

Some chopines were lightly indented under the sole, which gave them a slight "heeled" look; others were almost circular in the shape of the forepart; most had mules attached into which the stockinged foot slipped; but others had real shoes attached which fastened over the instep. This was largely the difference between the chopine and the patten . . the latter was held on by straps fastening over a separate shoe.

1. Extremely simple chopine with decorated bar of leather into which the wearer's own shoe fits with its flat heel.

2. Real shoes attached to the top of some chopines, with the fashionable toe and open cut-outs as seen in other shoes.

3. This chopine, typical of the extreme shape, has an attached shoe with a round toe; its platform base has a long tapering point.

4. A comparatively elementary shape could be studded with real jewels or depict a scene by an eminent painter commissioned specially.

5. A separate shoe of a basic shape following that of the foot, made of black leather and with an intricately cut-out vamp. The openwork vamp and tab show the contrast colour of hose. The shoe is typical of the type attached by straps to a chopine.

Chopines were a Venetian fashion which did not develop to any great importance in England. They are worthy of special mention because they are the first indications of the desire for a heel, which was not to develop fully for some years. They were rather more of a status symbol than anything else, as they were clearly indicative that a man had money when his wife needed the support of a servant on either side when walking. They were also proof of the fact that she had no intention of doing any work, or indeed of being anything but decorative.

41. CHOPINES (I)

1
2
3
4
5

1. The Victoria and Albert Museum has a chopine similar to this covered with white kid. About 18 inches high it has an attached mule. Its pointed toe was slightly tip-tilted.

2. High chopines appear in many forms among the fashionable. Worn only by women, this one has an attached mule, is highly tooled and ornamented.

3. Slim and standing nearly 24 inches high, this one is covered in cream leather. The attached mule is also made of cream leather.

4. Sometimes the chopine had a prow shape like the front of a ship, and a fluted platform. The mule has real jewels for decoration.

42. CHOPINES (II)

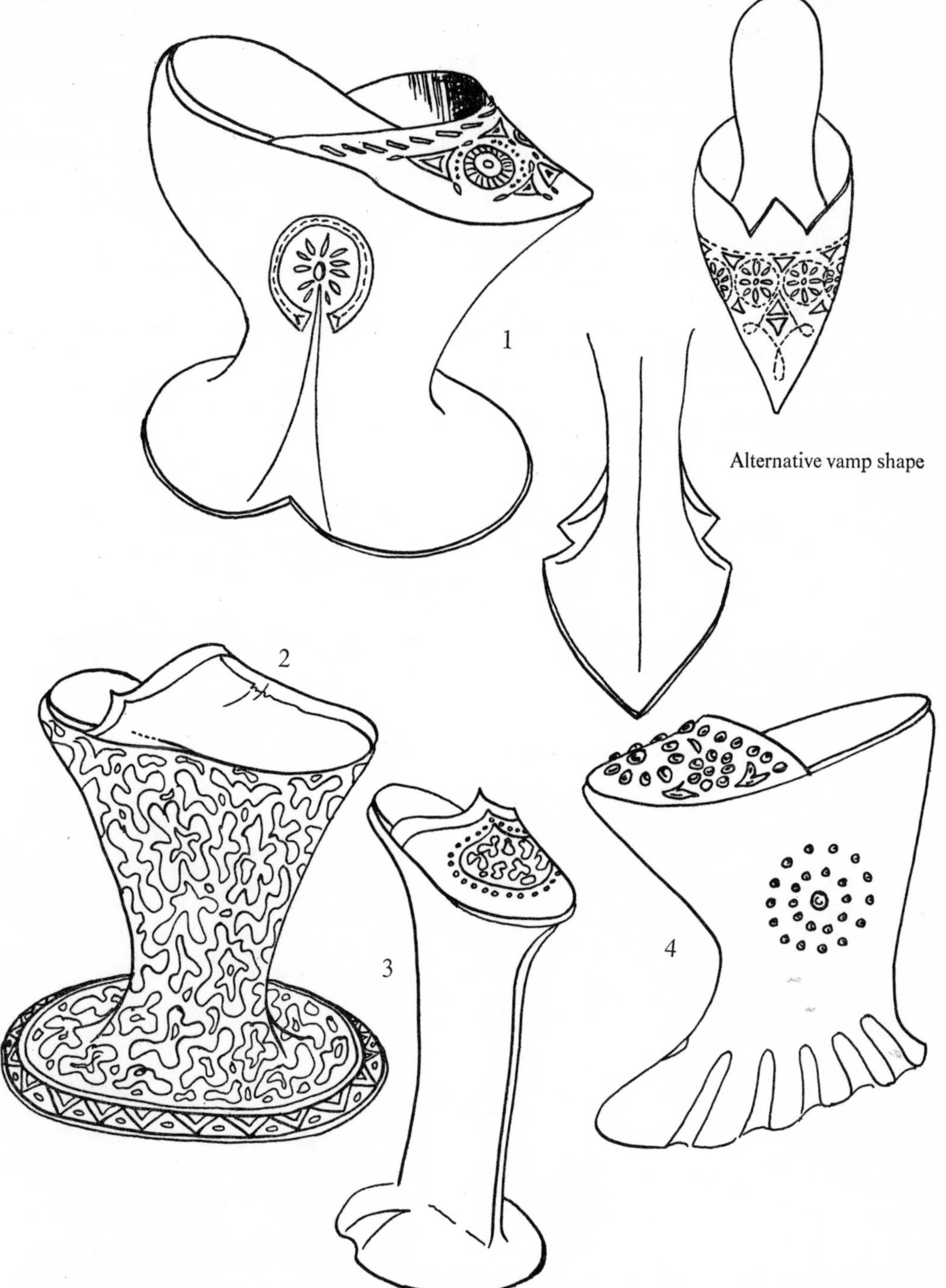
1
Alternative vamp shape
2
3
4

1. Venetian chopine made of cork covered in green velvet. Side view shows boat shape and wide spread at base. Decorated with frills of gold lace. Right-hand view shows sole shape. Third drawing shows square toe and alternative studded decoration round base.
2. Bound-foot shoe, the Lily Foot, from China. Made of silk and heavily embroidered. Note how the height of the heel supports the foot which walks on the toes.
3. Tabi sock and geta bamboo sandal from Japan. The toe of the sock is separated from the rest so that the straps of the sandal, made of padded velvet, may fit between them.
4. Embroidered silk and cotton pedestal shoe. Laminated leather cut to shape (or carved from a solid piece of wood) and painted white. From China.
5. Embroidered silk and cotton shoe with thick laminated leather "platform" painted white. For a man or a woman; from China.
6. Woman's sandal worn in the Far and Middle East, carved from pear or pomegranate wood and inlaid with ivory. Toe post is held by a peg underneath.
7. Red-lacquered sandal from the East, with red leather straps attached by brass nails. Carved bird's head and heel are ornamentally painted in gold and black.

43. CHOPINES (III) AND THEIR DESCENDANTS

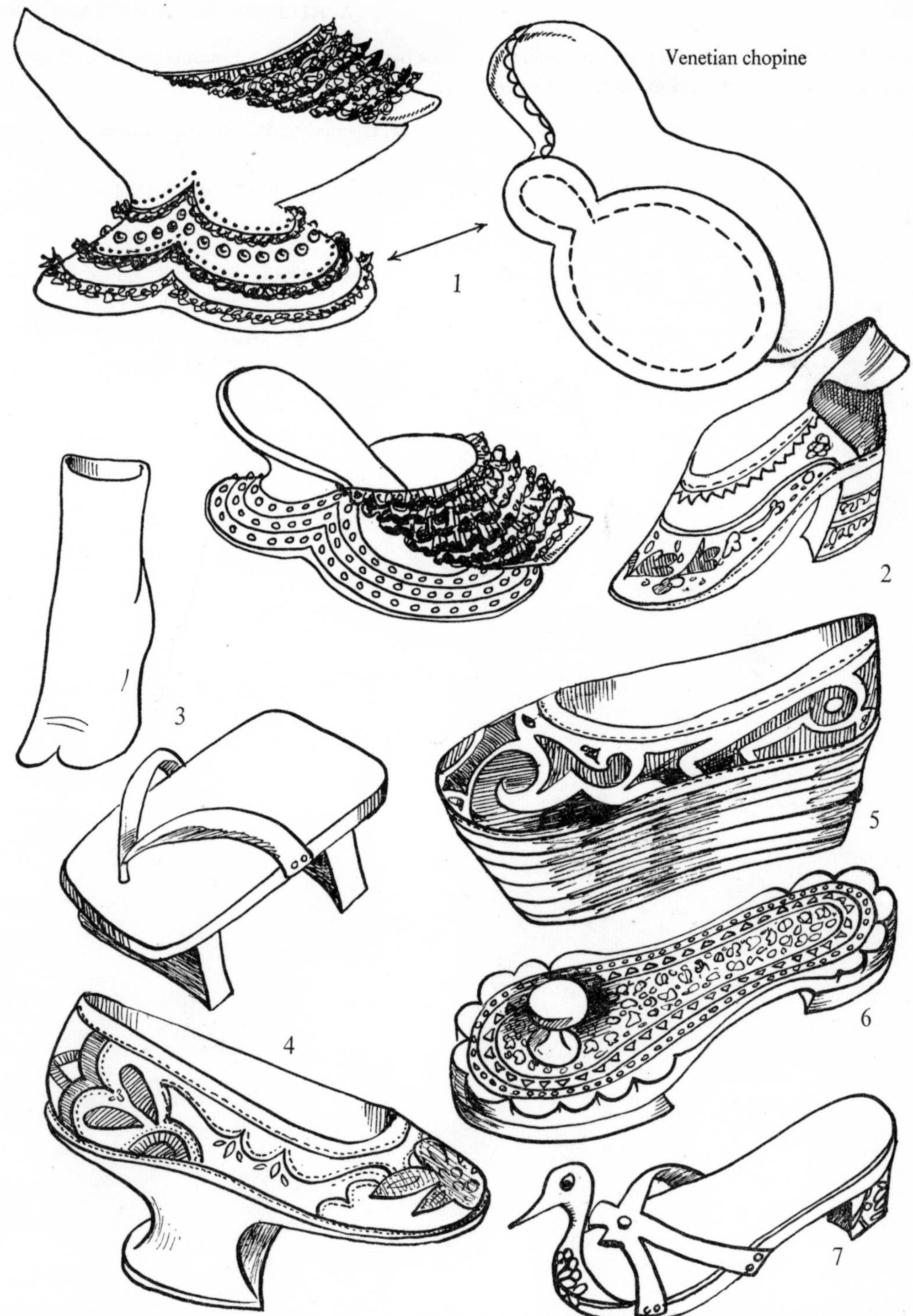
Venetian chopine
1
2
3
4
5
6
7

Though not related to the Chopine, the double-soled shoe has a similar effect of raising the heel. They are nearer in form to pattens and galoshes (see Georgian Period).

1. High straight heel covered in red kid on opened shoe, raised with double sole. Fastened with jewel through crude button hole.
2. Double-soled shoe with heavily decorated vamp, and shaped top-piece. Toe is long and waisted. Early 18th century.
3. Brocade shoe with large rosette and shaped heel.
4. High tabbed shoe with heavily-embroidered vamp. Note how stitching of heel continues down in a piping to the forepart (see detail in lower sketch).
5. A descendant of the chopine and the double sole is the modern wedge. This was one of the first to use Perspex. Inside was a white swan and green grass. A vulgar but interesting development.
6. A low wedge beach sandal moulded completely in rubber.

44. DOUBLE-SOLED SHOES

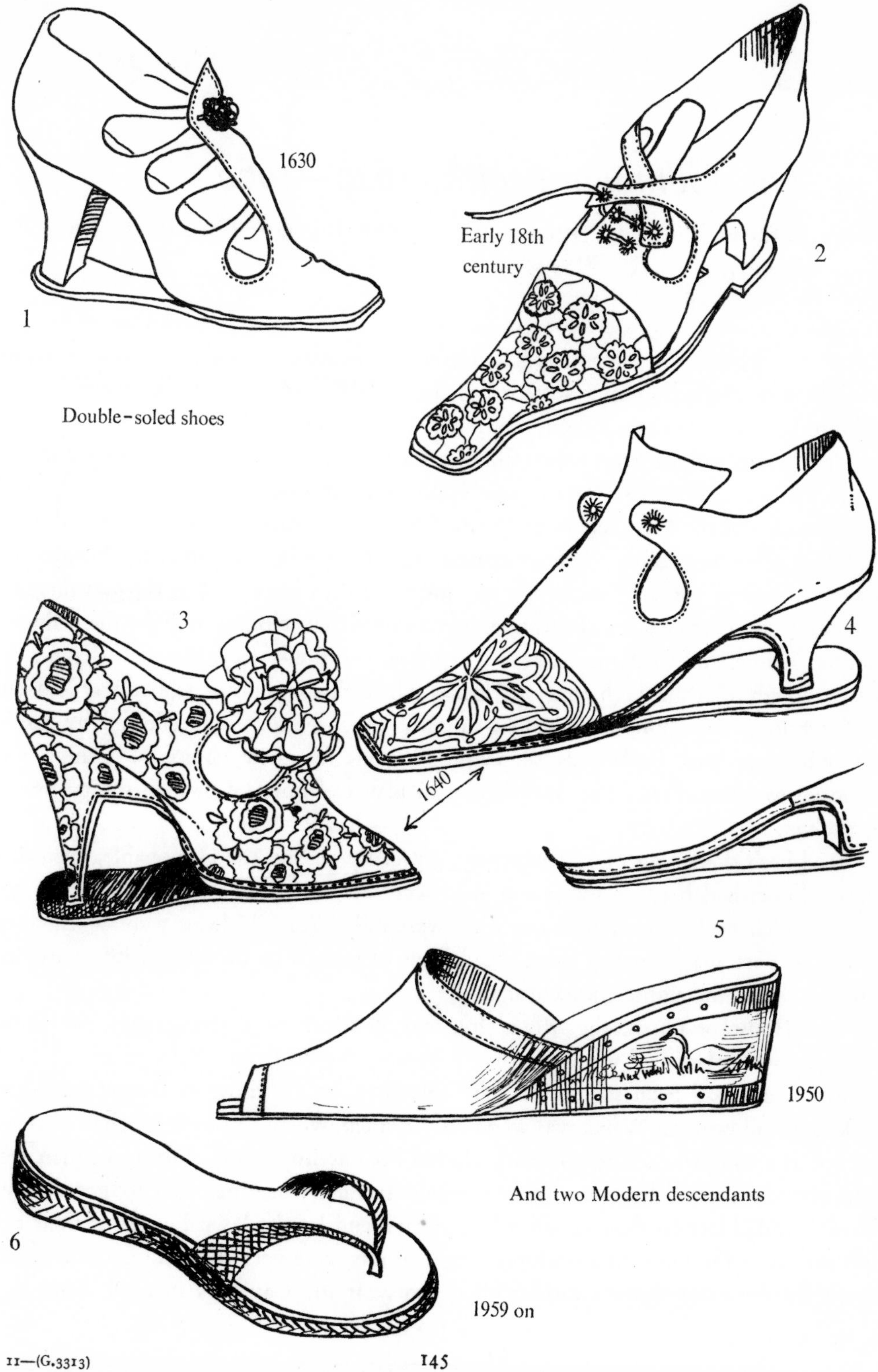
1630
1
Early 18th
century
2
Double-soled shoes
3
4
1640
5
1950
And two Modern descendants
6
1959 on

13

The Commonwealth, 1649—1660

Oliver Cromwell, Lord Protector, 1653–1658 Richard Cromwell, Lord Protector, 1658–1659

Without deliberately introducing it, Cromwell brought about a restraint in fashion which in turn created a better standard of design. His insistence on simplicity was not meant to be in the interests of fashion but there is no doubt that his reforms brought about that cleanness of pattern from which the best design evolves. It is worth noting that some of the extremes..plainness on the one hand and extravagance on the other..of the Roundheads and the Cavaliers, were intensified by their strong wishes to be as different from each other as possible. The accusation cannot fairly be levelled at the Puritans that they destroyed *all* pleasure in clothes, any more than it can be said of the Cavaliers that they indulged in it to excess. Both sides merely used their clothes to make their different opinions visible, and their means of self-expression naturally took different shapes. It is likely, though, that this is the only period in which this was done deliberately and with full intention; the opinions prevalent in most other periods are reflected by fashion only when we look back, because people's reasons for their choice of fashion were unknown to themselves. The spectators at a play see more of it than the performers themselves.

Red heels were seen more frequently, especially among the fashionable, even those whose clothes had become sober and who were in Cromwell's favour sported a little colour at their heels. From 1600 on, what were called "raised" heels were worn, as can be seen in portraits from this time. Red heels continued to be worn with court dress until the end of the eighteenth century.

The House of Lords, the Monarchy, and all forms of entertainment, the theatre especially, were abolished when Cromwell became the Protector. Gloom settled on the country which had been so gay and the colours worn by those in favour were grey, black, buff and brown. White was worn only as linen, which was very much in evidence, and not as a complete outfit. Military clothes became important, since most men wore them or were affected by them. A few rebellious men wore their hair longer than was allowed, added lace to their broad white collars, and let the lawn linings of their boot cuffs turn over the top into a scalloped edge. Boots were very much more close fitting, except for the extravagant swashbuckling footwear the Cavaliers strutted about in so arrogantly. They delighted in flaunting their long curled hair and their lace-trimmed ribbon-knotted clothes and as a result the Roundheads called them popinjays.

The Roundheads wore a great deal of leather, as armour, for physical protection of all kinds, and in the form of huge boots such as the one in Worcester Museum. This is a boot of the New Model Army and was found on the site of the Battle of Worcester. Although they were smallish, the men of the period must have been very tough to wear these boots, and when it is remembered that much of the rest of their clothing, their drinking bottles, their ammunition bags, etc., were also of the same heavy black leather their strength is indeed to be wondered at.

John Evelyn, the diarist, remarks on his surprise at seeing Venetian *Chopines*, and Giacomo Franco's costume book shows the extravagance of the Venetian costume from which they were derived. Although chopines were not seen to any great extent in Britain, because of the Civil War and Cromwell's dislike for fashion, the fact that Evelyn mentioned them as early as 1645 shows they did exist here. They were a development of the patten and were mostly of cork covered with leather or material. They could be of any height up to eighteen or even twenty-four inches.

Many books of the period mention clothes, but many records are lost because, in their excessive zeal, the Puritans destroyed many valuable paintings and books which would have depicted more clearly what was happening. They considered portrait painting, religious art, and a great deal of fashionable literature to be decadent, immoral, and inimical to the faith.

English art was so impoverished by these years that it has never entirely recovered. Art was mistrusted, and so were music and the stage. One has only to read Pepys to understand the difficulties of these years, which gave little incentive to fashion, yet which periodically effected great changes in the fashions of the time.

The extreme Puritan clothes had much in common with those worn by the Dutch, from which they came. The style of the tall black hat, banded by a leather strap with a brass buckle, was echoed in the blunt square toe of the shoe, also strapped and with a large square buckle. Note again the very close parallel between hats and shoes; this is a constant factor in most periods.

The austerely dressed man of the time wore a dark jacket, buttoned up high to a plain white collar, a broad buckled leather belt at the waist, knee breeches, and black stockings, with riding or plain black shoes. A woman dressed demurely, and the more extreme her Puritan beliefs the plainer her costume, although surprisingly enough the result was often very attractive indeed. It was considered seemly to wear always a snowy white apron, which indicated her domesticity. Royalist ladies echoed this fashion by mockingly adopting frilly, useless aprons with lace edging and flaring bows with trailing ends. The Puritan woman wore a tall hat like that of her husband and hid her hair neatly in a close-fitting, very becoming, linen cap; grey and black were the colours she favoured for clothes and shoes. The Royalists, however, wore long defiant ringlets and useless little caps of pretty materials, to match their dresses or lace, and on their feet pretty pumps of brocade with silver buckles and curving heels.

Buildings of this period were solid and plain, often unimaginative, similar to the Puritan clothes, for everything had to be utilitarian, functional, and serious.

George Fox the first of the Quakers (1624–1690), born at Drayton in Leicestershire, was the son of a weaver, but until he was twenty was a shoemaker and for his ride through the country on his mission, he made himself a suit of leather.

PURITAN

High steeple-crowned hats. Men's hair cropped. Woman's hair often hidden under mob-caps. Clothes shapeless with plain linen collars and cuffs. Colours generally black, brown and grey.

1. Wide-cuffed "bastard" boot, more of a French fashion than an English one, considerably influenced Cavalier styles. Of light coloured-leather and trimmed with lace, it has very extravagant shapes. Sometimes with pockets inside the cuff to hold a note or a lace handerchief.

2. Like other boots, the Cavalier boot has the leather stirrup-guard, made even wider now to match the cuff. The domed toe is seen on the square welted base.

3. A tall Dutch boot seen among traders in London. Made of brown buff with a collar of a lighter colour covered with white lace or broderie anglaise.

4. As the square toe lengthened and grew shallower, the bold cuff was replaced by a tall standing tab and "low shoes" were more fashionable. Fastened with a chased metal or jewelled buckle small and set high on a tab which turned back to show another colour.

5. A closer-fitting boot with a small contrast collar worn over silk breeches.

45. COMMONWEALTH (I)

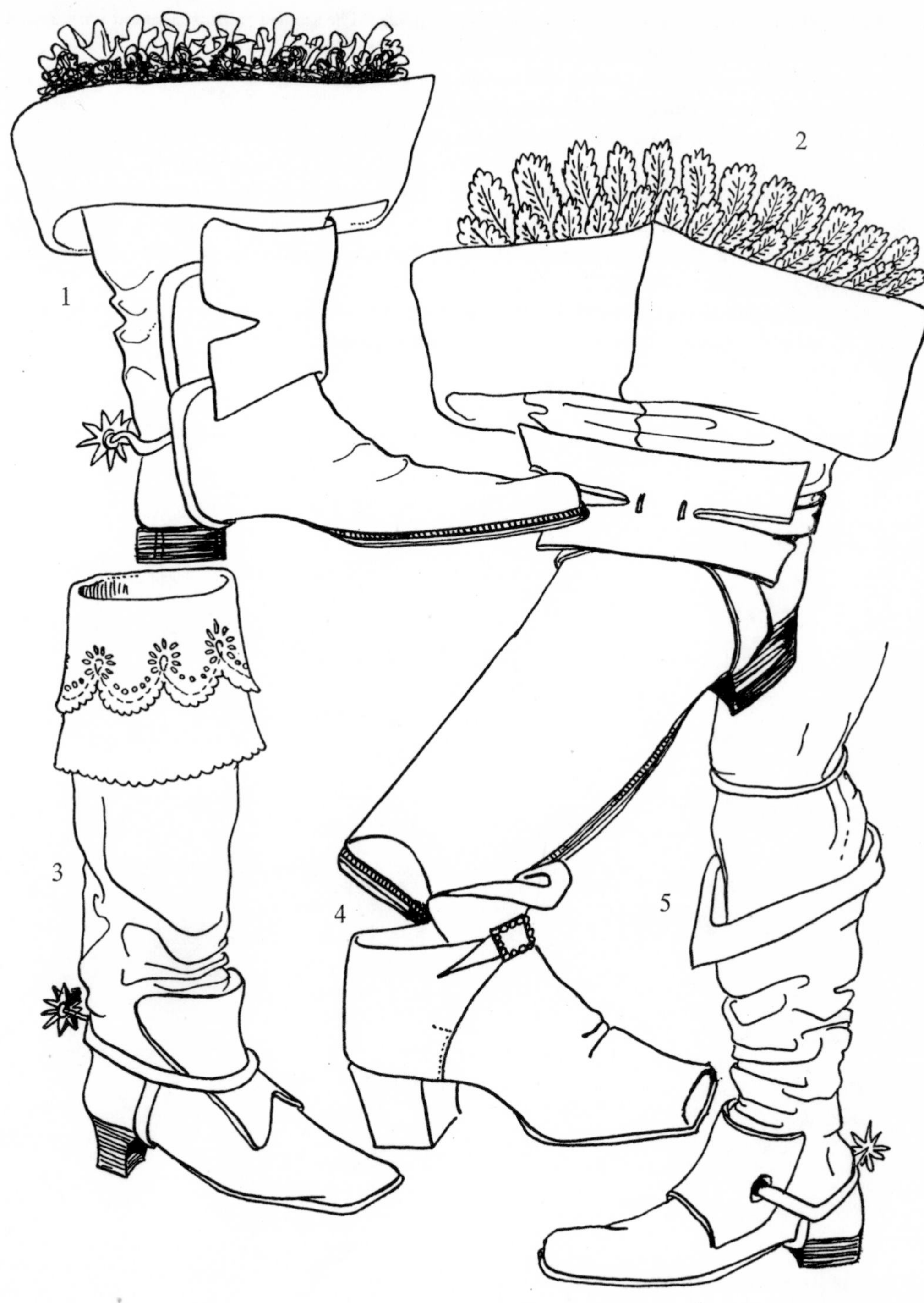
1
2
3
4
5

1. Ladies' kid shoe with wide strap and pronged silver buckle. The seamed front is indented with ironed creases. Note how the sole leather continues round the front of the heel.

2. Ladies' riding boot in black leather with stretch side gussets and high close-fitting front. Note the solidity of the heel and the jutting forward of its front.

3. A military boot in black leather, lighter than the jack-boot, but still having a heavy cuff and stirrup leather.

4. Ladies' silk shoe bound with a different colour and with a matching tie. The tall curved heel is almost wedge shaped and is covered in the same material.

5. The widest version of the bastard boot with its lace-decorated bucket top. Cavaliers put perfumed herbs in sachets in its folds.

6. Leather shoe with tall tab and widely knotted ribbon tie. Its curved decorated heel continues its leather covering up under the instep to the sole to form a thin inset or piping.

46. COMMONWEALTH (II)

1
2
4
Woman's shoes
3
5
French influence
6

1. Captain Lenche's thick black boot of the Civil War. Its toe at least 3 inches wide and 1½ inches deep. The stiff cuff covers breeches and is folded over a heavily-stitched leather stirrup-guard. A strong iron spur is attached to the guard. The heel is about 2½ inches high and made of built leather lifts.

2. A modest form of the undecorated bucket boot made of black leather, worn over silk stockings with knot of ribbons at the knee. Thick square toe is emphasized by a strong welt and built leather heel. The usual guard attaches the stirrup.

3. The usual form of Puritan shoe in black leather with a brass buckle and deep square toe.

4. The alternative version of the Puritan shoe with tall plain tab and buckled strap. The top edges unbound and unstitched but show the thickness of the leather.

5. A double silver buckle covered a high-cut shoe with thick round toe. Built heel and welt emphasized the bulky appearance of most shoes of this period.

47. COMMONWEALTH (III)

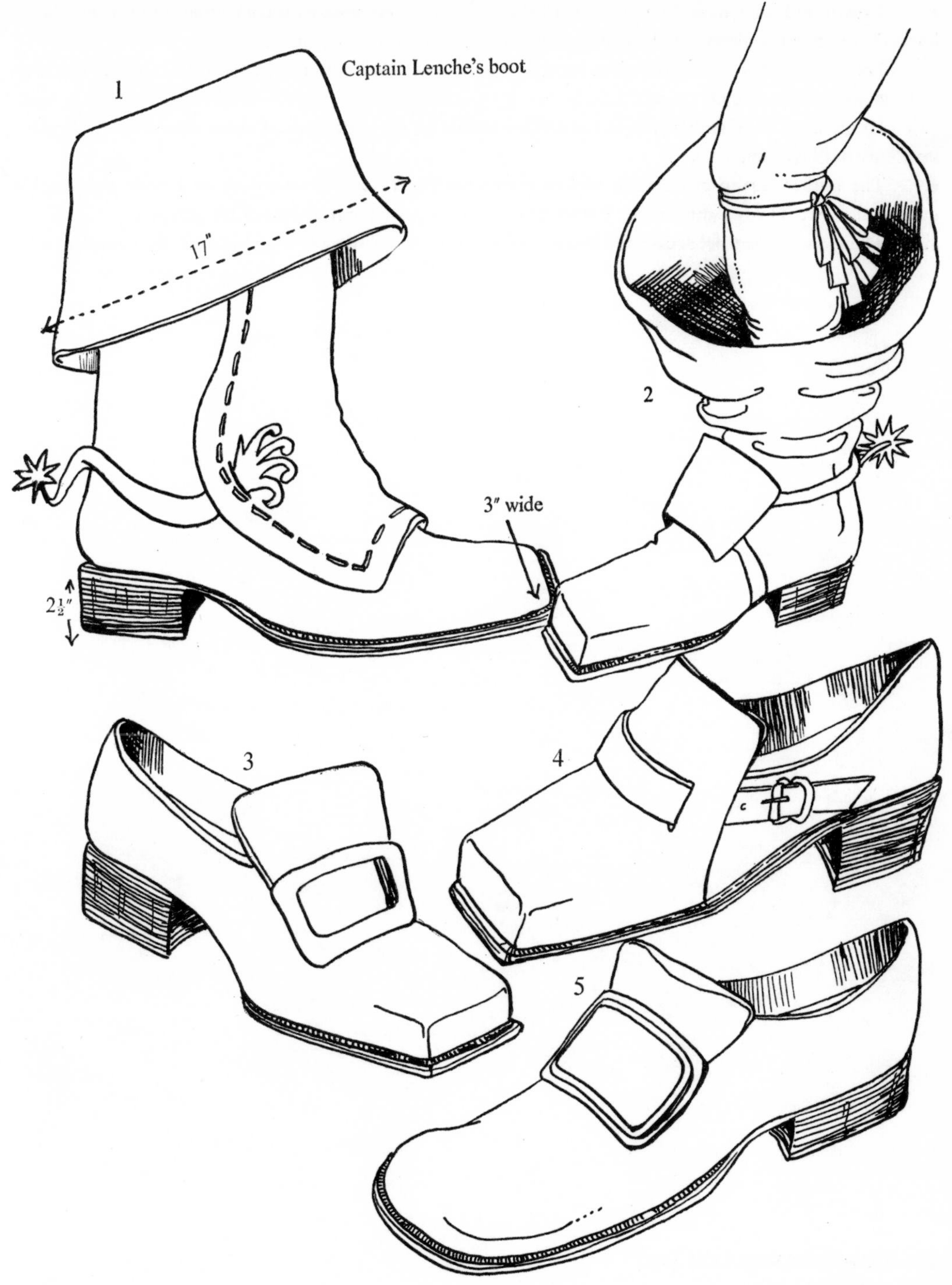
Captain Lenche's boot
1
17"
2½"
2
3" wide
3
4
5

1. Brown buff boot worn by the cavalier cavalry; plain in contrast with the clothes, softer than a jack-boot. With the same deep toe of the period and a wide stirrup-leather guard.
2. Form of jack-boot in black leather, for riding, with heavy welt and layered sole. Heavy upper stitching and stitched turn-back cuff.
3. Heavy black shoe with square toe and silver buckle set on leather tab. Puritan shoe worn with plain stockings and breeches.
4. The leather stirrup-guard took various forms ranging from a plain square to a wide extravagant quatrefoil shape. Held to the foot by leather knots and straps or the iron bars of the stirrup.
5. The shape of the sole, square and broad. Several thicknesses stitched together form the complete sole.

48. COMMONWEALTH (IV)

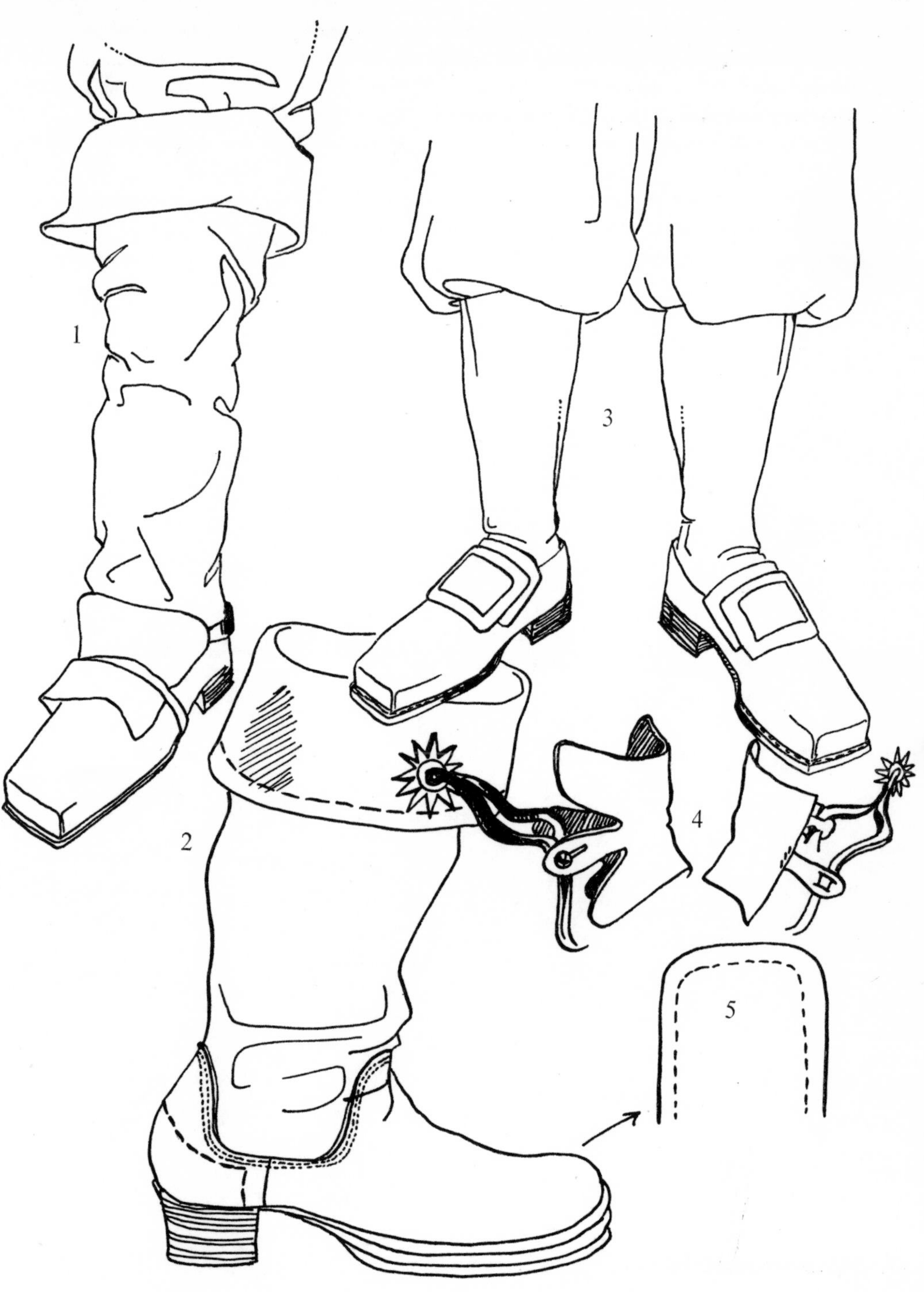
1
2
3
4
5

Postilion boot in thick black leather. Heavy iron wheel spur attached by leather links to boot guard. The boot's guard is decorated with handstitching and applied motifs. The knee-guard is separate and fits over the top of the boot.

(From the private collection of Dr. Dallas Pratt, Freshford Manor, Nr. Bath.)

49. COMMONWEALTH (V)

Detachable knee guard.

Boot of Cromwell's New Model Army. Found at Worcester.

50. COMMONWEALTH (VI)

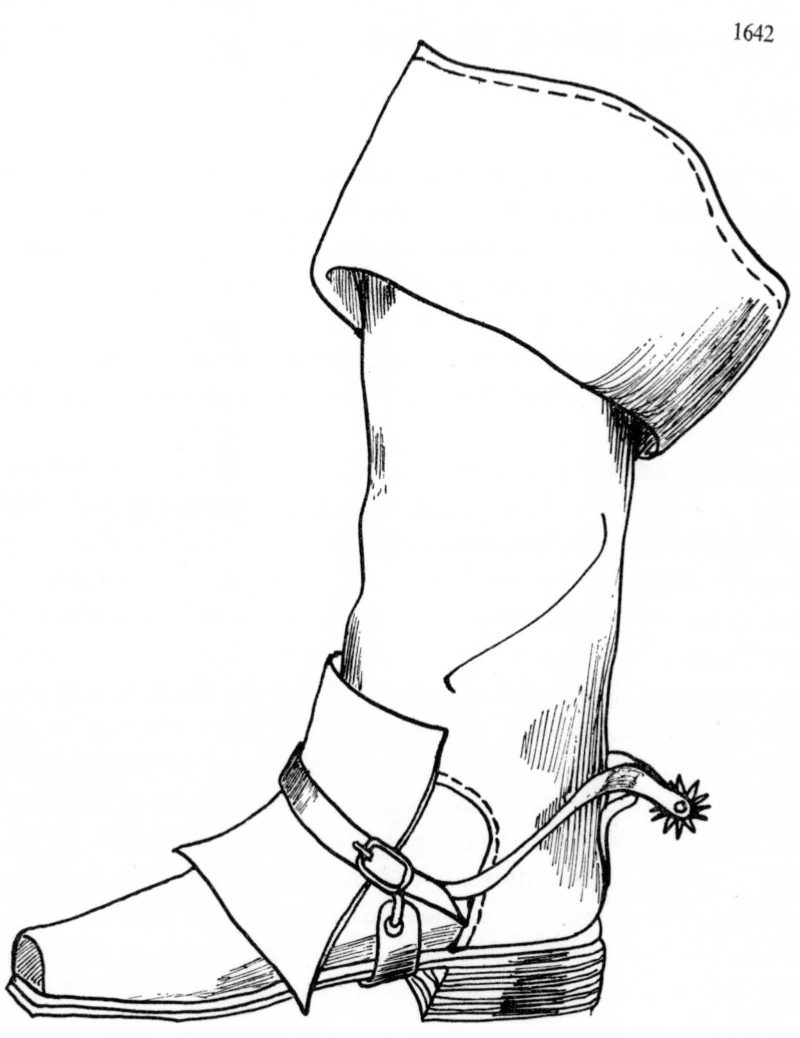
1642

14

The Restoration of the Monarchy, 1660—1688

Charles II, 1660–1685 James II, 1685–1688

THERE is a strong resemblance between the fashions of this period and those of the New Look which immediately followed the Second World War..not because they are alike in appearance but because similar social factors had brought about similar reactions.

After the oppression of the Protector freedom went to people's heads and clothes became extravagant again as the courtiers of the returning monarch came back from France, bringing new fashions with them. Descriptions of the coronation provide a clue as to how things would continue. Charles's numerous mistresses set the fashion styles for their contemporaries.

The fashions of England were now once more those of France, where the king had lived so long, and the name of our Louis heels dates from this period. Their curved fronts were to make the foot lighter-looking and more delicate and their shaping and stitching were to make shoes an even more important part of fashionable attire. Soles were slotted, to carry if necessary love-letters or notes of political intrigue and sachets of perfume were hidden in pockets within the deep turned-down cuffs of boots. Breeches were still as extravagant, but the decorations now below the knee in a deep flounce; these were known as "petticoat breeches." A falling band of lace in the form of a large collar sat round the neck, matched to the deep lace on the cuff, and the sleeves and body of the jacket were banded with ribbons which matched the wide tailored bows on the shoes.

Randle Holme, the Chester Herald, notes very interesting details of fashion in his diary, which is in the British Museum, and the paintings of Lely portray accurately women's clothes of the time. There are many portraits of Nell Gwynne, the most famous of Charles's mistresses, which illustrate the clothes and shoes of her era. And no less a person than Pepys, the best-known diarist of these times, tells us in great detail about the clothes he wore.

The courtiers of the France of Louis XIV were remarkable for their monstrous boots trimmed with lace: one has only to think of the Three Musketeers to recall them. But in spite of the costliness of the lace, the high quality of the leather, the enormous periwigs, and the rich fabrics used for the fashions of that time, there came about a gradual simplification. Buckles were commonplace on shoes, either big and square as in the Puritan period or small and set into wide ribbon ties. Laces for shoes were also becoming more common and were being worn by men and women alike. They had metal ends and John Bunyan, when in prison, kept his family from starving, by fixing metal tags on these laces.

Stockings and shoes had by now replaced tall boots, except for riding, and the vamps of shoes grew long and narrow with neatly-squared toes. High tongues and tabs emphasized this, and so did high-set buckles. The tab itself was interesting because, as well as standing high, it was often encouraged to fold forward to show a coloured facing, or to fold back over on to itself.

Fashion seems to have thrived in spite of the Plague and the Great Fire. Sir Christopher Wren, and Grinling Gibbons, who did a great deal of carving for him, were the great names in building and art at this time and the Great Fire, disastrous though it was, gave Wren the opportunity to rebuild the city churches which had been destroyed. The simple elegance of these buildings and of St. Paul's, his greatest monument, is part of the spirit of the times, which was already calling for a more refined look in fashion.

Coaches had been in use from the beginning of the century. Even in the sixteenth century broad-wheeled waggons, called stages, had been travelling between towns, carrying goods and passengers. Actual stage coaches began to run about 1640, so the need for protective footwear was becoming less as people travelled by coach rather than on foot. But the streets were still filthy and delicate shoes still needed protection, so pattens were still worn and were now metal-rimmed or -edged. Sedan chairs were seen by 1634 and experiments with springs were being made about the same times.

Descriptions of the costume of the regiment formed by Charles II are interesting. The Life Guards wore round broad-brimmed hats with white feathers drooping from the back. They had scarlet coats trimmed lavishly with gold lace, wide sleeves slashed in front from shoulder to waist and lace ran the length of them to meet the large ruffles at the wrist. They had wide scarlet sashes tied at the back and wore long flowing hair. Their boots were of jacked leather, which gave rise to their name jack-boots. Jacking was generally done on horse-hide; waxing and coating with tar or pitch gave it the black waterproof surface needed. Tankards, called "black-jacks," were made of leather treated in the same way. The word "blackguard" comes from the man who polished these boots for the officers, since he was generally dressed in black. The dressing on these thigh-high boots was the elementary beginning from which patent leather was much later to develop. A small shoe or slipper was sometimes worn inside the boot to protect the foot. Inside the top, which was sometimes detachable, there were pockets in which small objects could be stored.

Mules of Morocco leather were worn by both men and women, but women also wore shoes of pink satin, violet, beige, blue, and white. These had high heels and high-standing tabs and the workmanship was exquisite. They were called *Pantoffles*. Some had red heels, others were made of lace with a deep flounce over the instep. Women's fashions like these were very feminine, but some articles of clothing were interchangeable —muffs for instance; Samuel Pepys often borrowed his wife's. Many capes and outdoor coats were cut on similar lines for both men and women and women often wore the little flat-topped brimmed hat which was developing out of a combination of the tall Puritan hat with the befeathered hat of the Cavalier.

Fashion decreed small feet for women, so women who valued their appearance bound their feet with waxed linen tapes, which often caused them to faint with pain. This was a practice which was to continue in varying forms up to the end of the nineteenth century and the desire to take a size smaller in shoes than the foot actually needs still persists! Large rosettes continued to be worn, to the end of the century, by men and women. White or yellow square-toed shoes sometimes had red heels and huge red silk rosettes; a thin form of welt continued from the heel under the sole to form a kind of platform. Only a few leather heels have been found, heels being mostly covered with leather or fabric at this time.

Narrow square toes were shaped on a tapering last which had a slightly waisted look just above the little toe. The squareness of the toe was emphasized by its slight overhang at the tip which gave it a very pretty profile. The shoe as a whole was a graceful spatula shape.

Materials for women's shoes were varied, as the collection in the Bethnal Green Museum shows. These were made mostly from silk woven at Spitalfields in floral, leaf and natural patterns. They were bound with a matching or contrasting ribbon and the quality of workmanship is very much to be admired. They were made by the bespoke shoemakers, of which there were many.

Much new trade came to England at this time as a result of the settling here of refugee Huguenots, after the edict of Nantes had been revoked in 1685. The silk manufacturers of Spitalfields were among them. The leather-dressers, the tanners, and the paper-makers came to join others of their trades in Bermondsey, which had long been the centre of the leather trade. London people fled to Bermondsey from the Plague because the smell from the tanneries was considered a cure.

RESTORATION

Woman
Mop of curls over head and forehead. Bare shoulders. Bodice laced up at back with bows down the front and lace-trimmed neckline. Tubular sleeves front slashed with lace cuffs. Skirt divided down front and caught up at the sides with bows or clasps—could be higher or lower.

Man
Low-crowned hat decorated with plumes. Falling square-cut band at neck and breast bib. Shirt bulging at waist with deep wrist-ruffles. Doublet (short Eton), open front with short sleeves. Petticoat breeches, kilt-like, ribbon loops at waist and sides. Full breeches, knee-gathered, with boot-hose gartered at knee with large lace flounce falling over.

1. Buff-coloured leather shoe with high flaring or turn-back tab. The heel is covered in red leather. Long square-toed vamp now considerably shallower and carries a ribbon bow or tie as decoration.

2. High-cut black leather shoe with tall tab. The tailored collar and buckle are of the same colour but the heel is red. About 1660.

3. Tall tabbed shoe with wide tailored tie-bow. The heel is high and thicker, covered with red leather.

4. The double sole is seen frequently attached to a variety of different styles of shoes.

5. Large rosettes worn by men, women and children alike. Huge and made of ribbon or lace they often have a knot or a jewel in the centre. 1630.

6. Large soft bow of silk on pale leather shoe, often carries jewels as well. 1640.

7. Men's and women's shoes often similar, high cut, tied with soft floppy bows and with red heels. 1641.

51. RESTORATION (1)

Mid to late 17th century

1. Petticoat breeches mark a return to extravagant leg and foot ornamentation. Heels grow higher, tabs and ribbon ties more fanciful.
2. A low-heeled leather boot with small turn-back cuff split at the back.
3. The double boot. In buff leather with a lace edge to its bucket top, worn over white silk boot hose also with flared cuff and rosette decoration. The whole worn over silk stockings.
4. A boot with a decoration on its cuff of fine stitching. Unseamed high cut vamp with wide tailored silk bow and silver buckle.
5. A small bucket-boot worn over a tucked stocking with frilled lace top. Large leather stirrup-guard with tucked centre.
6. Ribbon knots took all forms and shapes: they were loose and soft or stiffly tailored and held with a jewelled buckle. Often they cost as much as the shoe itself.

52. RESTORATION (II)

1
2
3
4
5
6

1. Lady's shoe of beige silk with tucked vamp and tab. The tapered spatula toe is typical of many shoes, as is the covered seam at the sides. Thick stitched heel has small segment-shaped top-piece.
2. Embroidered silk shoe in many colours with silk binding, which picks up one of the colours. The narrow spatula toe is lightly padded beyond the end of the toes. Lined with linen.
3. Flat mule in leather, silk or velvet, had a metal-tipped square toe. There was a repetition of this toe in the late 1950s, called the Mandolin or Spatula toe. It came from France.

53. RESTORATION (III)

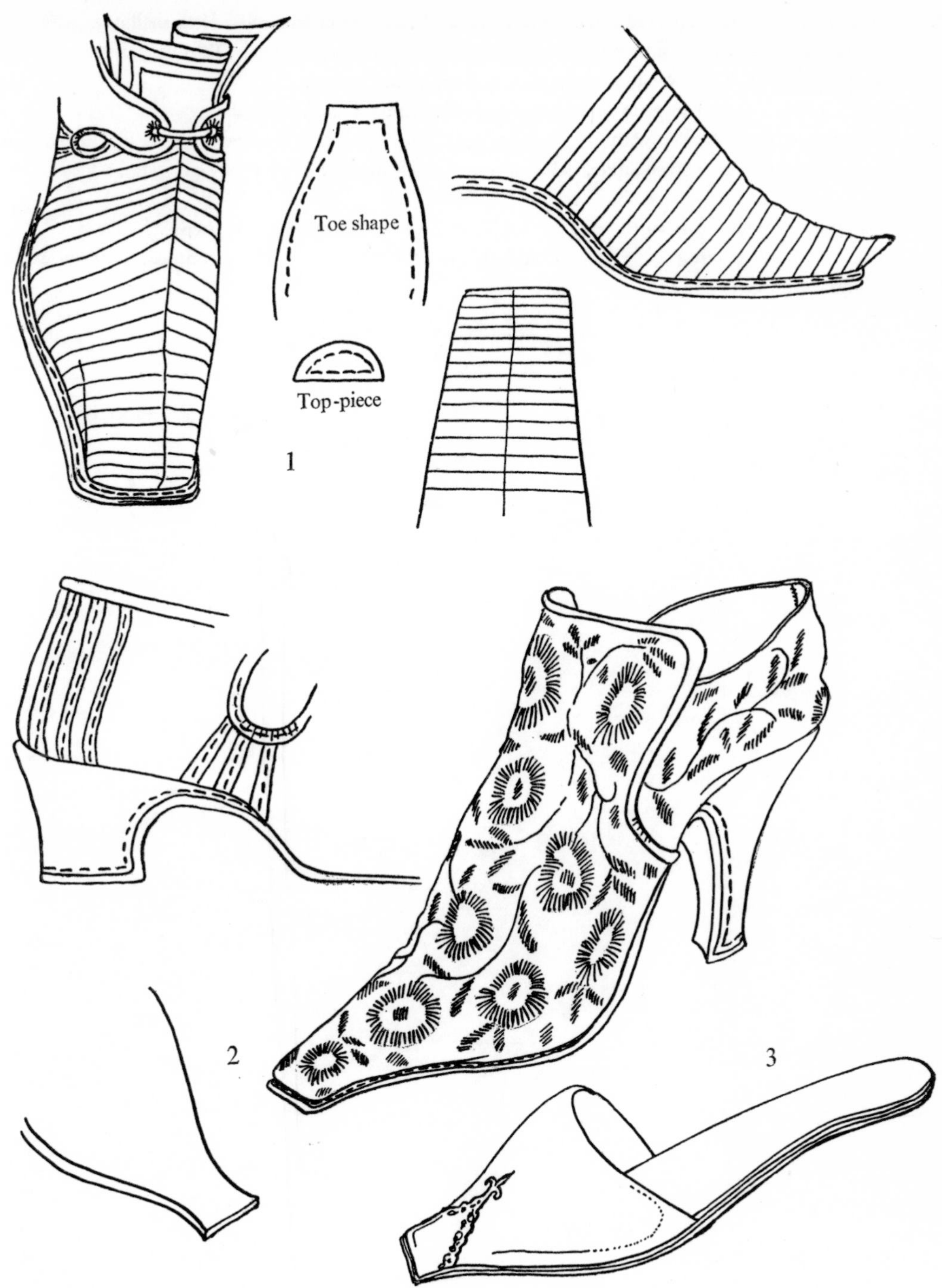
Toe shape
Top-piece
1
2
3

1. Satin mule with high covered thick heel. It has a pleated taffeta frill and a long shallow square toe.

2. Tall-tabbed black leather shoe with jewelled buckle, has a red painted heel. Tabs vary in being folded forward or backward. A tied version of this shoe was called an Oxford.

3. Lady's boudoir slipper in plain or embroidered silk, with gathered lace cuff.

4. Embroidered brocade shoe with long tapering toe. The high heel is covered with silk or kid and is so placed as to tip the foot to a steep angle. Most toes overhung the sole so that they projected a little at the tip.

5. Embroidered mule made from Spitalfields silk, with silk collar band and heel cover.

6. Silk shoe, plain or embroidered, with binding and heel cover to match or contrast. Note how the heel stitching continues to the toe.

54. RESTORATION (IV)

1
2
3
4
5
6

15

William and Mary; Anne

William and Mary, 1689–1702 Anne, 1702–1714

THESE MONARCHS were the last of the Stuarts and their reigns form the bridge between the fashions of their time and those of the Georgians, which differed from theirs as much as theirs did from the Tudors.

William, the son of William II, Prince of Orange, came to the throne because no direct Protestant heir could be found. He landed at Brixham with an army and came to London gathering men as he went. James fled the country, after reigning only three years, and William and Mary were crowned a year later. The tone of the new reign was set by the Massacre of Glencoe, the Battle of the Boyne, and the twenty-five year war with France. Thus it can be seen that fashion could hardly be expected to produce any great changes. Elaborate wigs remained, coats became more tight-waisted, with fuller skirts and big cuffs, turned back to show full pleated shirts. Breeches came to the knee and stockings were worn tight. Women's gowns were tighter-fitting at the waist, being worn over a whalebone-stiffened corset which was sometimes made of leather. Shoes were mostly in black leather with red leather heels, which were becoming higher and thicker. Shoe buckles had now replaced the wide starched bows and a great deal of ornamentation went into them, with the result that they were often more expensive than the shoes. Writers of the day frequently comment on the price of buckles.

Wide skirts brought hoops and there were bows everywhere, especially to loop up the drapes of over-skirts. Bodices were low and provocative. Fans were in common use. Children were dressed exactly like their elders, even to wearing the full wigs. Cuffs of men's coats and their centre fastenings were profusely buttoned. Patches and perfume were popular for both men and women; perfume had become popular especially on account of the plague, and orange or lavender pomanders were carried. But the great craze was snuff which was carried in beautiful little porcelain or silver boxes, the painted or jewelled tops of which were often to be repeated as shoe decorations.

Shoes themselves did not change much except that they had higher quarters, which were cut well above the instep. Toes were still shallow and square and buckles were generally square to match them. *The Tatler* mentions red heels in 1709; these had now become the mark of the dandy and are frequently seen in Hogarth paintings. It was a fashion that lasted for a very long time. . it was reported in *The Monthly Magazine* as late as 1806.

At this time we find what Fairholt calls a "clog," which was in reality a wooden sole fastened to the sole of the shoe, leaving the heel free. There were several rather similar soles which were called "wedges," meant to give height to those of small stature; these were worn by both men and women.

The whole of this period was marked by a stiff rigidity in its manners, its buildings and its clothes. William was very formal and formality became the keynote of these years. Nevertheless it was the era of the beau or exquisite, who appears in a woodcut on the front page of a pamphlet published in 1703 called the "Beau's Catechism." He combed his huge peruke in public and cropped his own hair very short underneath in order to wear the peruke to better advantage. Women's fashion went parallel to the fashion of their menfolk and they wore a tall combed-up head-dress surmounted with lace and ruffles, called a tower or commode.

The accession of a queen to the throne of England in 1702 made no great change in fashion and the formality continued in much the same way. In 1711 pictures of the period depict long-fronted shoes with high sides and high heels. These must have been of the kind that led Sir Thomas Parkins, in his *Treatise on Wrestling*, to say "Let us leave off aiming at the outdoing of our Maker in our own true symmetry and proportion; let us likewise, for our own ease, secure treading and upright walking, as he designed we should, and shorten our heels." Some heels had become so high that it is difficult to see how people walked in them. Boots now had light-coloured tops to them, often in tan, with legs of black leather. These could be polished at any street corner by the little boot-blacks who were so common until the present century.

Fashion magazines abounded from then onwards, but fashion was also the subject of satire in many magazines and papers, even those not directly concerned with it.

WILLIAM AND MARY

Woman

Fontange head-dress. Laced corset under slender peaked bodice. Front of skirt pulled back to reveal decorative underskirt. Printed calicoes widely used.

Man

Very long, curled periwigs over short hair or shaved heads. Full-skirted cassock coats over fancy waistcoats. Fine lace shirt cuffs showing at wrist. Breeches (culottes).

1. Black grained leather military boot with knee guard which can be turned down, flesh side out. Deep round toe.
2. Lady's silk-embroidered slipper with pointed toe. Taffeta frill and knot.
3. Satin slipper with ribbon binding to facing, and matching heel cover. Deep lace frill and silk rosette.
4. Self-stitched beige silk shoe with matching heel cover. Silk ribbon tie and back frilling. Thick heel extends right under arch.
5. Embroidered silk pantoffle worn by men and women. Shallow square toe and exceedingly high tab, bound with a matching coloured ribbon.
6. Thick high heel covered in the same brocade as the shoe, stitched at front and base. Note crescent-shaped curve at front of top-piece.
7. Most heels heavily curved whatever their height. Some, as in the lower sketch, tipped the shoe at steep angle owing to the wrong placing under the arch for their height.

The double sole often had a scimitar shape at the heel swinging to the outside.

55. WILLIAM AND MARY; ANNE (I)

Heavily curved heels covered in brocade

1. Embroidered silk mule with pointed toe and curved heel. Ribbon binding at top and taffeta double frilling.

2. High curved heel and slightly rocked sole to this frilled mule with its peaked vamp. Embroidery in gold thread follows the square shape of the narrow spatula toe.

3. Men's high-heeled shoe with tall unseamed tab.

4. Another heavily embroidered mule with a ribbon-bound top-line.

5. Men's high-tabbed shoe cut to cover the ankle. Because tab is unseamed it wrinkles over the instep. Undercut leather heel and wide square flat toe are typical of the period.

6. Large coloured silk rosette on a man's leather shoe. Laced under the rosette, it has deep side openings.

56. WILLIAM AND MARY; ANNE (II)

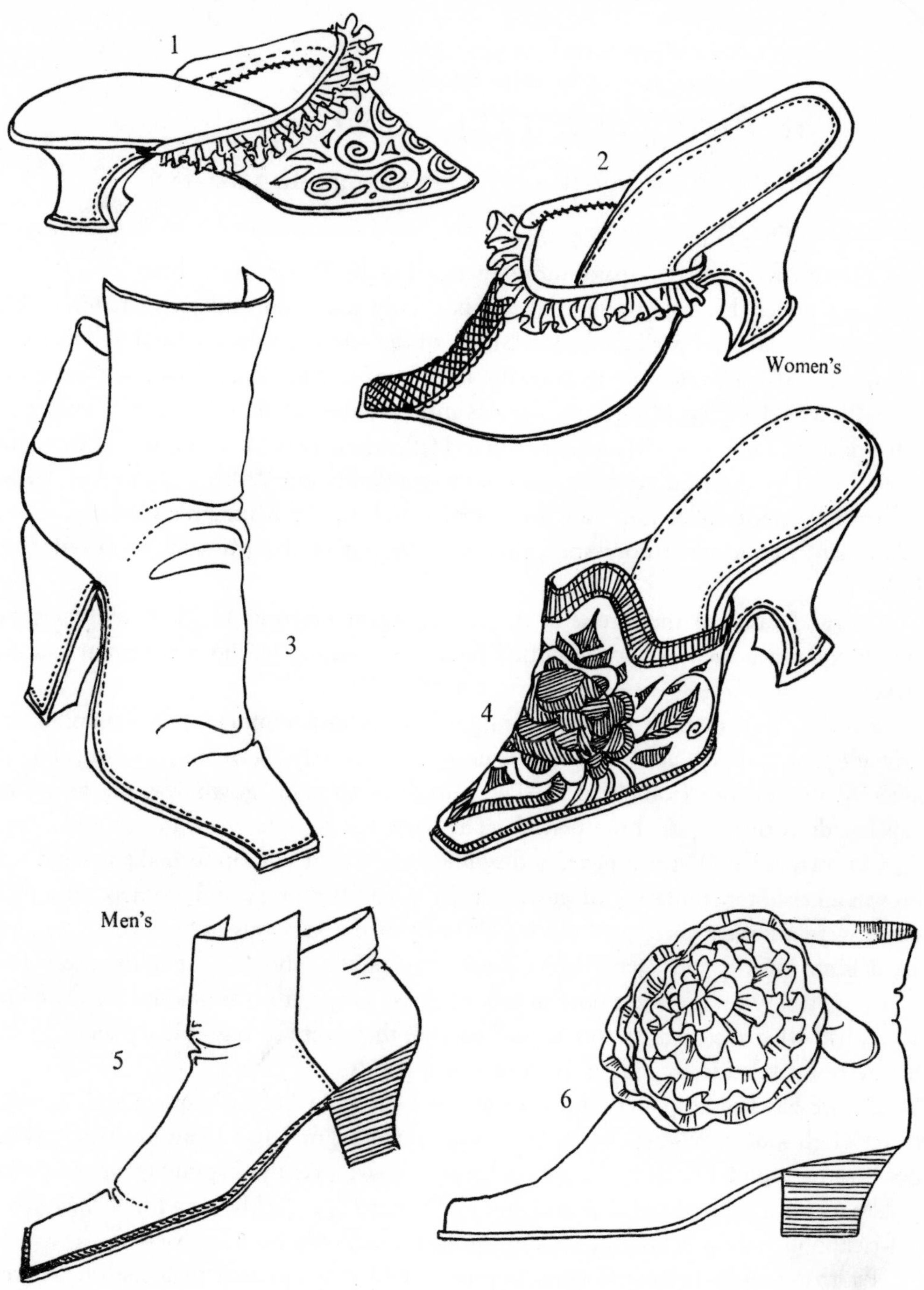
1
2
Women's
3
4
Men's
5
6

16

The Georgians, 1714—1820

George I, 1714–1727 George II, 1727–1760 George III, 1760–1820

The Georgian period spans more than a hundred years and there are so many details and styles that it is possible to mention only the main outlines of fashion. The student will be familiar with the better-known of the costume museums and will therefore have much first-hand reference to draw upon. These museums are worth a detailed study, especially Mrs. Langley Moore's in the Assembly Rooms at Bath. . a perfect setting for such a detailed collection. Manchester's Platt Hall, where may be seen much of the actual material used by those eminent costume historians Phillis and Willet Cunnington, houses another important collection, and the Victoria and Albert Museum's Costume Court makes many of the allied domestic exhibits in the rest of the Museum come vibrantly alive.

George I came to the throne as direct descendant of James I. He could not speak English and did not cut a very dignified figure so anything he did was certain to cause offence.

It is clear then that the first two Georges had not much influence on the fashions of their adopted country, as their own fashions were heavily Germanic, and the English preferred the fashions from France. The square, or straight, gown was the somewhat shapeless dress that typified the period. The back fell straight from the shoulders in a pleat, known as the Watteau pleat, and swung gently over a hoop to make it stand out; this was an elaborate imitation of shepherdesses' garb. Both men and women wore shoes which were a lighter version of the buckle shoe of the previous period; high-standing tab, delicate buckle, and flaring heels, made very pretty footwear for both sexes. Red heels were still worn but were now mostly reserved for great occasions and for the court. Jackets had what were called "bootcuffs" because they were so big. Henry Fielding said they were intended to be the receivers of stolen goods.

Square-blocked deep toes came back into fashion again and high square heels matched them. High square tongues, lined with another colour, matched them in shape. When toes became rounder heels and tongues became lower. At the beginning of the period buckles were small but they became bigger again after 1740. Jackboots with bucket tops or half-jackboots ending below the knee were now worn only on horseback.

By 1750 toes had changed again to points and by comparison their high heels were massive and clumsy. Tongues were high and square until about 1750. Elegant overshoes, called "clogs," were now being worn, but they were not what we know by this name. They had come from France and were made to match the shoes so that they looked all of a piece. Pattens with high metal rings supporting wooden soles were worn in the second half of the seventeenth century and were to continue in varying forms until the Victorian age. Dr. Willet Cunnington mentions these several times in his books, so there must have been many examples. They appear also in a satirical cartoon in 1770. Pavements were still not as we know them and roads were unsurfaced and muddy, but the gentry seldom walked, so pattens were mostly worn in wet weather by the lower classes. A collection of pattens was frequently to be seen awaiting their owners in the church porch on Sunday.

Heels varied considerably in height and were lower in the seventeen-sixties, and became flat in the seventeen-nineties. Red heels were worn by the beaux until 1760 but went out of fashion until 1770. In that year they were revived by Charles James Fox, the eminent Whig statesman.

Low shoes and mules were called slippers and were often made of brightly-coloured Moroccan leather.

Hessians were worn in 1795. These were short riding boots cut to just below the knee and close-fitting, rising slightly in the front, the peak being decorated by a tassel. They were called after the troops of the same name (many other fashion names at that time were taken either from the names of prominent people or from popular regiments). Another boot, worn mostly by labourers and country people from 1785 onwards, was the *Highlows*, a calf-length boot laced in front. Short boots were worn only out of doors and not in the house as before.

Pointed toes for women's shoes returned in 1790 and with them high Louis heels. Buckles disappeared as a decoration about this time and ribbon rosettes replaced them. Beautiful embroidery on shoes was a commonly found decoration. Some of the uppers must have been cut and especially embroidered, for they matched the materials of dresses exactly and the designs fall so gracefully on to the toes or quarters, or are symmetrically placed on a vamp.

For the earlier part of the century Hogarth's works provide many helpful illustrations. His "Harlot's Progress" shows a typical pair of high-heeled buckled shoes. And one of Goldsmith's Essays, in 1759, describes the buckled shoes of his cousin Hannah, who revealed her high-heeled shoes under the shorter front hem of her dress. Little heels were now very pretty and were cut under the shoe in a kind of wedge. They are mentioned as a novelty in 1753, so this must have been about the time of their introduction. Buckles were ornamented with costly jewels, some representing the fortunes of their owners, who seemed to have no fear of losing such precious "gewgaws." Those worn by the Honourable John Spencer, at his marriage, were said to be valued at £30,000.

Beau Brummel discouraged the tendency toward lavishness in men's clothes towards the end of the century by asserting that exquisite cut and plain wool cloth were the only style and fabric fit for a gentleman.

Fabric was now in great use as shoe material. Pleated silk or satin was very fashionable; sometimes the pleats were all over the shoe and sometimes they were an insertion over the instep. In some cases ribbon panels formed the vamp, repeated in a panel edging the breast and top-piece of the very curved and in-set heel. As heels became lower they tended to sit more under the arch again and it was as though all the years of experiment to find the correct position had been wasted.

These flat shoes were more like slippers and had a small curved wedge-shaped heel which ran the length of the shoe, its cover tapering off at the sole into a tiny welt. The fronts were low, making the vamp very short. Sometimes the toe was delicately pointed and tip-tilted. The vamp was tied with the ribbon bow, which had now replaced the buckle. The Duchess of York was famed for the smallness of her foot and in 1791 Foret published a coloured print the exact size of her foot. It measured $5\frac{3}{4}$ inches in length and across the sole at the instep her shoe measured $1\frac{3}{4}$ inches. This of course set a fashion and small feet became the aim of every beauty. The shoe in Foret's print was made of green silk ornamented with gold stars, bound in scarlet silk and with a scarlet heel.

In 1800 the shoes of the old fashion with high heels and buckles came back again and of these many examples are preserved. But laces began to take the place of buckles and tied shoes became so much the rage that the bucklemakers were alarmed at the loss of trade. They petitioned the Prince of Wales to help them by discarding his own laces and returning to buckled shoes, but even though he did so, the turn of fashion was not halted.

The tall boot in black leather with a brown turned-down cuff lasted throughout the period. Sometimes made with a white top, to match white breeches, it was a fashion which stood the test of time; it is still the accepted boot for huntsmen.

The first daily newspaper was printed in 1702. Some of the early papers were printed with a blank page inside, so that Londoners could write their own notes and comments on it after buying the paper and send them to their friends in the country. No doubt, the wider diffusion of fashions was encouraged by this means of spreading the news of the latest modes.

The series "Cries of London," by Tempest, tells us a great deal about the clothes of the later period. So do the portrait painters such as Gainsborough and Reynolds.

Manners during the eighteenth century were a strange mixture of elegance and coarseness. The elegance was mostly artificial, having been learned from books of etiquette written for those who had made money quickly and now wanted to learn gentility.

The French Revolution

During the reign of George III, immediately before the Revolution, fashion was having its last fling in France before being radically changed in 1793. Heels rose to extreme heights and women took to using long slender walking sticks because it was difficult for them to keep their balance. The back seam of a slipper was often encrusted with jewellery, a fashion which was called the "*venez-y-voir*," or "come-hither." A favourite colour was blonde, which was considered very smart for ladies' slippers and was called Queen's Hair colour. The Queen of France had such an extensive wardrobe that she had matching accessories for each dress and her shoes were so numerous that they required an index with details of the colour and style of each. Rich needlework decoration was very fashionable and, in France, the lily was the most popular design.

During the Revolution dress in France became steadily more sombre. The colours used were the basic ones. Silk slippers in pigeon-grey, or a reddish brown colour, were worn. Leather shoes were for the lower classes, but when out riding women wore clothes and leather boots similar to those of their men-folk. As in Britain, ribbon ties began to replace buckles, especially since anything suggesting luxury was frowned upon as being in the style of the hated aristocrats.

The French Revolution had great influence on English trade. The total replacement of buckles by ties, in both England and France, caused the Birmingham buckle trade to pass out of existence before the end of the century. It was to be replaced by the manufacture of costume jewellery, but later buckles were made once again, as well as other brass wares.

The influence of the former women of fashion, such as Madame Camargo of the French ballet (who had such small feet that her shoes were copied by the court so that her shoemaker made a fortune) was replaced by the more down-to-earth influence of the citoyennes themselves. High-heeled fashions were worn only by the exiles.

1790–1804 was the Directoire period, which took its inspiration from the paintings of the day, based on the art of ancient Greece and Rome. A return to the wearing of classical clothes brought about the revival of the shaped Greek sandal, which was criss-crossed up the leg, as is seen in the paintings of Jacques-Louis David. High-cut draped dresses suited these sandals, which were made in blue, white, gold, or silver, with ribbons or straps of leather. Blue, white, and red were fashionable colours for French shoes after the Revolution, and the tricolour rosette was often worn on them.

After the upheaval certain luxuries returned and shoes were again made in velvet, silk, and moiré, soft kids and satins. Colours in favour were red, black, and apple green. The flat sandal lasted for more than half a century, in England too, and was often made at home.

Stockings became an important fashion article because of the semi-transparent nature of the dresses, and long flesh-pink tights were worn. Some ladies carried their trains over their arms to show silk-covered legs to the knee. Some daring women appeared without stockings and sandals and compromised by wearing jewelled anklets and toe-rings. Madam Tallien created a sensation by appearing barefoot in sandals, her toes bedecked with rings, her legs banded with gold straps above and below the knees.

The bourgeoisie in Europe still wore heavy black shoes with stout leather soles and trimmed with a large silver buckle. . a style which survives till now in national costumes. The poor often went barefooted and nails for their boots were a luxury; peasant footwear consisted of clogs, sabots, and sandals.

America

The American War of Independence brought new influences to bear on fashion, many of them military. The hussar boot with its pointed front and tassel became a popular style, as we have already seen. In England and America it was called the Hessian boot, as it came from Hess and was worn by the Hessian soldiers George III used to fight the Americans.

This fashion brought boots back into favour for a while. The top-boot or jockey boot with its turned-down top appeared again after its first appearance among the young bloods of the seventeen-thirties. When reintroduced to France in the seventies it was not an immediate success, but by the nineties it was widely worn. This boot was usually made of grain leather, the flesh side being left brown and the outside stained black. Often white chamois was used for the turned-back cuff. The seamless boot made from the leg of the animal was very fashionable, but shoemakers later disguised the back seam of other boots with a special paste which made the boot appear seamless. Boots were polished with white of egg and lamp-soot.

In America there was a temporary return to straight shoes, because the army needed to be shod quickly and well. But this did not last long, and the chief result of military needs was an emphasis on the mass-production of shoes.

EARLY GEORGIAN (1714–1740)

Man

Wig curled at sides, parted in centre and drawn back with black ribbon at the nape of the neck. Frilled shirt. Long embroidered waistcoat with pockets. Frock coat with wide cuffs. Shaped breeches, finished with narrow band at knee.

Woman

Lace cap. Hooped petticoat under Watteau sacque; box pleats at back hanging from shoulders; front opened over embroidered bodice; large cuffs turned back to show under-sleeves.

MIDDLE GEORGIAN (1740–1780)

Man

Tricorne hat. White wig. Frilled shirt. Cut-away coat, shorter waistcoat. Skin-tight breeches, buckled at the knee. White stockings.

Woman

Hair high, egg-shaped, curls and ringlets at neck. Dress with fichu neck and fitted bodice and sleeves. Sleeve and dress ruffles. Skirt divided and gathered into panniers with bustle to show ankle-length underskirt.

(From a fashion plate of 1781, Bertarelli collection)

LATE GEORGIAN (1780–1820)

Woman
Hair curled in wanton disarray. Small round poke bonnet trimmed with feathers. Pleated ruff. High-waisted dress with puffed sleeves and narrow pleated skirt. Long gloves. White stockings.

Man
Top hat. Curled hair. Stock at the neck with length of material knotted around it. Coat with high padded collar, double-breasted, tails. Sleeves well over wrist with no cuff. Waistcoat and fob watch. Pantaloons fitted into calf-length boots.

1. Bucket-top boots still worn but refined down a little.
2. Embroidered brocade shoe with ribbon binding, thick heel and pointed toe. The cross-over front sometimes carried an ornamental buckle or a jewel.
3. Tooled and decorated clog or patten worn over the shoe above it. Made completely of leather, or leather and wood. The toe shaped the same as that of the shoe, to support it. Laced over the shoe's instep with ribbon ties.
4. Man's shoe with red heels and tall turned-down tab.
5. Gentleman's boot of soft leather, strapped above and below the knee. Worn with or without spurs.
6. Lady's silk shoe with pointed toe and elegantly wedged heel. Braid embroidery on the frilled vamp.

57. GEORGIAN (1)

1
Bucket-top boot
1760
2
1700
3
4
Red heels
1730
5
6

1. Leather riding boot, probably French, but worn in Britain. Laced well above the ankle and tied in a neat bow. Tape boot-straps for pulling on. On its vamp a silk ribbon rosette.
2. Pale-coloured kid shoe with matching ribbon frill and rosette. Lined with linen.
3. A silk shoe with ribbon rosette under a flat button decoration. The vamp ribbed with narrow braid.
4. Stitched silk shoe bound with ribbon, with a plain silver buckle. High arched heel which tips the shoe forward on to its short pointed toe.
5. Another shoe which tips on to its toe because of a very high heel. Black silk bound with black ribbon. Lined with white silk.
6. An embroidered velvet shoe with ribbon around top-line and tab. Beautifully shaped demi-wedge heel.
7. Turn-of-the-century use of buttons on a spat shoe in beige and black.

58. GEORGIAN (II)

1
2
3
4
Turn of the Century
7
5
6
1714-1820

1. A patten for a lower heel with strong canvas front which ties over the shoe. The sides of the heel platform are studded with small brass nails.

2. The shoe has a high heart-shaped tab and a thin undecorated silver buckle.

3. This mule, worn by men or women, has a tall tab, and is lined with a different-coloured silk. A stitched heel and a pointed toe.

4. Delicately embroidered mule for a lady, in white silk and pastel colours. The vamp visibly stitched to the upper.

5. A silk shoe with ribbon-bound edges. A long pointed toe lightly padded at the tip. Sometimes this type of shoe has a prongless buckle.

6. There are many shapes of tabs and many kinds of buckles, highly decorated and often jewelled. They cost as much as £6 per pair.

59. GEORGIAN (III)

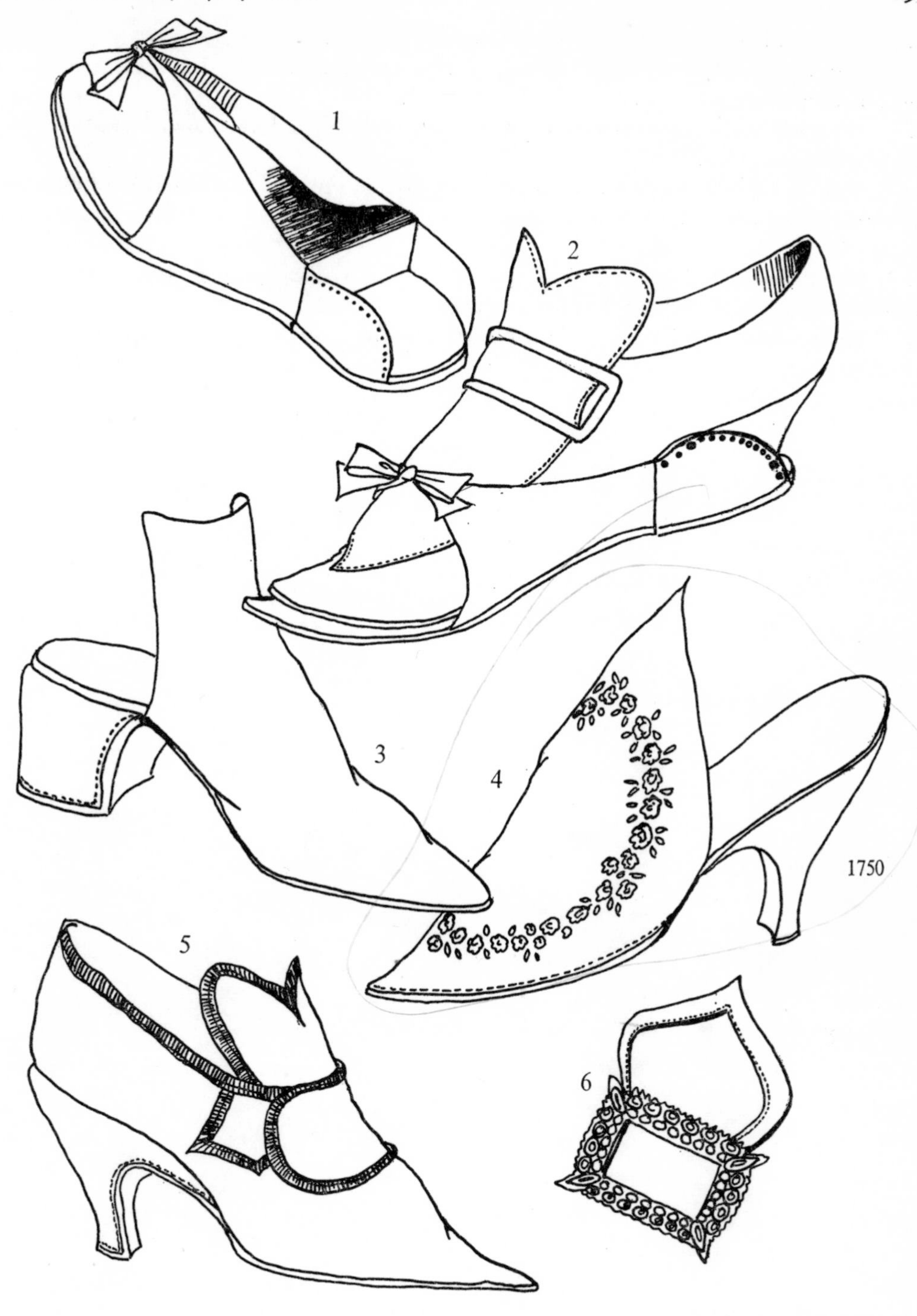
1
2
3
4
1750
5
6

1. Pattens, or leather clogs, frequently worn over delicate shoes.

2. Very high-heeled shoe in beige kid with pointed toe which overlapped its sole. Appliquéd and embroidered panel on the vamp.

3. The patten was so shaped as to be able to take any of the higher heels. Covered in leather, silk, or velvet, and hard wearing.

4. A young girl's silk slipper with a drawstring top-line. Its vamp frilled with small folded silk petals. The heel was so waisted that it had to be covered in two pieces. The upper part of the heel cover continues to the sole.

5. High curved stitched heel on black silk shoe. The tab and overlapping bar are bound with ribbon and the topline has a double-stitched frill of the same ribbon.

6. Silk shoe with deep ribbon-bound top-line and matching bow. Vamp decorated with self-coloured stitching.

60. GEORGIAN (IV)

1
2
3
4
5
6

1. The thick heel was well set under the arch in most shoes. This mule had a padded and covered insole, and embroidered silk vamp bound with ribbon. The covering of the heel was extended into a thin piping which continued under the shoe to the toe. The sole was thick and slightly convex. Its heel had a ridge down the centre back, and the sole was channel-seamed and pointed.

2. A thick solid heel to this shoe was covered in the same material as the upper and a plain version of it continued under the sole and stitched. Overlapping front carried a buckle or buttons. The whole bound in matching ribbon. The thick padded sole forms a kind of platform. Lined with cotton or linen.

61. GEORGIAN (V)

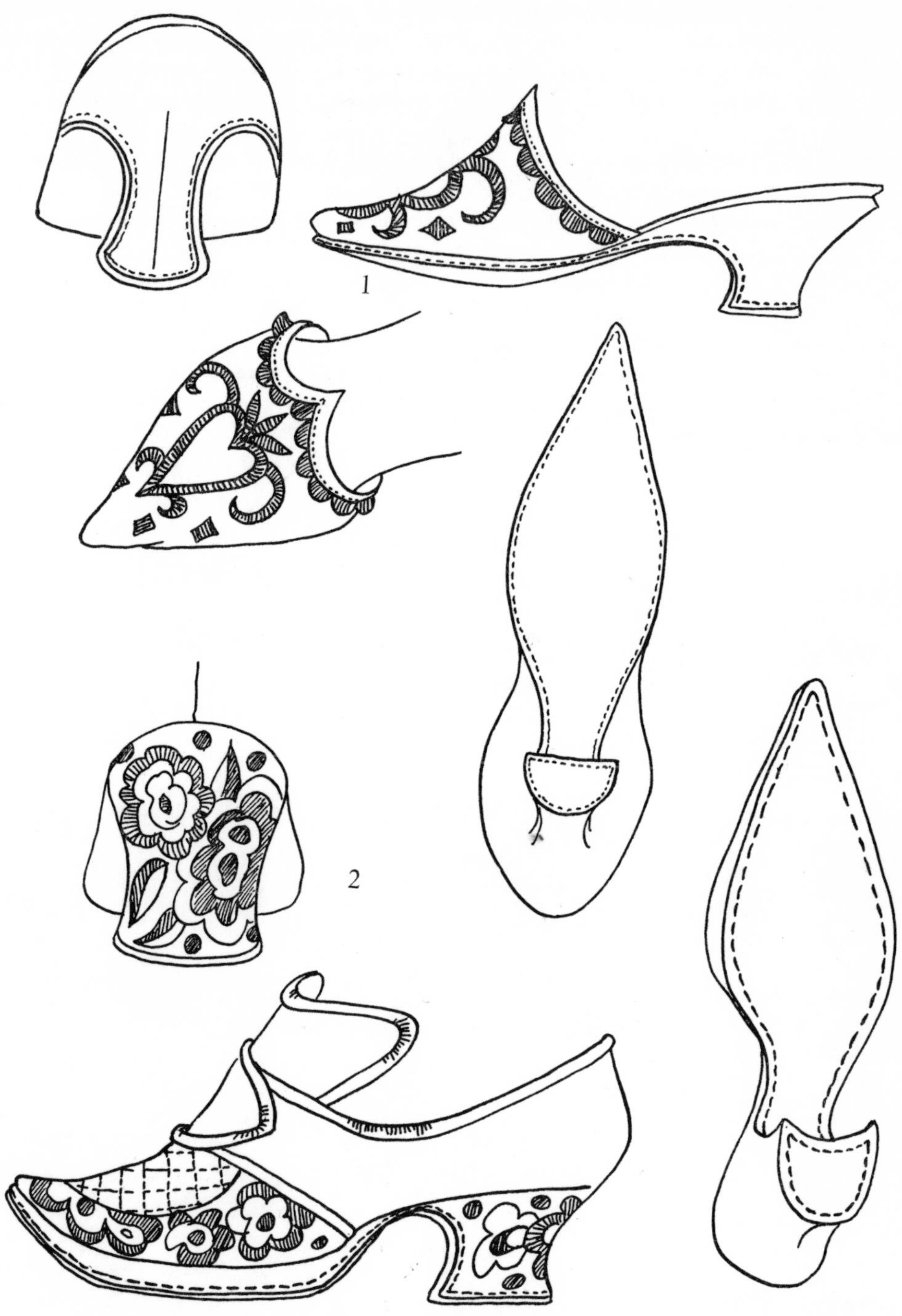
1
2

1. A low-heeled kid slipper in beige with an overlay of olive green kid. The top bound with ribbon which also covers the side seams. The toe flat to the ground and pointed. The heel a shallow curved wedge covered in kid, stitched at the bottom. A soft, suede-finished sole narrow in the waist, and of thin substance.
2. A day shoe in cream kid with a pointed toe and high vamp. The top, bound with ribbon, and trimmed with a satin bow. The kid-covered heel projects at the back and has a small top-piece, and extends under the narrow waist.
3. This shoe illustrates the length of the vamp and the height at which sit the ribbon-bound lap-overs.
4. Deep self zig-zag embroidery overlocks the edges of the facings and tongue of this shoe, which is fastened by hooks. The top of the tie front covered by the flaps. The vamp of pleated or stitched silk has a small kid toe-cap at the point.
5. Contrasts of toe shapes often arose at this period; the round toe balanced by a round silver pronged buckle supporting the cross-over lappets.
6. Handstitched eyelets form the holes for rolled tape or leather ties.
7. Spitalfields silk form the materials from which many of the shoes in the Bethnal Green Museum are made. The ribbon binding picks up one of the colours. The heel is heavy and stitched as are most heels of the period, and projects slightly at the seat.

62. GEORGIAN (VI)

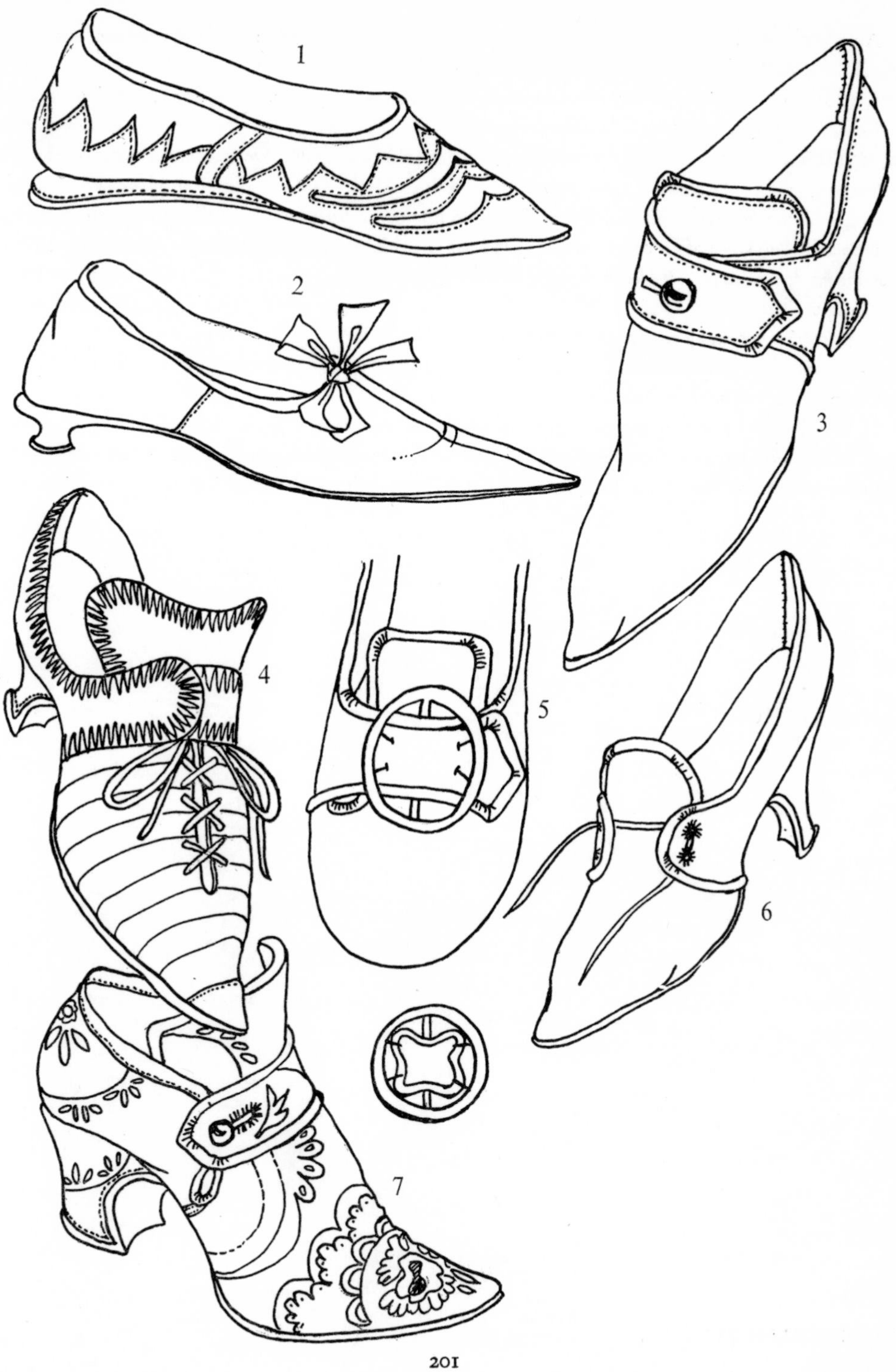
1
2
3
4
5
6
7

1. An embroidered or brocade slipper with a court topline, its side seams covered with the same ribbon that faces the top. Low curved heel covered in cream kid.

1a. Is a version of the same shoe with the embroidery all over the vamp. Both lined with linen and with slightly tip-tilted pointed toes.

2. Men and women wore clocked stockings which gave them more fit. Delicate and intricate embroidery sometimes continuing as far as the knee was a feature of the period. Many stockings in black or white thread are on view in the Museum of Costume at Bath. With them were worn flat slippers which looked like ballet slippers—they were often called dancing slippers. Very light in construction and made of kid they had various throat decorations. Cut very shallow and often heel-less.

3. Another version of 1 and 1a showing the semi-wedge shape of the heel. This criss-cross stitched court often carried a brooch or buckle.

4. Beads were a favourite form of decoration, which were all painstakingly sewn on by hand. Tassels were a favourite form of trim.

5. A finely striped silk slipper with hand embroidery at the toe.

6. A patten looking more like a mule was often worn with these delicate slippers. It had a low covered wedge over which the heel of the shoe fitted and overhung at the back. High fitting, it was secured by a lace at the front.

63. GEORGIAN (VII)

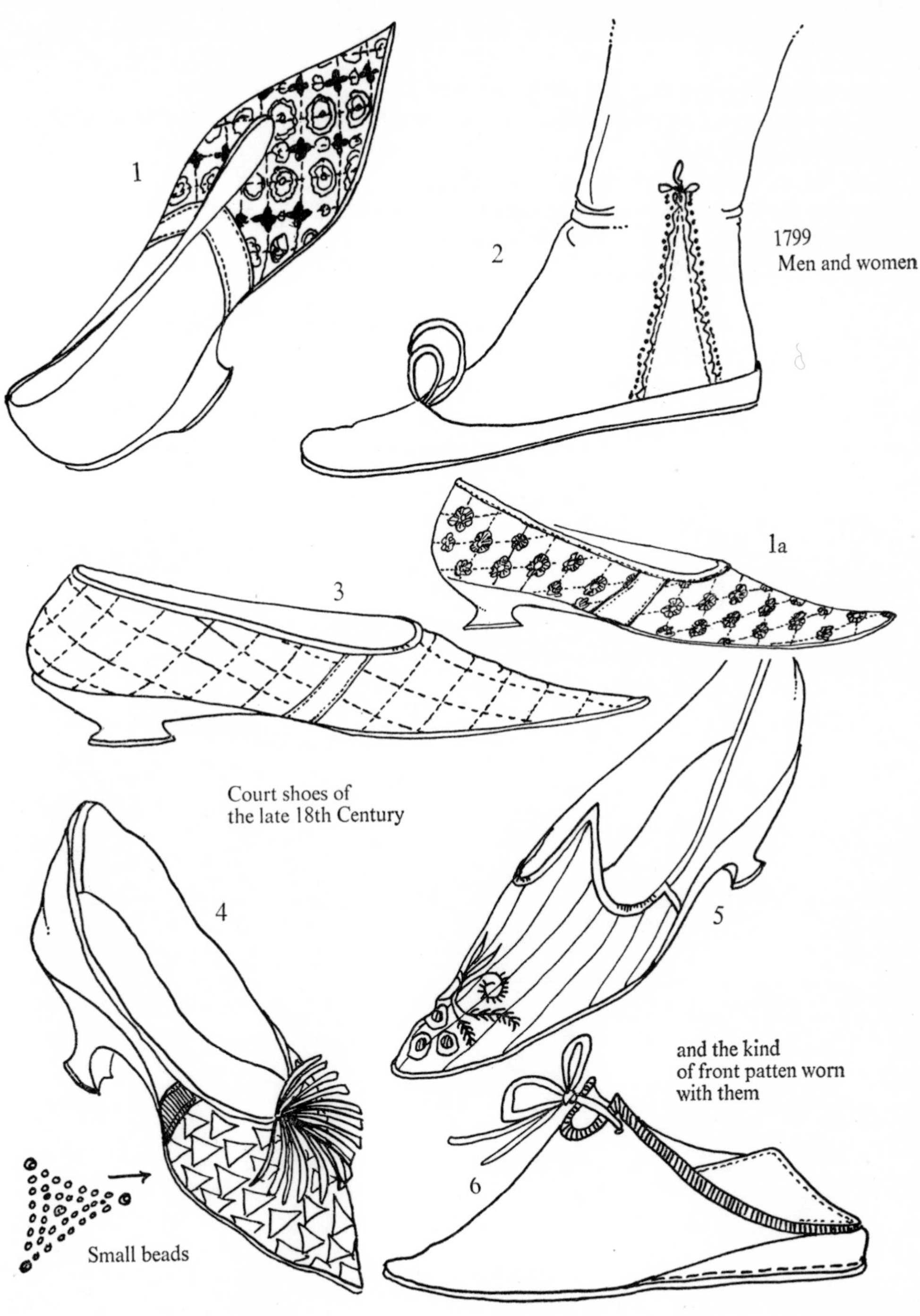
1
2
1799
Men and women
1a
3
Court shoes of
the late 18th Century
4
5
and the kind
of front patten worn
with them
6
Small beads

1. This shoe, from the portrait of Jonas Hanway (1780), shows that the toes of men's shoes were not so pointed as those of women. Black leather, with silver buckles and red heels, worn with white stockings and velvet breeches.
2. Woman's embroidered shoe with silk-bound top-line and waisted heel.
3. Heel so high that the foot was walking on its toe. Black satin bound with black braid. Embroidery which stands away from fabric.
4. Low, red, very waisted heel, covered with leather.
5. Kid shoe with very pointed toe and up-tilted toe. Edges frilled with satin.
6. Kid shoe bound with braid has a shank button and high tab.
7. Pointed toe mule with a frilled and jewelled top-line.

64. GEORGIAN (VIII)

1
2
3
4
5
6
7
Men's shoes were not as pointed as women's

17

The Romantics, 1820—1837

George IV (Prince Regent, 1811–1820), 1820–1830 William IV, 1830–1837

GEORGE III LIKED music, furniture, and gardens; he also liked collecting and making buttons and putting watches together. The creation of model farms on his estate at Windsor earned him the name of Farmer George. It was his collection of books, mostly books on arts and sciences, that served as the foundation of the Library of the British Museum. But he was highly neurotic and he spent the last nine years of his reign in seclusion. His son George IV, having been the Prince Regent during these last tragic years, succeeded him in 1820.

The Regency period is most clearly typified by all that Brighton stood for, with its pavilion and other elegant buildings and its fashionable season. When he was a child, it was said of the future George IV by his tutor that he would be either the most polished gentleman or the most accomplished blackguard in Europe..and possibly both. He set up his own establishment at Carlton House when he was twenty-one and the "First Gentleman of Europe" proved indeed to be both as his tutor had forecast. He was the leader of gay London fashionable society, patronizing the arts, setting the fashion in clothes and styles in architecture. His extravagance became a byword throughout European Society. He had many mistresses from whom many well-known families now claim descent, but this aspect of his life ended when he secretly married a twice-married Catholic widow without his father's consent. Poor Mrs. Fitzherbert found her marriage illegal and she herself was excluded from her husband's public life. When he died, he was succeeded by his brother because his only legitimate child, Princess Charlotte, had died in 1817.

With so frivolous a monarch it is not surprising that fashion had a changeable aspect at this time. At the beginning of the reign there was little change from the flat heels and pointed toes of the previous era. Shoes were made of soft kid material to the colour of the dress trimmings. Half-boots which fitted closely to the leg were worn by women of dashing *ton* and these, like those of the men, were drawn on by means of boot-hooks inserted in the loops at the side. There were stockings of silk or cotton, generally white, and there were also examples of stockings with divided toes, in the Japanese style. Double-soled sandals, called "comforts," and slippers of dark "mulatto" colour were often mentioned in the many fashion magazines for women.

In spite of the superficial frivolity of the time manufacturing towns were growing in importance and machinery was coming into its own. The cleavage between rich and poor was profound.

Regency Period

An analysis from contemporary fashion magazines might read as follows:

1811 Coloured day shoes and half-boots in grey, beige, or black. Roman sandals for evening, elegant little slippers with entirely flat heels in silk or kid.

1812 Half-boots laced at the back. Slippers slashed across the front in a brief revival of Tudor fashions, square throat line. Wellington coats, mantles, boots, and Wellington slippers.

1813 The Wellington mania having subsided, everything now takes its name from the beloved Regent. Sandals no longer fashionable. Evening slippers in white satin with ruched silver rosettes. White stockings.

1814 Sandals and kid slippers for carriage wear. Jean boots for walking. Ribbed stockings with clocks at 7s. 6d. to 10s. 6d. a pair.

1815 Scarlet morocco slippers. Wellington boots and demi-boots. Invisible soles of plaited horsehair, covered with velvet, worn inside boots. Evening sandals of green kid with crossed ribbons.

1816 Walking boots at half height made of satin and fitting close to the leg, laced tightly to give shape. Silk half-boots for carriage wear. White satin embroidered with pearls for evening.

The ballerina line for shoes was very important since there was great interest in the dance and many fashions took their inspiration from the stage. Worn with nearly all costumes, the flat ballet shoes were made in all kinds of colours and materials. In 1833 we find references to the black fishnet stockings which were often worn with these ballet shoes, over pink silk tights. They were meant to give the impression of bare legs but without revealing bare flesh. The shoe had little or no heel and a very waisted sole. In some examples the heel was very ingeniously made and concealed within the shoe so that the ball of the heel rested in a concavity.

Many shoes had interesting decorations, intricately stitched patterns on a scalloped-edged toe-cap overlaid on to an otherwise plain shoe. Brown kid was a favourite colour and material. Decorated with fine beading, embroidery, and stitching, many of these shoes were works of art.

A further analysis reads:

1830 This is the era of Romance and Sentiment. There is a backward-looking tendency and fashions are taken from other periods and romanticized. Shoes had higher heels and were cut into open sandal shapes and fastened with three or more instep bows.

1831 Carriage clogs for ladies and gentlemen, made of cork or leather and worn over the shoe for its protection between door and carriage. (Thus the patten returns to fashion.)

1833 Shoes were less square at the throat though square toes were still long and thin. Silk and fancy leathers were used a great deal. "Prunella" shoes were so common that no lady would wear them. (This was a kind of woollen stuff used for making shoes and of a prune colour.)

1834 Cloth boots worn over slippers for the theatre; carriage boots made of velvet, trimmed and lined with fur; black satin slippers for evening. Fashion authorities complained: "When will English women realize that white satin is not becoming?"

1836 Black silk shoe or black velvet buttoned with gold for "promenade dress." Black tassels on the insteps of boots the favourite trim. A great deal of braiding either round edges or in frog patterns down the front.

ROMANTIC

Man

Beaver top-hat. Hair longer, curled in front of ears. Coat with high padded velvet collar, deep revers tapering to low down. Sleeves gathered at the shoulder. Stock at neck. Waistcoat. Trousers long-legged extending over insteps.

Woman

Large hat lavishly decorated, tied under chin. Hair parted in middle with curls down side of face, and back knotted high on head. Dress with wide accentuated drooped shoulder-line, all fulness drawn down to waist and held by wide belt, neckline round with ruching. Skirt wider and shorter.

1. Black kid square-toed boot with elastic sides. Plain or decorated with intricate stitching.

2. Brown kid ankle boot with inside ribbon lacing through stitched eyelets, with a ribbon bow half way along its vamp. A light leather sole and single lift heel.

3. Some shoes reverted to being cut on the "straights" principle, especially backless mules of this type. They took on the left and right shape through wear. Heels were often very curvy and covered with the same material as the upper.

4. A child's side-gusseted shoe with lapped-over buttoned front decorated with a silk tassel. The overlaid vamp is decorated with ornamental stitching, often in a lighter colour.

5. A man's side-laced boot in black kid with small heel made of leather.

6. A woman's shoe in brown kid with lightly-curved leather heel. The boot comes to just above the ankle and has a tape for pulling on at the back. The long vamp is decorated with a knot of silk loops. The square toe is shallow.

7. A peaked kid shoe with elastic gussets, with an asymmetrically-cut vamp decorated with a silk tassel and ornamental stitching. The curved heel is covered and stitched.

65. ROMANTICS (I)

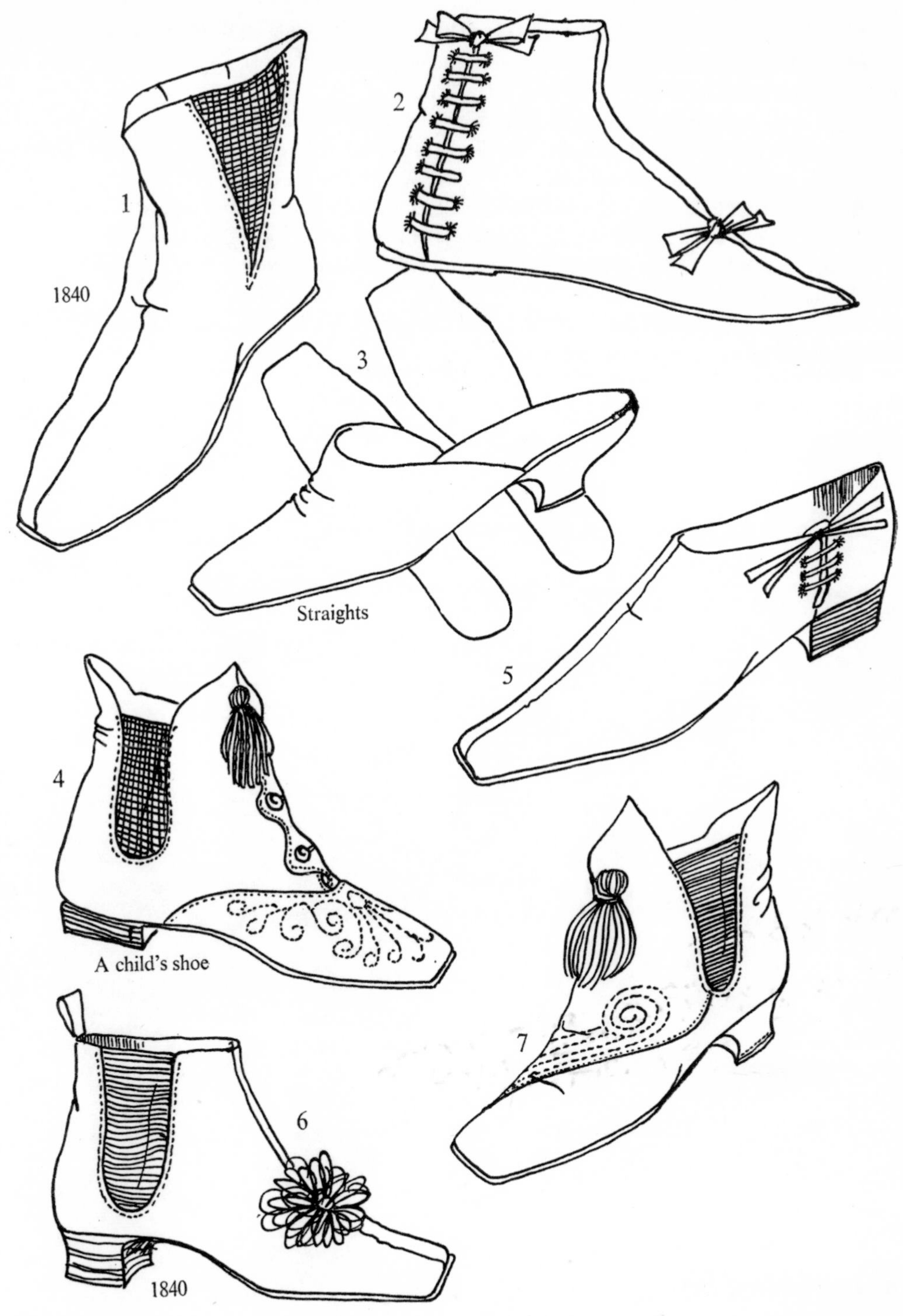
1
1840
2
3
Straights
5
4
A child's shoe
7
6
1840

1. Black satin shoe with flat sole and square toe. The bound topline is bound with black ribbon and the throat trimmed with a tailored bow. The ribbon laces come up from the sole, often covering a seam, and lace several times round the ankle. Lined with beige linen.

2. There never was a greater contrast in men's and women's clothes and shoes were no exception. This man's Wellington boot in shiny black leather, fits closely round the calf and wrinkles at the ankle. The deep round toe has a square-edged welt and sole.

3. Navy-blue satin indoor slipper, self-bound round its peaked vamp and back and with a zig-zag cut bow. A light flat sole and a linen lining almost universally found in this type.

4. Black canvas side-laced boot, with small wedged heel and black patent toe-cap. Lacing often on the inside, through stitched eyelets.

5. Calf-height, tight-fitting boot in buff-coloured canvas with black kid vamp and black ribbon laces. Flat and heel-less or with a very thin leather heel.

66. ROMANTICS (II)

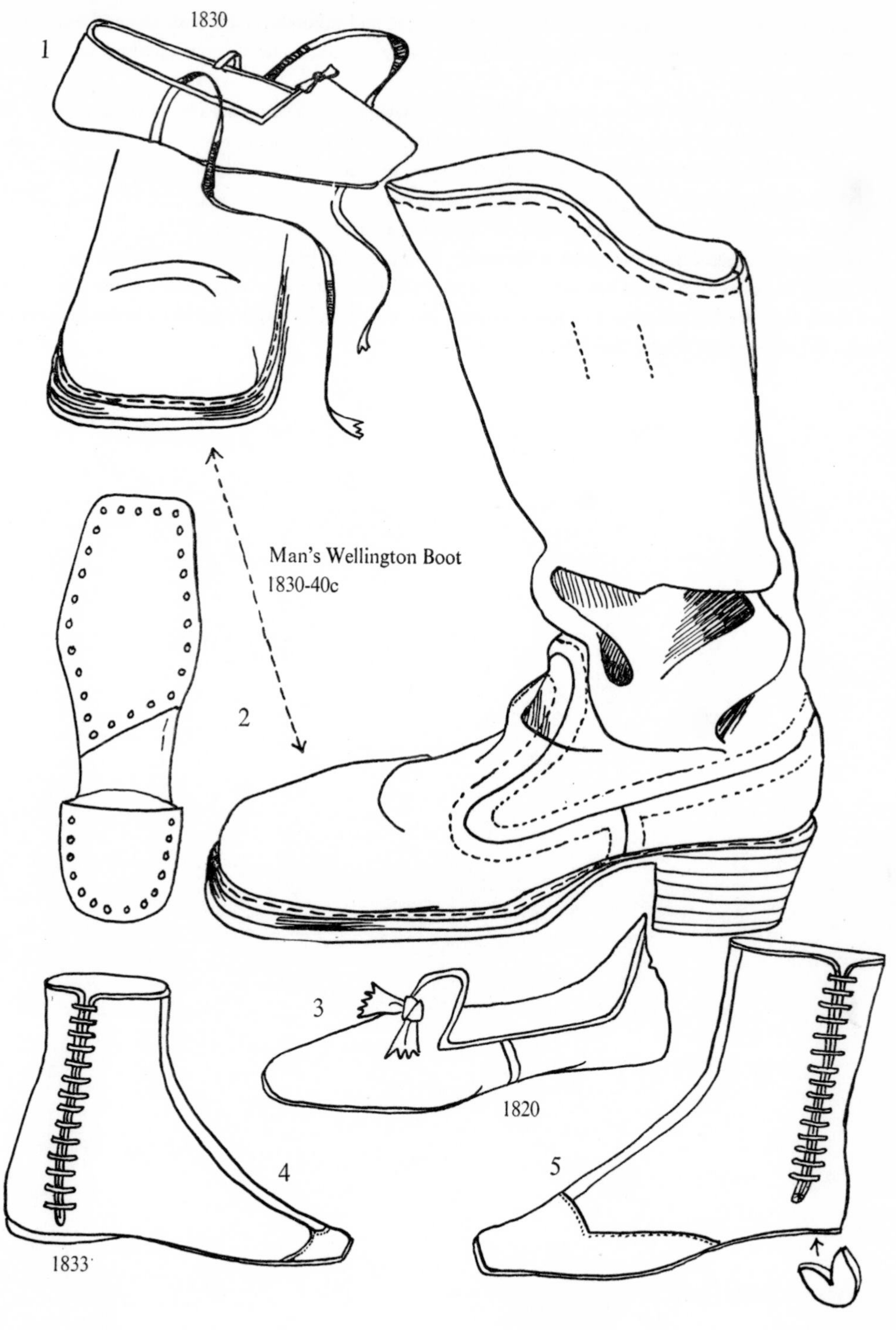
1830
1
Man's Wellington Boot
1830-40c
2
3
1820
4
1833
5

1. Cloth gaiters, white or beige, worn by country people and others over black shoes and breeches.
2. Black leather shoes with square toes with laces showing or hidden under trousers whose cuffs cover a large part of the shoe.
3. A riding boot in black well-polished leather with a leather heel and square toe. The turn-down cuff was of brown leather and there were tape loops for pulling-on at each side.
4. Trousers with instep strap under foot, cuff over shoe so that the shoe was completely covered at back and sides. Sometimes worn over or inside Wellington boots.
5. Man's buttoned shoe with bound edges, for informal wear.
6. Woman's or child's boot in canvas with leather toe-cap. The back peaked for pulling on.
7. During the latter part of the century clogs developed from pattens and were worn in the mills. They were of thick black leather nailed on to a thick wooden sole which had an iron edge like a horse shoe on sole and heel. Worn by quite young children.

67. ROMANTICS (III)

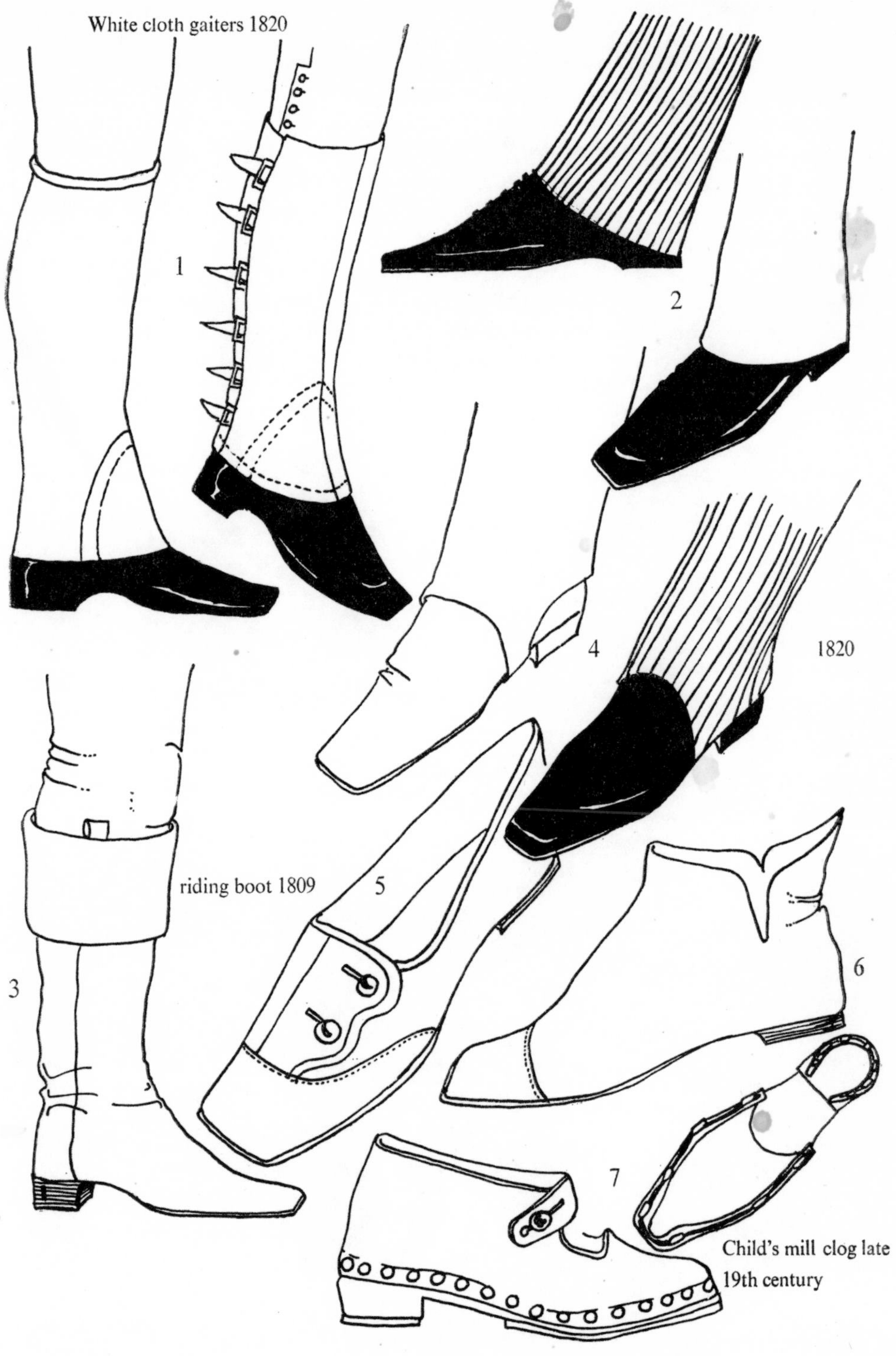
White cloth gaiters 1820
1
2
4
1820
riding boot 1809
5
3
6
7
Child's mill clog late
19th century

18

The Victorians, 1837—1901

Victoria, 1837–1901

It is pertinent here to quote from "The Noble Gentleman," written in 1647:

"Nothing is thought rare
Which is not new, and followed: yet we know
That what was worn some twenty years ago,
Comes into grace again."

That "twenty years" is important, because from the Victorians onward we find that each generation takes up a fashion that is new to it but commonplace to its elders, yet shocking because it appears in a new light.

An almost year-by-year account compiled from many fashion papers and magazines gives the best survey of the shoes the Victorians wore. It must be remembered that this is one of the longest reigns, which, though influenced greatly by the Queen herself, saw several generations coming to maturity.

1837 In this, the first year of the young Queen's reign, fashions had a young look in keeping with her age. Flat-heeled black kid boots laced at the inside. Toes slightly pointed with patent toe-caps. Fancy silk buttons used as decoration on shoes and clothes. Coloured enamel buttons used also.

1839 Fine white stockings fitting closely to the leg, though the leg is not talked about. Well-fitting shoes cut to the shape of the foot.

1840 The year of the Queen's marriage. Toes were pointed, but there were some with the point chipped off into a narrow square. A pretty example was cut in white satin, a boot with a cerise satin galosh and laced on the inside. It was close-fitting and its top was above the ankle at slightly lower than mid-calf. The Romantic period in clothes came to an end about this time and the crinoline took over until 1860–5.

1843 Elastic was used a great deal in the sides of shoes, making lacings and other fastenings unnecessary. This was an insertion in one or both sides, cut deeply, and seen on both men's and women's boots. There are advertisements in the magazines of the time for Hall's Patent Elastic Boots. Elastic garters were also made and, like boots, were made of silk, cashmere, and wool.

1844 Rubber galoshes were worn in winter by both men and women and were cut to fit over shoes. Some had holes for the heels to come through so that the forepart fitted closely over the upper.

1846 Buttons on clothes were cut from amethyst, turquoise, marcasite, or cut steel, and these were repeated on shoes for evening wear.

1847 White silk was used extensively for evening shoes, with curved heels covered to match the shoe. Evening boots in white satin had a small toe-cap of black satin. Some of these were also elastic-sided, but this form of adjustment was generally in day shoes. Slippers of velvet in all colours were popular, dark red, lined with red flannel, being the favourite. Rubber overshoes improved and in current magazines we see "Godfrey's improved overshoe; a sock or slipper to wear over a lady's boot or shoe in wet weather; of waterproof material." Its headline reads "Patent India Rubber Galoshes."

1849 Dress boots of coloured silk for evening, silk or satin slippers with small buckles or a rosette. For walking, boots made with cashmere tops and kid vamps, matching the colour of the dress. For promenade, shoes with a small matching rosette. The American Mrs. Bloomer tried unsuccessfully to persuade English women to adopt a more rational costume in which it was possible to lead a more active and functional life. She advocated trousers gathered at the ankle. which were known as "bloomers." The name has survived, but not the garment.

About 1850 the Pre-Raphaelite Brotherhood was formed. This was a group of artists, including Rossetti, Millais and Holman Hunt, who felt that contemporary art and design were over-ornate and decadent. They wanted to return to the style of the times before Raphael, when art was pure and undiluted. This bold attempt to return to nature affected the appearance of clothes, bringing new natural dyeing processes and a simpler cut of clothes into favour. These fashions were not of course adopted by everyone and were laughed at by many, but nevertheless out of the Movement came the beautiful designs for which William Morris is known and many forms of decoration we take for granted today.

1850 Half-high heels, but small and set on the end of the last, often built in leather lifts. Elastic-sided boots. The Pre-Raphaelites brought back into favour natural sandals under flowing skirts.

1851 The year of the Great Exhibition. Clothes showed a nationalistic trend and were faintly military and masculine. The Exhibition was the fashionable place to be seen in, and the amount of walking involved there brought lower heels back into fashion.

1853 Boots of stuff with small heels and laced on one side; evening shoes of stuff also, or black taffetta with a small bow on the vamp, ballet-shaped, with or without laces, low or flat heels.

1854 Evening shoes had higher heels.

1858 Hoop skirts reached their utmost width in this year and wits said that doors needed to be made wider. Balustrades had already curved outward to accommodate what appeared to be a permanent fashion. Bold curving lines in every kind of decoration and in architecture. The use of sewing-machines had made dressmaking so much easier. They had chain-stitch at first, but lock-stitch was developed toward the end of the decade. This mechanical improvement made shoemaking easier also and shoes, as well as clothes, were made faster. Tight lacing was on the way out. Kid boots were now buttoned at the side and needed button-hooks.

1859 Elastic-sided boots for day wear. Evening shoes with or without small heels and rosettes. There was a great deal of choice in heel heights, shapes and colours, as well as in toe shapes, which a look at any shoe collection of the period will confirm.

1860 The crinoline now had less importance. Garibaldi jackets of scarlet cashmere reflected the tendency to call garments and shoes after well-known people. Chenille hairnets were decorated with stars, rings, or coins, and some of these were also used as shoe decorations.

1861 Colleen Bawn cloaks of white grenadine with a large cape caught up in the middle of the back with two rosettes. Colours increased in importance, and there was a wide choice, the most frequently named being: havannah, black, white, mauve, violet, green, blue, with red for stockings; "cuir"-coloured shoes, and blue, violet, green, scarlet, black, white, more or less matching the clothes, although some liked a shock of colour under a sombre dress. Shoes had high heels and stockings were patterned or spotted. Growing prosperity encouraged a development of genuine English styles, not simply copies from Paris. Chamois-leather foot-socks, as supplied to Her Majesty, were supposed to cure rheumatism and wash-leather underclothes were advertised as having the same effect. Messrs. Wells of Nottingham offered new patent stockings in which the seam and the stocking were knitted in one. Cork soles lined with wool were also used in boots.

The death of Albert, the Prince Consort, in 1861, plunged the whole country into mourning. Black became the only acceptable colour from the December of that year and this mourning style was to continue for some years, being moderated only as the Queen allowed her own to diminish, which she did only to a limited extent.

1863 A note gives the price of elastic boots at 8s. 6d.

1864 High peg-top heels on boots and shoes for day wear. Toes nearly square. Evening shoes and boots, white for white dresses, blue or pink. Heels one inch high.

1865 Masculine influence shown in coats and jackets, waistcoats, cravats and boots. Croquet boots in morocco kid, with fancy stitched and punched toe-caps, coloured ribbon laces, peaked before and behind at ankle and with a tassel for decoration.

Satin evening shoes with steel or jewelled buckles and pointed toes. Buckles large and square. Heels 1½ inches high.

1866 Heels still 1½ inches high and nearly square toes, rosettes or bows on instep. Boots of black morocco, buttoned and with tasselled tops. Lacings had tassel ends.

1867 "All girls transformed into guys," said a contemporary fashion magazine. Boots had rounded toes, high-laced boots had a tassel at the top and bows on the vamp, made in leathers of every colour. Kid walking boots had patent leather toes. Buttons were the fashionable method of fastening, so button-hooks were essential and decorative. Elastic-sided boots were not now worn for dressy occasions. Polished boots of military cut were high-legged, with pendant tassels and high coloured heels.

1868 This year imitated the mode of Louis XV, Regency, Pompadour, and Watteau periods. Clothes took ideas from the past. It was the year of the bustle and the Grecian bend, of tight-lacing, tight-fitting gloves and shoes and, consequently, the "vapours." Cromwell shoes with large square brass or silver buckles covering the instep, worn especially at croquet, which was the fashionable game. Buttoned elastic-sided boots, high-laced boots of kid or satin, still had a tassel or bow on front. Broad square toes and well-fitted ankles attracted more attention now that skirts were a little shorter.

1869 Indoor shoes for day and evening made of kid or satin with large instep bows in the same material. Heels were 1½ or 2 inches high. Barbaric designs on jewellery reflect the influence of the "back to nature" cult. Dark red-gold colours and Moorish crescents used as decoration on shoes as well as clothes.

1870 Shoes, not boots, *de rigueur* for evening; white satin or kid embroidered in gold, silver or coloured silks. Boots of black satin, with high heels, worn for indoors; shoes also worn indoors, bronze-coloured or adorned with coloured rosettes.

1871 Dolly Varden hats and the same look in clothes of chintz and floral-patterned materials. This look called for barred shoes with button fastening, of *ingénue* appearance.

1872 Military trimmings like braiding and frogging, ground-length skirts again. Not much mention of shoes, though they must have caught some of this military influence. A great deal of mourning black still worn, though changing.

1874 Shoes matched day dresses for colour as mourning subsided.

1878 French fashions no longer slavishly followed by women of fashion, who by now had many more magazines to draw upon for ideas. Willet Cunnington's books give a comprehensive list of these.

1879 Aesthetic fashions important, especially with reference to colour. Shoes as well as clothes made in dull greens, peacock, and rich deep reds and browns. Clothes were worn in genteel disarray, with ideas taken from the picturesque. Fashions were called after the things or people of the day, such as the Jersey dress which recalled the name and figure of the Jersey Lily, Mrs. Langtry. (It was named for her shape not for the fabric's knit, its "jersey" name comes from "jarnsey" the type of knitted sweater worn in the Channel Islands.) "Pinafore" dress comes from Gilbert and Sullivan's *H.M.S. Pinafore*. The expense of dressing had trebled in forty years. The aesthetic styles do not seem to have been mentioned in the "glossy" magazines for smart women.

1880 The Rational Dress Reform Movement was important because it was the first movement of any kind in which women took an active part. William Morris said that "no dress can be beautiful that is stiff, and drapery is essential," Artists were now becoming interested in dress design, but there was a falling-off of quality, material and workmanship. The medieval appearance of clothes brought simple boots and sandals back again. Pilgrim-type simplicity brought buckled shoes and low heels. What was called "high art" costume was fashionable. Beads used on everything, as shoe embroidery also. No two people dressed alike. Tartans, brought into fashion by the Queen's love of Scotland, was used even for the tops of boots which looked like spats. Evening dresses were made of hand-painted materials, some of which we find in shoes also. They must have been made especially for shoemaking as the design fitted the pattern so well.

1882 There was no limit to colour this year. Silk stockings were elaborately embroidered. Great use made of machine-made lace, in clothes and on boudoir slippers, and of tortoiseshell. Gloves and boots had 16–18 buttons.

1883 Suede or bronze glazed kid for dancing; some had very pretty hand-painted toe-caps. Pointed toes on shoes embroidered with fine beads. Louis French heels in again. Boots were not now seen in town on well-dressed women.

1884 The Calcutta Exhibition brought ideas from India and a great deal of Indian muslins, other materials with printed designs, jewellery, buckles, silver, etc. Shoes for day wear were Oxfords laced closely and high. Button boots in patent leather with 12–16 buttons with kid or satin tops. Plain or Louis heels covered to match the shoe, some with a metal insert above the top-piece. Coloured clocks on stockings. Stockings themselves ribbed and in many colours, but also black cotton for day. For evening plain coloured open-work.

1887 Red stockings studded with a swallow pattern. Paris said to have lost some of its hold, Americans preferred London.

1888 Sarah Bernhardt with her stayless figure appeared in Directoire and Empire styles in sandalled feet. These styles swept Europe and because they shortened the hem to the ankle, brought shoes into focus again. They brought about the disappearance of the bustle.

1889 Subdued quiet colours, related to nature. Green was said to be popular because of the wet weather. Greek clothes worn damply, so that they clung to the figure giving an appearance of nakedness. Day shoes had a black and white magpie appearance, and were made of black patent and white buckskin. Cromwell shoes in again with high-cut fronts, buckles, and large tailored bows. Evening shoes were pointed, had small bows and medium heels; in bronze or black. Black stockings for day and evening.

1890 Higher heels, jet clasps, "frog" trimmings. Shoes excessively pointed making the vamp long and slender, small feet seldom seen. The popularity of sport made special sports shoes necessary for women as well as men.

1892 A fashion magazine forecast in this year that trousers would be worn everywhere by women in fifty years time. This was not far wrong.

1898 Shoes laced and buttoned in front, pulled tight to show shape of ankle, had rounded toes till this year when the American pointed toes came into fashion on all footwear.

VICTORIAN

Left (1885)

Hat high, sloping crown and narrow rolling brim dropped in the front. Ribbon ornament. Hair pulled high on head and coiled. High-necked dress fastened down the front. Bustle at back standing out from the figure at least one foot. Skirt full, just clearing the ground.

(From photograph Princess Louise, Duchess of Fife, by W. D. Downey, 1889)

Centre (1850)

Hair smooth and parted with knot at the back. High-necked bodice with narrow collar fastened with brooch. Pagoda sleeves with full white undersleeves. Skirt gathered over several petticoats and crinoline.

(From engraving by D. J. Pound, 1861)

Right (1880)

Hair piled high on head. High neckline, bodice fitted smoothly from neck to low hip-line. Sleeves tight-fitting with cuff of ruching. Skirt tightly draped with fulness pulled behind. Overskirt outline or underskirt.

(Skirts so tight that it was only possible to hobble along)

1. A cream satin shoe with soft satin bow and elastic ankle-strap. Self-covered curving heel.
2. A striped velvet house mule for a man to wear with a smoking jacket. Silk fringe outlines its bound top.
3. A young girl's pump with a flat tailored bow, in kid, or satin.
4. A woman's close-fitting ankle-boot in shiny brown kid. Its laces are crossed over hooks. The decoration is very fine stitching, and the intricately cut toe-cap is in self-coloured leather.
5. A very soft kid court shoe with a high-cut front decorated with a jewelled brooch. The collar is cut from the same leather in slightly darker colour.
6. Cream satin wedding slipper with very curved heel. Its double decoration is in twisted rouleau cut from the same satin and set on hidden bars. The ends are ornamented with small pearls.
7. Young girls wore pantaloons of linen and lace which showed below their long full skirts. Ballet-shaped shoes, made of satin or kid and laced over flesh-coloured stockings.
8. A flat-heeled pointed-toed pump made in cream satin with a folded tailored bow of the same satin.
9. Beige cloth top of spat-like shape on black kid. An ankle-boot laced up the outside with ribbon.

68. VICTORIAN (I)

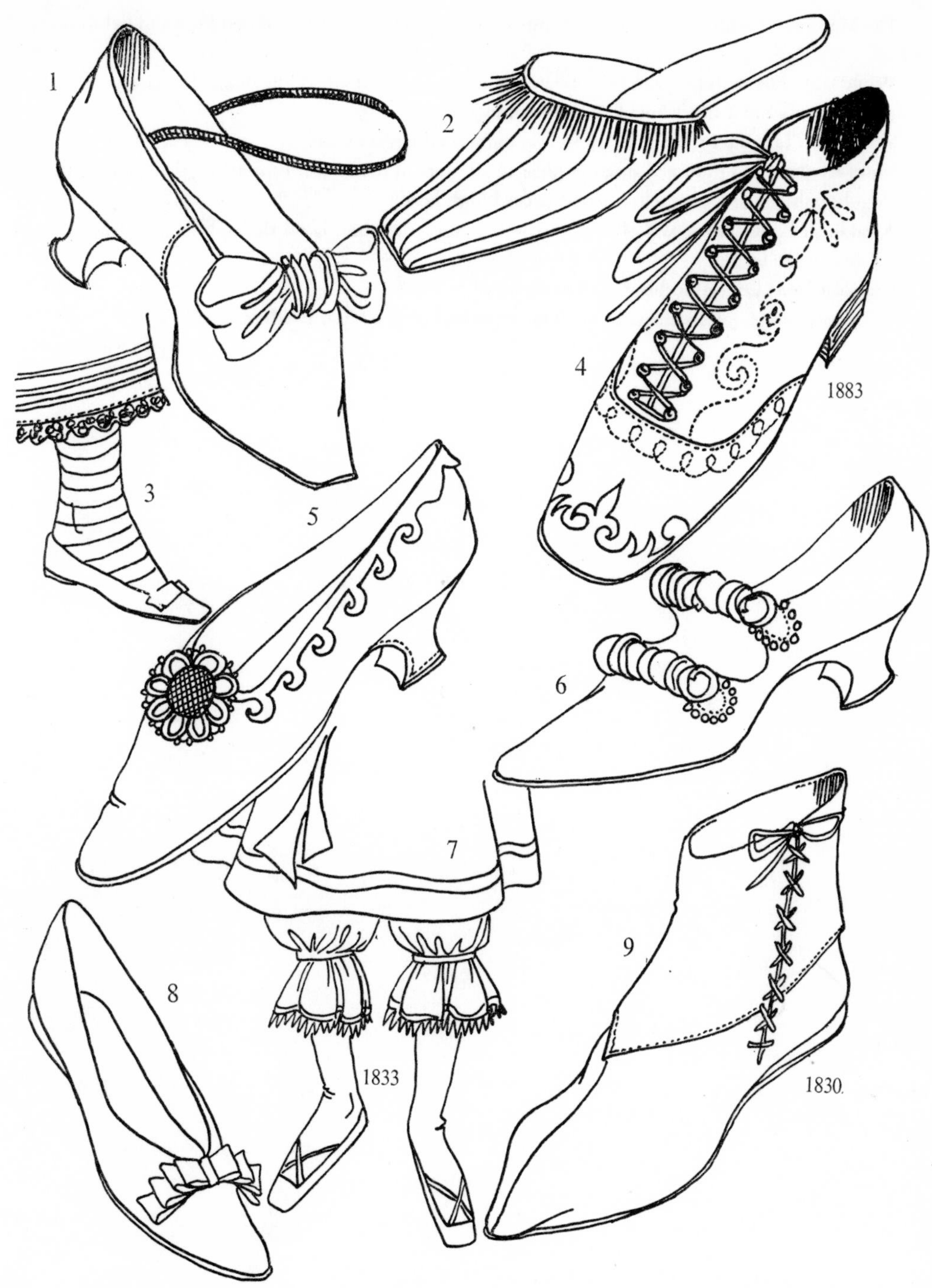
1
2
3
4
1883
5
6
7
8
1833
9
1830

1. Tan kid Oxford with decorative punching and wide taffeta ribbon tie. Round toe and lightly-curved built heel.
2. White satin shoe with big satin bow extending to beyond each side of the shoe. The centre of the bow is edged with pearls and a silver buckle holds it all together.
3. Shaped and buttoned strap in beige kid on high-sided tabbed shoe.
4. Multi-strapped and buttoned shoes popular in all types of materials. Especially good-looking in light brown highly polished kid with self-covered curved high heels.
5. A mid-calf boot with separately cut cap and counter. Ribbon laced through hand-stitched eyelets, and lined with beige linen.
6. High-cut laced Oxford in black or brown kid.
7. White silk shoe bound with satin at all its edges and with a big soft white satin bow.

69. VICTORIAN (II)

1
1872
2
3
4
5
6
7

1. Wellington boot in black leather with deep turned-down cuff in tan leather. The leather or tape knee-ties knot through the loops on the inside.

2. Another popular boot of the period in black calf with additional upstanding collar put on with a concealed seam. Some boot legs were cut seamless.

3. Tall boot with separately-cut vamp and seamed leg. The inside top is cut higher to protect the leg when riding. Kid-lined.

4. Typical ballet-type shoe of the period with loops inside the shoe for the laces. The square-cut vamp has a small brooch at the throat.

5. Buttoned ankle-boot in black kid with bound top and button-tabs. The vamp and quarter-line is heavily embroidered with silk stitching.

6. Expensive, heavily frilled and decorated kid boot with elastic sides. The lap-over front takes a double bow of taffeta frilling which blends with the frilled and padded front decoration. Mock buttons decorate the front and sides.

70. VICTORIAN (III)

1
2
3
4
5
6

1. Cream satin shoe lined with beige linen. Very curved heel covered to match in the same material. The topline is bound with ribbon and the vamp decorated with a soft satin bow.

2. A popular kind of bar shoe in kid or in material. Vamp and quarter shoe with a low self-covered heel. A soft bow in satin decorates the vamp.

3. Ballet-shaped shoes like these, generally in soft black kid, were laced over net stockings worn over flesh-coloured stockings.

4. A high boot made of kid with a braid-trimmed front and bead-decorated vamp, with button fastening on the inside leg.

5. All forms of delicate embroidery, often incorporating small glass and pearl beads and frequently seen on evening and wedding shoes.

6. A child's boot with elastic on the outside only. The vamp is appliquéd kid on to kid in the same or lightly-contrasting colour. The toe is square and shallow.

7. Man's cloth-topped spat-type shoe in beige felt and black kid. The elastic is at the sides, and the top is buttoned down the back.

71. VICTORIAN (IV)

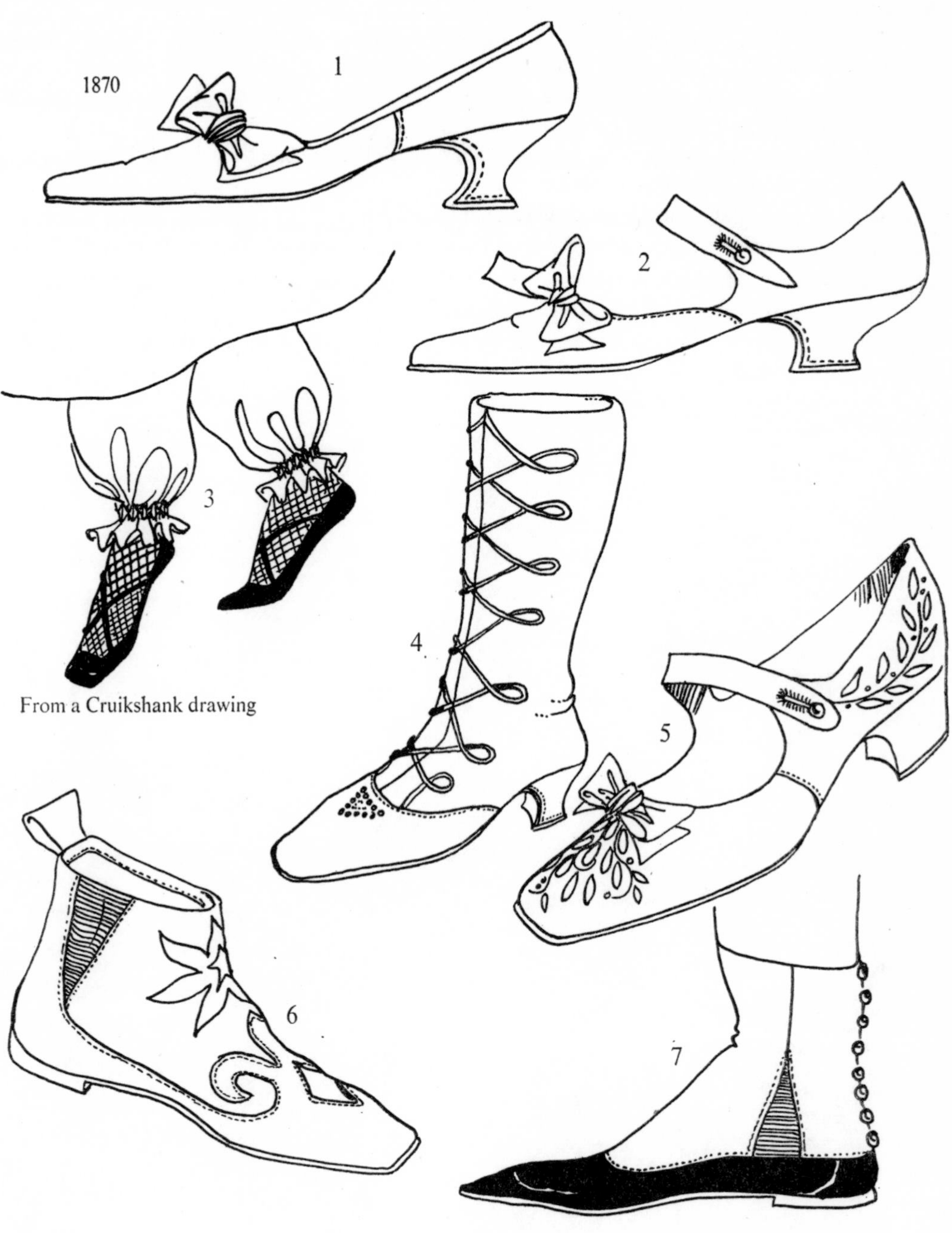

From a Cruikshank drawing

1. Cloth-topped boot with black kid shoe and heel cover. Satin ribbon bows, the top one decorated with a brooch or jewel. Buttons fasten it on the inside.
2. White satin shoe, bound with satin ribbon and with looped rosettes also of satin. The rosettes carry a jewel or a brooch and the curved heel is covered in the same satin.
3. High button boots very popular during this reign, their height and number of buttons varying with fashion. In coffee-coloured kid with pearl shank buttons.
4. A tartan-topped kid shoe showing the fashion for Scottish things. Lightly pointed and tilted toe.
5. An embroidered tabbed shoe in soft kid.
6. Velvet slipper with flower decoration lined with beige linen.
7. Cloth-topped boot with brown kid, brown kid facing and pearl buttons. The button holes are stitched.

72. VICTORIAN (V)

1
2
4
3
1868
6
1868
5
7

19

The Edwardians

Edward VII, 1901–1910

THE PRINCE OF WALES was sixty years old when he became king, and since he was a grandfather before he ascended the throne, naturally he had no "youthful" influence on the fashions that started the century with him. However, he had already exercised some influence over fashion before becoming king (hence the Prince of Wales checks and the Prince of Wales feathers), and his wife, Alexandra, Princess of Wales, had set a fashion in clothes. During his reign there were many social changes that the old Queen would have resisted, and many of these were to benefit the lower classes, thus making fashion much more democratic and accessible to all than it had been. In spite of his age when he came to the throne, Edward cared for personal appearance and set the fashions of the day which gave his reign that Edwardian elegance for which it is famed. His was a short reign but the Edwardian period lasted in effect until the outbreak of the Great War in 1914.

Characteristic of this period were the fashions given prominence by the Gaiety Girl and the Gibson Girl in the theatre and music-hall, as well as the fashions worn at Ascot, to be seen in contemporary illustrations.

Improved transport facilities, and in particular the motorcar, however, were beginning to make a significant difference to fashion in the next few years. Wide skirts were replaced by narrower ones, shorter because of the growing vogue for bicycling and for other sports. Shoes were by now machine-made and therefore more readily available. The whole aspect of fashion showed a revolt against Victorian restrictions, which had become even narrower since the Queen's widowhood. Under Edward frivolity was encouraged and new ideas in fashion were fostered.

Women's hats were enormous, so wide that for motoring they were tied on with veils. They were elaborately decorated with flowers and feathers. Towards 1910 the ankle-length hobble skirt became very narrow indeed, focusing attention directly on the feet. Toes were pointed, the heels high and waisted, the upper often of the one-bar button type; the colour was often beige, though shoes generally matched dresses.

Mrs. Pankhurst's campaign brought a totally different conception of women's position in England at both ordinary and professional levels, and women's emancipation was to show very soon in the clothes they wore during the war years. Until their clothes were freed by this emancipation, women's shape was similar to that of a pouter pigeon.

Heavily draped and looped skirts were lifted at the side or front to show a white stocking, high heels and pointed toes. The court shoe became very popular. For outdoors, spat shapes were popular, cut in the same shape as the genuine felt or wool spats, worn by men. (Spats were an abbreviation of the earlier Spatterdashes.) The colours of men's spats were generally beige or grey on a black patent or brown shoe. For women, a buttoned cloth-topped boot in the same colours was cut to just above the ankle. Tie shoes of all kinds cut very close to the leg were popular, laced with ribbon with metal tag-ends; light broguing and stitching edged the vamp, toe-cap, and counter. Beige or bronze colours were very popular for these. When cut higher they echoed the curving shape of the figure. Marcasite buckles, cut steel, and paste diamonds were very fashionable.

Bar shoes were popular, sometimes cut with three or more buttoned bars high on the instep. The boot button had remained more or less unchanged since its invention with a metal looped shank at the back, which facilitated its stitching on. Toes were deep in silhouette, sometimes round, sometimes pointed, always narrow and elegant. To wear boots and shoes a size too small was considered smart. Large flat soft bows of draped ribbon were seen on all kinds of shoes; nearly all heels were curved and set somewhat further under the instep. High-necked blouses with boned lace stand collars echoed the high curving "neck" of the boots seen everywhere.

Machinery had made stitching much simpler and it was now used in intricate detailing as decoration on boots and shoes. Some of this work was very fine and beautiful, and in several colours.

While hems grew shorter and freer, shoes became easier to wear and, as more women were drawn into the war in either factories or the forces, more practical. Spats for women were made buttoning down the side, for winter wear, worn over dark-coloured shoes. The bar shoe became increasingly fashionable and there are many versions of it available for study. Men wore boots rather than shoes, black and brown being the usual colours; a form of bright tan was called "yellow" and was considered vulgar. A great deal of light broguing was seen on all kinds of shoes. Two-tone shoes in tan and white, brown and white, and sometimes daringly dark red and white were worn by both sexes (these were later called "co-respondent shoes"). Heels were growing much higher, were still curving, and were sometimes in a contrasting colour.

Clothes for women were in directly contrasted styles. . the severe military uniforms, or near uniform of the associated services, and the frivolous clothes worn on leave. Patent leather was very popular for wear with them.

Little girl's clothes were very much shorter, being cut to above the knee. Long white or black stockings worn with white or black barred shoes were the accepted wear.

Instep bars appear about this time as a logical development from the buttoned strap. These were of varying widths, some quite wide, and were brogued to match stitched and punched toe-caps. Sometimes these were set on an elastic on the inside, which was lasted in when the shoe was made, to facilitate fit. Elastic was in growing use but was now moved to the front of the shoe, enabling a much higher cut to be achieved. In this style it was generally concealed behind a decorated tab. Any shoemaker's catalogue of the period will show many of these.

Opened-up sandal-shoes begin to appear after the war. These had closed in toes and quarters with open sides and high-set T-bars. This is a style with many versions and one which has continued in varying guises ever since its inception.

EDWARDIAN

Woman (left) (1902)
Hat very large and covered in feathers or flowers. Hair piled high. High-necked gown with wide pleat over the shoulder and down the sides, back and front. Waist belted and dipped at front (Gibson style). Renaissance sleeve with full puff at wrist caught into a cuff. Long flowing skirt over padded hips with tucks at hem.

Man
Shirt with attached cuffs, separate collar. Coats fairly long and fitted snugly. Trousers cuffed at bottom.

Woman (right) (1914)
Small head-hugging hat. Bobbed hair. Pleated ruffle at neck. Jacket with blousing at waist. Hobble skirt.

Turn-of-the-century fashion spans the link period between the Victorians and the different clothes and shoes which began to appear with World War I, so that we get a little of both in this short reign.

1. High-laced boot of the Gaiety Girl, worn in many versions by most women. The dancers wore an ornate, over-decorated boot, stitched intricately with rows of coloured stitching and with coloured insets of other leathers. Toe caps were lightly brogued, and vamps were often scalloped. Plainer versions were in brown or black or beige. This was the boot that later became the basis of the popular skating boot of the time. Laced to mid-calf.

2. Some boots of a similar shape and height were fastened with a dozen or more shanked buttons and hand-stitched button-holes. These were often in patent for the vamp and quarter with soft kid or cloth for the leg. Toes were pointed and long with the tip lightly curved. The heels were either straight as in sketch 1, or curved as in sketch 2, and in heights up to 2 inches.

3. Both these types of shoes had a narrow-fitting sole and a horseshoe-shaped top-piece, both of leather.

4. Scalloping was a favourite form of decoration, large or small, and was often combined with a scooped top-line. The stitching on these boots, though done by machine, was very small and delicate. A boot like this, cut without a galosh, was often in soft kid.

5. Buttonhooks were an essential. They were short and plain or very ornamental depending on the user's taste. Some were long, which enabled the user to fasten her boots without bending down. Buttons were plain pearl, or black, all with a metal shank, or made of silver and very ornamental.

73. EDWARDIAN (1)

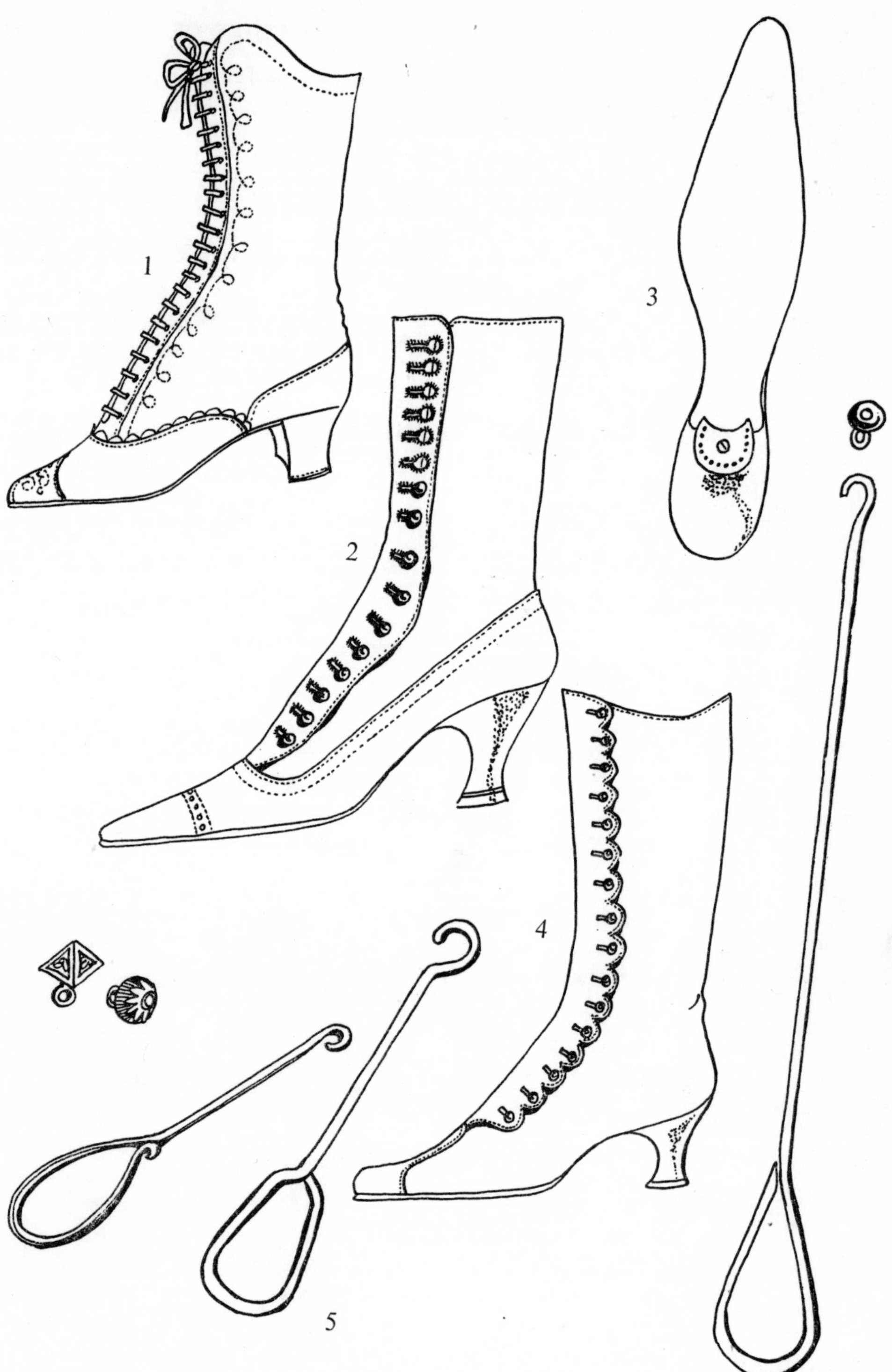
1
2
3
4
5

1. Button boots were as fashionable for men as for women but men had an additional help to fastening at the back in the form of a tape loop, with which they were pulled on. Low leather heels were usual. They often had striped linings.

2. A child's leather gaiter was often fur-lined and with an elastic under the foot. The whole covered the shoe completely and was fastened with buttons and hooks like those of their elders. Children's skirts, however, were short and gaiters reached up to meet them.

3. Some kid boots for women, cut to mid-calf, were buttoned on both sides of a centre seam. Small toe-caps were lightly brogued on all kinds of boots and shoes.

4. This high-heeled buttoned bar-shoe was the start of a fashion that was going to continue for forty years in one form or another, often changing only in the shape of the toe and the height of the heel.

5. Pointed-toe court shoe with large decorative tab, high-cut front and thin high heel. Garters were worn to show under short skirts at the knee.

6. Rather heavy-looking kid shoes with gusset concealed under the decorative tab were popular with the shortening skirt. Piping was a fashionable method of neatening edges. Curved heels and pointed toes looked right with shortening skirts.

7. Gaiters were worn by women as well as children. Made of wool or felt and worn over shoes, their tops were hidden under full skirts. Buttons were still the method of fastening, and they had striped linings similar to those in men's boots.

74. EDWARDIAN (II)

1
Man's boot
Child's gaiters
2
3
4
5
6
7

1. High fronts of all kinds were fashionable, and so were side-lacing and rather top-heavy looking Louis heels. This semi-boot was made of kid with a patent vamp.

2. Gusseted high vamps often concealed by decorative buckles of glass or marcasite, giving a long vamp effect.

3. Soft-looking court shoes of kid were to be a constant shoe fashion from here on. This had a tab cut in one with the vamp forming creases on the front.

4. Criss-crossed vamps in varying forms were used on all types of shoes. Generally they had elastic gores on the inside. Often in two colours, black and white was popular, with brown and beige also very fashionable. Long foreparts had gently rounded toes.

5. Punched and finely stitched tabs of all kinds were featured on high-cut shoes of this period. High Louis heel with low-set curve gave an illusion of slenderness.

6. Women's shoes often copied men's in both cut and colour. Apart from looking lighter, the design was the same, featuring fine stitching and worked eyelets. Heat-pressed creases were popular, so were braid and tape laces.

7. Spats had a very long run of fashion for men. They were generally in light beige with worked buttonholes and shank buttons, but were often also made in light grey or white. All had elastic under the shoe's arch.

75. EDWARDIAN (III)

1
2
3
4
5
6
7

The House of Windsor, 1910 onward

George V, 1910–1936 Edward VIII, 1936 George VI, 1936–1952 Elizabeth II, acceded 1952

THE FIRST HALF of the twentieth century brought more changes in fashion and ways of life than Britain had ever seen before. The First World War broke the connection with the Victorian and Edwardian epochs because it was a war fought not only by professional soldiers and everyone was in some way involved. George V's modesty and good judgement had a steadying influence and the fashion of the early period shows a change from the careless gaiety of the Edwardians. The new reign was not one of Puritan sobriety but it was less casual and took serious things more seriously. The levelling of classes, the emancipation of women, aided by the shortage of man-power in war industries, caused women to increase their demands for equality and independence, both of which were to have wide effect on fashion. By 1928 women were given equal suffrage with men and their clothes reflected the new freedom.

Skirts grew shorter as more freedom of movement was needed for the increasingly active life women were now leading. Shape became relaxed, waistless, easy to fit. The use of bias-cutting made fabrics more pliable, and silk and lisle stockings made the now clearly-revealed legs more attractive.

Men's clothes took their lead from the popular and fashionable Prince of Wales, who set the style for such fashions as Oxford bags and plus-fours. Prince of Wales checks and tweeds were also popular, as were soft caps and wide-brimmed trilbys. Their shoes matched what we would now term the "gangster" look of men's clothes, being pointed, made of bright brown calf or cut from white nubuck with brown cap and counter trimmings. There were also cloth-topped boots which laced closely round the ankle.

Women's shoes also exploited the new freedoms and a great many varieties of styles were experimented with. Though the basic shapes had pointed toes and high-cut vamps, set on curving "lavatory bottom" heels, the upper designs were limitless. New ideas were no longer confined to the upper and monied classes, and fashions were often set by the "flappers," the bright young things who danced the Charleston, the Black Bottom, and the Itchy-Coo.

Skill in shoe manufacture had improved tremendously so that many more shoes were produced by the new methods and prices were low and within reach of everyone.

Motoring had brought its own fashions which were rapidly becoming part of the everyday scene: foot-muffs, carriage boots, and warm-lined overshoes were for many an essential. For the first quarter of the century men retained the high shoe or laced boot pattern for footwear for many occasions; turned-up cuffs to trousers revealed brightly patterned socks, which were worn with boots and shoes alike. Some boots were still buttoned but many were laced through eyelets at the bottom of the facing, finished through hooks at the top. In the summer they were replaced by white canvas or buckskin boots or shoes, some trimmed with tan, brown, or black; these were the typical "co-respondent shoes" of the twenties.

Kid or felt tops known as spats were worn by smart and formal young men, generally to match gloves in a pearl-grey or white. Women wore them on occasions also. They had many interesting variations and were often to return in later periods.

A shoe made in polished tan calf was inelegantly called a "yellow boot." It had a deep boxed toe known in Europe as the American toe or the "bulldog," and was a very popular fashion. This was one of the styles made by machinery for a widening market. Brogue-style decoration was also done by machine and was a form not necessarily used only for sports shoes.

Many shoes for men and women were made on the turn-shoe principle, that is, made inside out. They were very soft and flexible. For men this was used mainly for evening shoes. Some evening shoes were made of patent which, trimmed with a flat grosgrain bow, became highly fashionable. An Oxford made also in patent with laces of military braid became a leading shoe fashion.

Rubber and crepe soles were frequently used for sports and country shoes, the methods of attaching them having now been perfected. They were first used for footwear intended for bathing and for sports wear. Ready-to-wear boots were now more popular, and as the industry and machinery developed they were made both quickly and cheaply. This was especially important in the rapidly-increasing American markets. Although more and more of them were bought, it was still considered the correct thing to have one's footwear bespoke-made. Many of these bespoke shoemakers still exist in London, with names and addresses which go back a very long way.

Many styles were copied from the Army, adapted from the field boot which became a basic shape seen in many types of men's lace-up boots and shoes. In America this particular style was known as the Blücher, after the type of shoe which that General had introduced for his soldiers.

With women's footwear it is the wide choice of materials which impresses us most. In an age which as yet had no synthetics to speak of, the list of materials available was considerable. Reversed calf, that is, suede dressed on the flesh side, was growing in favour and throughout this period we see many shoes which use it in combination with kid, patent, or satin, with attractive effect. It considered mostly of buck or antelope, but could also be made from goat or lamb. Colours in favour were sand, beige, brown, and grey. A great deal of bronze kid was worn and so were all types of lizards and snakes. Kid, patent, or suede were the most important materials for shoes, though all kinds of cloth, satin, crepe, gabardine, *peau de soie*, and sharkskin were also used to good effect. There was slight reaction against these as a fashion immediately after the war, however, as they had been used as substitutes for leather when it was in short supply.

Great names in dressmaking became *haute couture*, with its strong influence over clothes of all kinds. This was the time of Paquin, Vionnet, and the Callot sisters. It had been due to the influence of the prudish Madame Maintenon in the reign of Louis XIV, who would not allow men to control fashion because it was "not decent for men's hands to touch a woman," that these great names had all been women. But men had come to the lead in recent times and it was not until the twentieth century that women became their equals again as fashion designers. Then came Coco Chanel, who started an era of casual dressing in which she has never been surpassed. Even today her shoes are almost as important as trend-setters as her clothes. It was her beige and black sling-back court which brought the return of the open shoe.

This was also the the period when Paul Poiret's tailored clothes of 1910–14 were extending their influence far beyond that of their early years. It was he who had made corsets less tight and taught women to wear unrestricting clothes and to walk freely. He had first shortened skirts to ankle-level, thus revealing the foot and making the shoe important. The war accelerated this tendency and the foot began to develop a special importance of its own. Walking skirts, culottes, and cloaks were introduced, all of which drew attention to the feet, which were encased in light kid with gently rounded toes and curved heels. His shapes and colours caused a scandal when they were first introduced, but as he was the first designer to travel with his mannequins, spreading French ideas round the world his authority spread wide. He was extravagant in his personal whims as well as in his designs, and his flair for publicity was equally remarkable.

In the thirties, to the beginning of World War II, extravagances of fashion flourished, and shoes were affected as much as other items of dress. A platform lifted modern women from the ground and added to her height. Made glamorous by Carmen Miranda, it was studded with diamanté or nail-heads, or covered in different colours of leather; it was sometimes six inches in height. Ankle-straps of all kinds were to fluctuate in and out of fashion for several years. High wedges increased heel-height and were often cut out in different shapes like modern sculpture. High, thick heels and T-straps were also features of this period. Many of them return spasmodically to today's fashion in modern interpretations.

The war years of 1939–45 saw rationing and utility marks, a curtailment of material in clothes, and a heavy restriction in shoe-making materials. Substitutes were a necessity and fabrics such as gabardine took the place of leathers.

Wedges became commoner but were now made of cork and left uncovered. Peep-toes and big chunky trimmings decorated the very popular court shoe. Shoes in general were heavy-looking and not made more attractive by the leg-make-up which was sometimes used instead of stockings. Influences were derived mostly from filmstars, who were now the fashion-leaders, and great designers such as Adrian rose through the medium of films. American influence was very strong indeed, even the G.I. uniforms of the war starting fashion trends of their own. As always happens, fashion had anticipated the war and had been aware of the impending cataclysm, demonstrating this in a faint military echo of square shoulders and shorter skirts. But Paris was divided, offering frou-frou and femininity with an echo of the gay nineties in button-boots, veils, long gloves, tight corsets and a revival of the crinoline. At the same time, however, there was in Paris a sudden shortening of the skirts.

Not only in fashion, Britain was reduced to necessities and shoes were very scarce. The most popular was a classic shoe with a leather heel, probably because it wore well. Punched shoes of all kinds, courts, ties, ghillies were made in whatever leather was available. Because of the restrictions on design and materials and because factories were engaged on war production new methods of manufacture took preference over fashion, which tended to stand still for a while.

This state of un-fashion continued until the end of the war, when, released from many restrictions, ideas exploded in the New Look. Christian Dior dropped the hem-line to ankle-length and completely changed the look of clothes. With coupons still needed to buy both clothes and materials in Britain, this new and generous cut of skirts was hard to achieve. Immediately, the Edwardian look which Paris had been trying to achieve before the war came into being, and along with long, full skirts came high button boots, "buttons and bows," Edwardian boaters tied on with veilings, parasols, and all the trappings of a previous age. Naturally everything was overdone; from having too little, fashion now had too much.

Once in a generation comes a great designer who changes the look of everything whose name is known even by the man in the street. The designer of the post-war era was Christian Dior, whose New Look is still talked about and which started a chain reaction of "looks," which is still a term used to describe a different influence.

The shoe designer of this period was Ferragamo, who changed the look and the fit of shoes. His autobiography describes the origins of this world-famous Italian shoemaker, whose business is now carried on by his daughter Fiamma.

FROM THE FIRST WORLD WAR TO THE 'THIRTIES

Left (1914)
Wartime worker. Hair cropped and covered. Bloused overalls.

Centre (1925)
Hat small and tight down on head. Hair, boyish bob. Coat with fur collar and cuffs with long flat revers. Low waist. Tiers of diagonal ruffles to form skirt above the knee. Silk stockings.

Right (1932)
Large beach hat. Hair softly waved. Blouse with tie. Sleeveless jacket and wide lounging pyjamas.

SECOND WORLD WAR YEARS

Left (1941)
Trilby-type hat. Hair smoothed back into roll all round head. Two-piece mannish suit with square padded shoulders. High-placed lapels and single-breasted. Box-pleated skirt. Shoulder-bag.

Right (1947)
The "New Look". Sloping shoulders on very fitted jacket with small nipped-in waist. Skirt very long, to within 12 inches of the ground.

1. Russian boots were one of the most significant styles of the 'twenties. Made of leather and cut to just above mid-calf height, they fitted well but wrinkled round the ankle, which was a feature of their appearance. They had round toes and low heels.

2. In Paris the skirt went very short and was cut well above the knee. The boot rose higher to cover the knee; it was made of kid and was fairly tight-fitting though without fasteners. Toes were rounding slightly.

3. The court shoe had a high-cut throat-line and very often asymmetric decoration was an important feature. Beige kid and beige lizard were the usual materials used.

4. T-straps were one of the main shoe fashion details and the variations on this theme were very wide. Intricate and detailed cutting made cleverly cut motifs on the vamp and sides. Pale green kid with matching lizard insertions and a button fastening are featured in this round toe shoe.

5. A man's tall elastic-sided boot cut to cover the ankle. The extended welted edge runs through to the heel.

6. A long-vamped court shoe—in America, a pump—with straight top-line and inset throat panel of a contrast or toning collar.

76. FROM THE 'TWENTIES TO THE MID CENTURY (I)

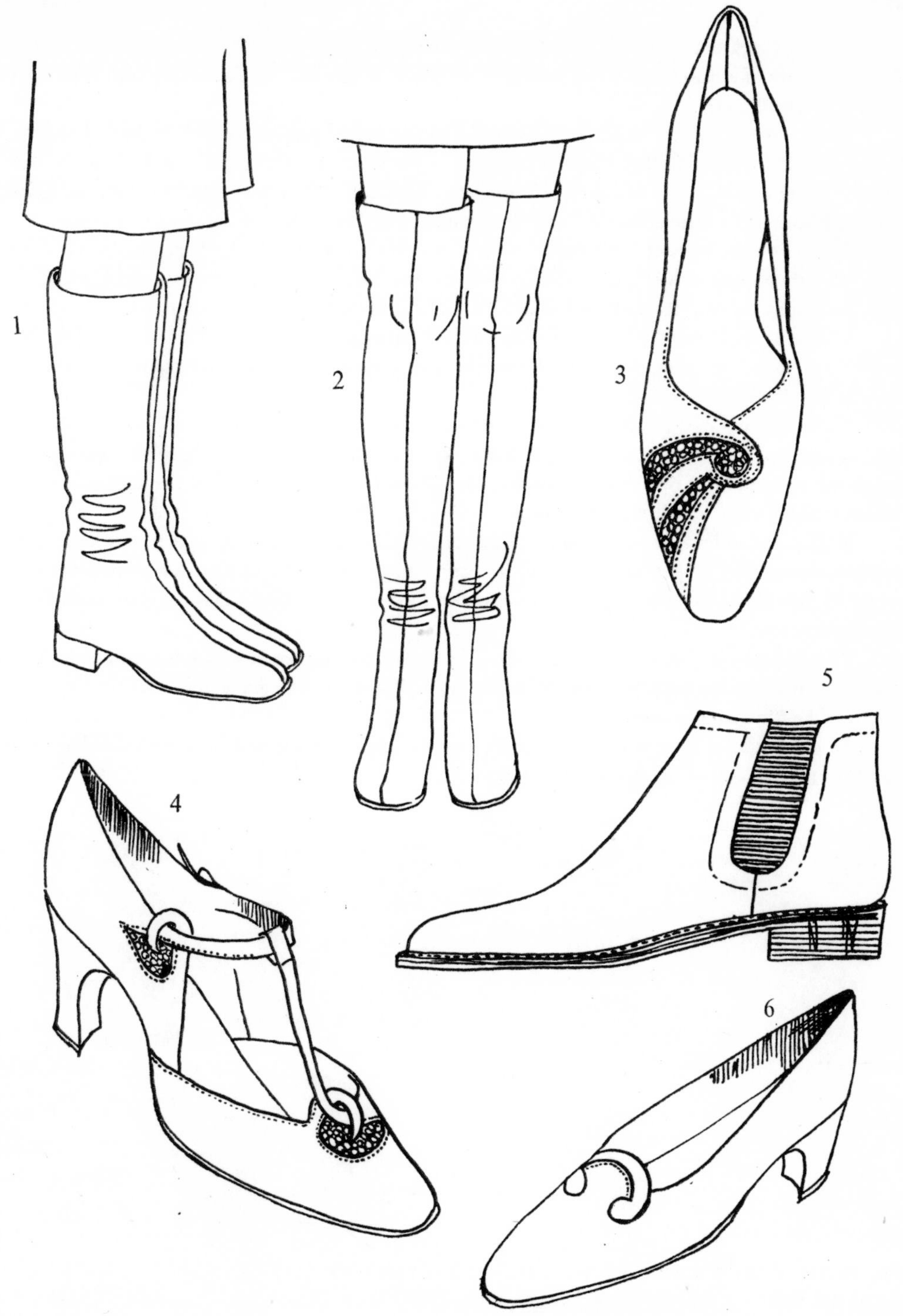
1
2
3
4
5
6

Ever since the Greek drama, which introduced the Cothurnus, there has been great importance attached to shoes as a means of elevation. It is not surprising, therefore, to find that the fashion for high heels and platforms is a recurring idea.

1. There comes a point at which the heel cannot go any higher because the arch of the foot and the last do not permit it. When further height is required, or the same but with a different look, it can only be achieved by the combined use of a deep platform and a high heel. The most recent use of this aid to height was in the 'forties as a natural reaction after the period of low-heeled fashion enforced by the war.

2. Spread over the years of the 'forties various shapes evolved which gave heels themselves more importance. Layered wedges offered a great deal of design scope, which was interpreted as summer and winter wear, for beach or town. Its elasticized sling back was also the beginning of a new trend.

3. As soon as the higher wedges were accepted their variations were legion. This was called the "flying wedge," the "loop," or "flying buttress." It used the same sculptured lines as do the groups of Henry Moore and is in the idiom of the period.

4. Another feature of the 'forties was the open toe, a fashion which has continued up to the present time, with varying degrees of opening. In 1939 Edna Woolman Chase, Editor of *American Vogue*, protested against the promotion of open-toe and open-backed shoes for street wear when she addressed the Shoe Fashion Guild of America. It was of no avail.

5. In 1967, for a film based on the life of Catherine the Great, there appeared the newest version of the platform, designed by Roger Vivier. It will be seen to have a great deal in common with its forerunners but for its forward-jutting edge repeated in the walled toe-shape of the last. This is a clear example of the twenty-year cycle.

6. The extremity of platforms, and therefore of heels also, was reached in sandals like this, six inches high at the back, made of black silk and embroidered in gold. It had a gold lining and sock. Dated 1941, it can be seen at the Museum of Costume, Bath.

7. An extraordinary shoe in clear vinyl with an elastic back and a gold-kid-covered slim high wedge. Dated 1949, it was one of the first shoes in plastic.

77. FROM THE 'TWENTIES TO THE MID-CENTURY (II)
(WEDGES AND PLATFORMS)

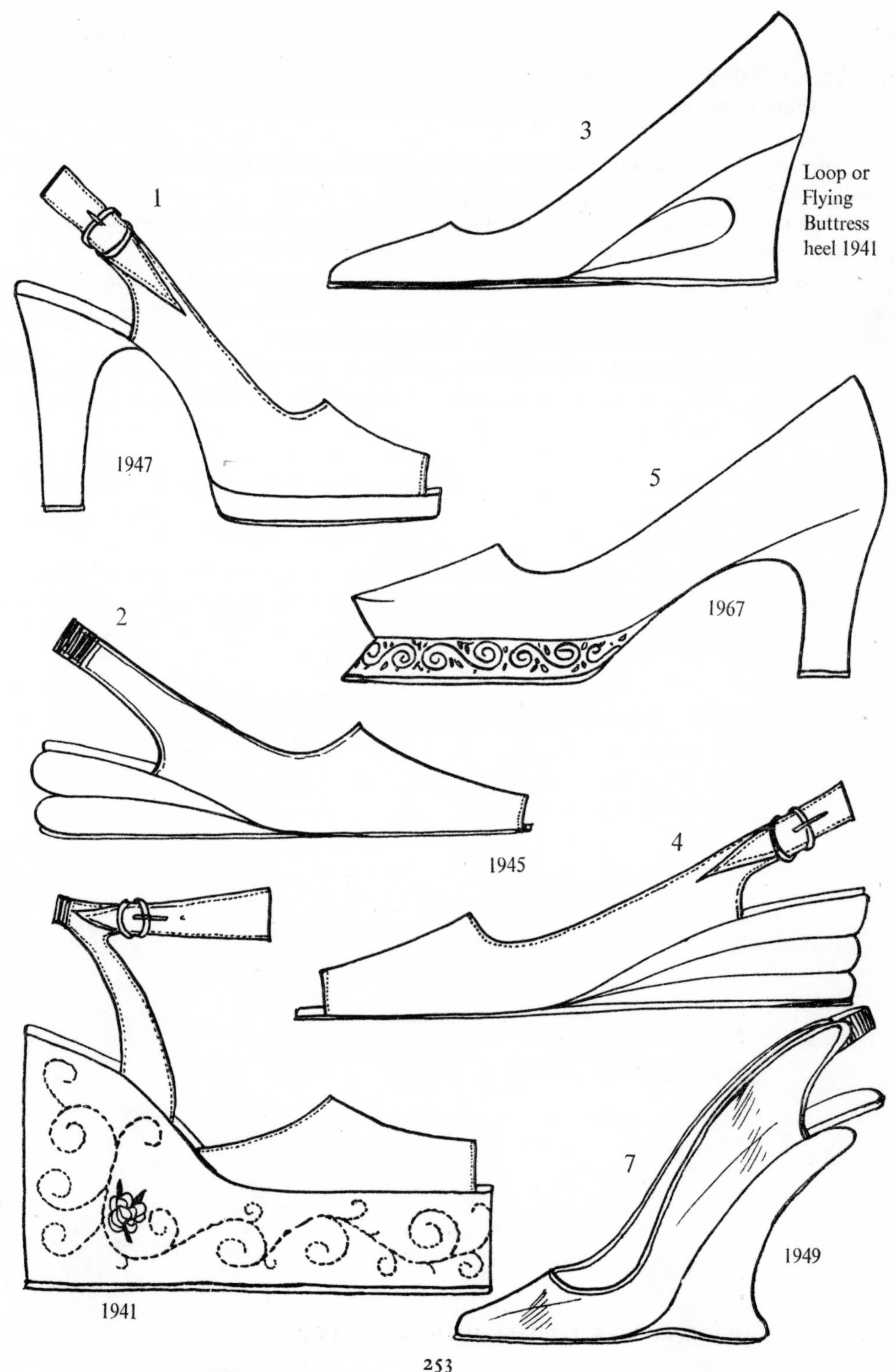

1
1947
3
Loop or
Flying
Buttress
heel 1941
5
1967
2
1945
4
6
1941
7
1949

1. High heel thick at the top and waisted toward the bottom. High-cut vamp outlined by double-rouleaux strip. T-strap supported by double-rouleaux strips. Buttoned at side with shank button. Made of kid with kid or lizard strips.
2. High-cut opera court with saddle outlined with braiding. Middle-height curved Louis heel. Made of kid.
3. High-cut open-waisted sandal with strips of lizard decoration set into a low T-strap.
4. Open-waisted d'Orsay court made from soft kid and lined with patterned silk.
5. Three bars of beige kid, buttoned to matching saddles, on a very finely-punched kid upper. Thick curved Louis heel. The lasts of these shoes are long in the forepart and gently rounded.
6. High-cut T-bar shoe with double-strapped front and short vamp.
7. Man's co-respondent shoe in white buck and brown calf. Also in lighter shape for women's shoes.

78. FROM THE 'TWENTIES TO THE MID-CENTURY (III)

1
2
3
4
5
6
7

1. This basic bar shoe is one which set the style for a large variety of shoes at this period, and has recurred in many patterns ever since. High-cut vamp and top-line bound with kid or ribbon. Shank-button fastening. Thick curved "lavatory bottom" heel. This shoe was very much favoured by Queen Mary.
2. A similar shoe with crossed button bars, trimmed with brooch at throat.
3. Sandal of woven leather with hand-stitched rand often rolled up round the foot into a moulded shape on the mocassin principle. Imported from Czechoslovakia.
4. The tango pump. Made of white satin with matching ribbon ties fastened at the top-line with small clusters of diamanté.
5. This kid ankle-bar sandal has suede insets.
6. Twenty years later the bar fashion is repeated. In 1950 the open-waisted sandal decorated with coloured overlaid strip and fastened with a shank button, was a popular style.
7. This crossed-bar pattern with two side elastic gores is also a repeating pattern.

79. FROM THE 'TWENTIES TO THE MID-CENTURY (IV)

1920
1
2
1917
1916
1928
3
4
1924
5
6
1950
7

1. Man's four-hole Oxford-toe shoe with plain toe-cap. The toe tapering off almost to a point. A younger man's shoe which goes with long coats and wide trousers. Contrast this with . . .

2. . . . An older man's shoe of the same period which is really a half-boot with a more rounded toe. A cloth or suede top on a black patent or brown calf vamp. These fasten with shank button, and fit close to the ankle.

3. Woman's shoe of the same period showing high-cut lines and curved heel. Generally made in black kid with patent toe-cap.

4. When the 'thirties dawned, clothes had become much more easy and casual. This Norwegian moccasin was unlined and in soft leathers. It was worn by all classes, especially in America.

5. The Riviera sandal with its very simple cut was another indication of growing freedom from convention in footwear. Many styles based on this pattern had straps which slotted through the insole. A plantation crepe sole was one of many soft soles which added to its comfort. Worn by men and women.

6. High cork wedge covered in different colours. The elastic form of sling-back becoming commonplace.

7. The "New Look" was an echo and a re-echo of many past styles. Suede tie-shoes with large peardrop eyelets were popular.

80. FROM THE 'TWENTIES TO THE MID-CENTURY (V)

1
2
1918-20
3
4
Norwegian Moccasin new in 1936
6
Riviera Sandal
1938
5
7
New look 1945-6-7

1. High-sided court shoe with small peep-toe and high heel. Its trimming consists of two wooden blocks covered with leather.
2. Wedged court shoe with thin platform and peep-toe. Note the high cut of the sides and throat. Made of gabardine and suede.
3. Typical of the cross-over sandal of the period decorated with an imitation jewel in the centre. Thick platform tapers off toward the back, supported by a high thick and straight heel. The ankle-strap crosses at the back.
4. High-tiered wedge sandal for resort wear, made of straw. Decoration on the front is in the form of a small hat; the button is of plaited straw. Imported from France.
5. Another straw sandal in a conventional tie pattern bound with tape. Cork wedge and platform.
6. Thick high wedge on straw tie-shoe. These were used as conventional shoes when leather grew scarce.
7. High-heeled strip sandal. The strips were made of straw, kid, or plastic.

81. FROM THE 'TWENTIES TO THE MID-CENTURY (VI)

1
2
3
4
5
6
7

During the period following the war of 1939, the main characteristic of shoes from this time was the gradual narrowing of the toe and the slenderizing of the heel, which grew higher. All upper design was planned to fit in with this theme which was applied to all types of shoes.

1. As the heel grew higher so did the front of the shoe to meet the longer hemline, now settled for a time at mid-calf.

2. One of the longest running fashions of the period was the built-in concealed wedge of the 'fifties. An entirely different construction with the quarters and heel-cover cut in one, seamed down the centre back, and with a wooden wedge heel concealed inside. The small sketch *2a* shows another shoe shape also made by Brevitt with a more curving back line and an arched sole. It is called the "Bouncer," is still made and has never been surpassed.

3. As the heel increased peaked fronts became popular for court shoes. Well cut and invariably without trimming they often had a lightly-walled toe, and were called Jesters.

4. There were many cross-currents of fashion after the war and contradictory silhouettes often appeared together. This shell court which began to be seen in the mid-'forties, had a deep throat line which lowered the top-line almost to the toe nails.

5. The T-bar is a basic pattern for shoes which is hardly ever out of fashion. It has appeared in varying forms since the turn of the century as a modern shoe shape. Important throughout the 'twenties and 'thirties it re-appeared strongly in the 'fifties, and again in the mid-'sixties.

6. The walled toe "dutch boy" of 1939 is another style whose cut has remained in fashion for a very long time. At its first appearance it was accompanied by a dipping top-line and a completely round heel which gave it a wooden "sabot" look. During the war period it was made frequently in gabardine or cavalry twill or one of the other substitutes then fashionable.

7. The early 'forties saw an increase in the design of toe shapes and heels as lasts sought an affinity with hems. The Sultan toe with its tip-tilted bump was used in combination with a high top-line and nail-heads.

8. This sling-back court is almost dateless. It appeared during World War II and has continued in more or less the same shape ever since. It is brought up to date by the height and shape of its heel, which in the 'forties was thick and about 2 to 2½ inches in height, and by its toe, which then was generally open. It had a high-cut sweetheart throatline which was ribbon-bound, the ribbon being either left plain or carrying some kind of bow or other decoration.

82. FROM THE 'TWENTIES TO THE MID-CENTURY (VII)

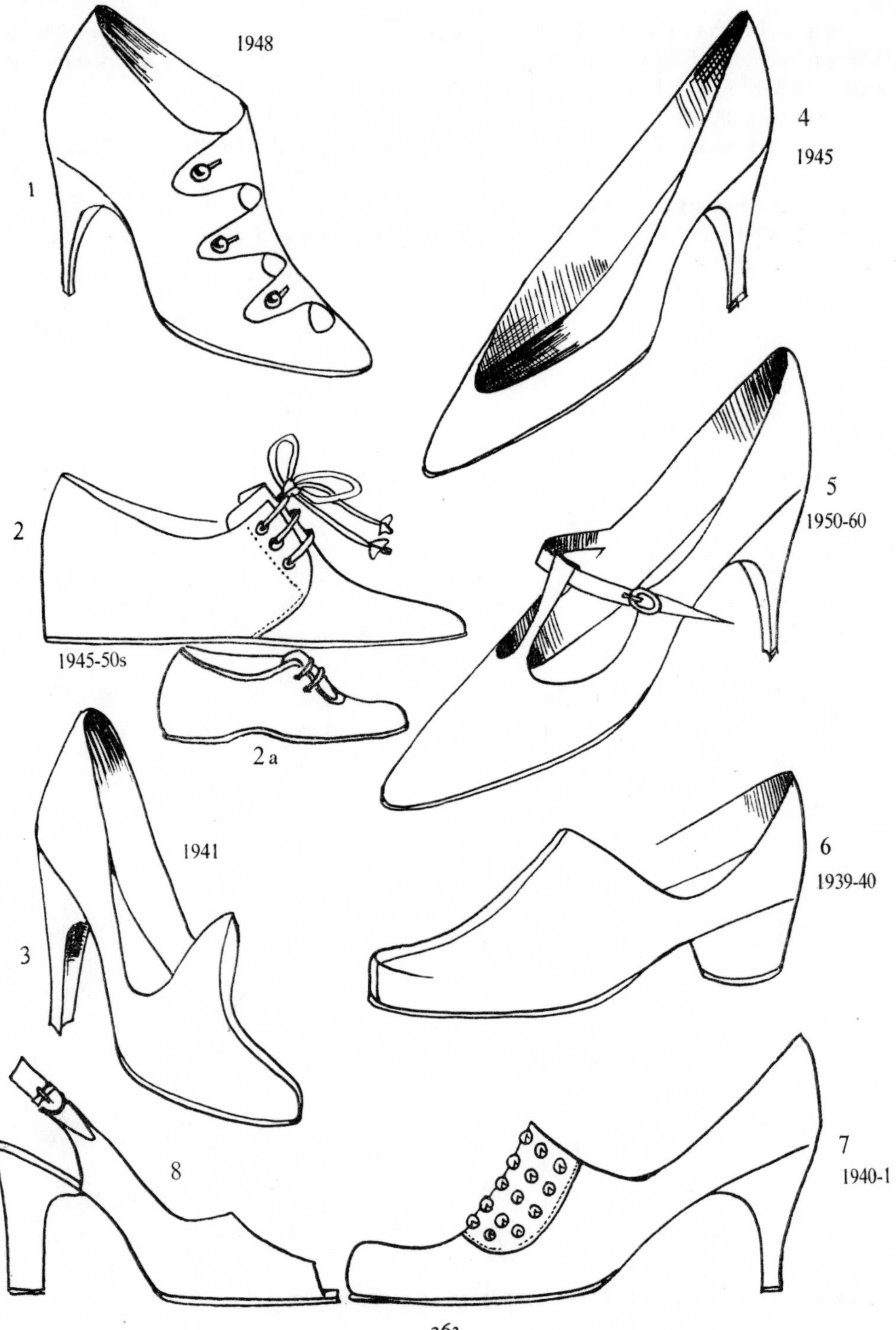
1948
1
4
1945
2
1945-50s
2 a
5
1950-60
1941
3
6
1939-40
8
7
1940-1

1. Sling backs were replaced by lattice backs which offered a group of new ideas as alternatives to the closed back court. High-set ankle-bars were often linked to semi-open backs and counters cut so that the bar appeared to be part of the strapping.
2. Asymmetrically-cut court shoes with one open side became popular.
3. Slip-lasted methods of manufacture provided new looks for sandals. This "wishbone" shape was very frequently used.
4. Elasticized material was extensively used in fitting shoes, especially in those for older women. The toe was still round and deep, though beginning to fine down; the heel was of medium height and was thick with a straight back.

83. FROM THE 'TWENTIES TO THE MID-CENTURY (VIII)

1
2
3
4

21

The New Elizabethans (the Nineteen-Fifties)

BY THE FIFTIES the extravagance of the New Look was over, the overdone appearance of clothes was tidied up, and elegance returned. Close-fitting waisted suits for men and women, shorter skirts trimmed to pencil slimness, court shoes and their variations formed a basic part of every shoe collection for several years. It was amazing how many different kinds of shoes could be made from one shape, and, as standardization was a growing factory trend in order to simplify production and keep prices stable, the court shoe remained a favourite.

The low shell-shape vamp was popular but in a more becoming shape than the uncompromising one of the forties. The foot was encased in a glovelike guard which was to drop lower in the next few years. The way in which the vamp was filled in provided scope for many new ideas. Nail-heads of all sizes and shapes, mostly in gilt and silver, and diamanté, provided decoration round throat-lines and tabs. The shape of the shoe was plain and unfussy and depended for its dressing-up on decoration such as these. They stressed asymmetric lines, studded platform, and even covered heels.

In 1954 the coming of the "Regency" toe suggested that the tendency might be for lasts to become squarer, but in fact the point was coming and was not to be displaced for several years. Toes in general were soft and unblocked but new developments were making use of a different kind of puff which was not so stiff. The toe was deep and round but during the middle of this period, about 1955, it began to fine down. Round toes, on short lasts, lent themselves to the classic style of punching, which was very much in vogue for all kinds of shoes. Skirts were becoming shorter and at the same time heels were becoming higher. Ankle-straps, though out of fashion in Britain since the forties, came back with rising hemlines and were worn with either low or high heels. A new kind of "shell" shape formed a casing round the foot, leaving the top bare, often latticed with straps. Heels had become very fashionable again, and from 1950 were decorated with jewels, stitching, tucks, and lace. Transparent heels overlaid with gold filigree, transparent wedges enclosing plastic aquaria, hand-painted heels in oriental designs. . all were to come and go quickly.

Skirts were not shortening as quickly as they had lengthened and this slowness resulted in a slack period in shoe fashion, which offered only variations on a theme. It seems as though the fireworks of the New Look had used up too much energy and there was a need to cast around for new ideas. Many short-lived styles appeared, like the turned-up Turkish toe on a low-wedged shoe which was made with a platform. This was called the "Gondola" last, which also had its high-heeled version.

In 1955 lasts had begun to fine down and toes began to have a less bulbous look. Heels too were more slender to match the slimmer shape of clothes. Mock platforms had taken the place of the real thing, and sling-backs now included latticed backs. Back interest became a new focal point in clothes and shoes and the "*suivez-moi*" look was revived for the first time since the last century.

Casuals and naked sandals and rope-soled canvas shoes became an increasingly important part of summer wardrobes as people began to go abroad again for holidays. The influence of Italy and Spain increased and Britain bought shoes from all over the world. This was a period when London's shoe-stores could really claim to stock all that was good in world fashion. Dolcis had as their slogan "The world of fashion at your feet," and it was justified.

Pointed toes were now accepted and were to reach their longest and most pointed in the "Needle" which the Americans were to exaggerate still further and call the "Needle-needle." Eventually, of course, this was to reach its extremity in the "winkle-picker," which reached such absurd extremes that girls could not place their feet squarely on the step of a staircase but had to walk up sideways, the toes being too long for the tread. And when any fashion reaches this stage of absurdity it heralds a coming change, as we have seen before.

The change came in the "chisel toe," at the beginning of the sixties but, as with any fundamental change, it was some time before this settled down to a definite and wider shape.

Shapes of lasts were slimmer, providing a "straight-down" look to the legs and feet, making both look longer.

Aniline leathers, through whose translucent surface the perfection of the leather, including its growth-marks, could be seen, came in as a strong new fashion. Of course there had been aniline dyeing before, but it had never attained the importance it did in this era. From now on it became a fashion in its own right and introduced new ideas of colour for shoes, but it required high-quality, unblemished leather, since there was no thick pigment to conceal any faults and blemishes in the surface. It was some time before the public learnt how to wear it most effectively.

New materials in general were improving the looks of shoes. In particular there was one called "pointelle," which consisted of hundreds of tiny plastic sequins stuck by hand on to a black or white fabric. Another was lace over gold or silver kid, and another was woven from Cellophane strips into a kind of silk grosgrain.

Paris had by now fully regained its place as the fashion centre of the world and shoe designers like Roger Vivier were making footwear an important item of fashion again.

Boots trimmed with leopard fabric had a hat to match; heels were made from mock bamboo and had vamp trims of the same wood; straw shoes were now fashion and not the utilitarian article they had been originally; embroidery from India made beautiful velvet sandals; cork-soled sandals for town had uppers made from soft "cushy" calf; flat ballerina shoes were popular for all ages; moccasins with hand-laced vamps were made under licence from America; woven vamps for soft shoes and for formal shoes from Spain; pointed toes from Italy. . all these showed how London had become the shoe market of the world.

Lurex, a new thread, untarnishable, unbreakable, wove and knitted glitter into fabrics for clothes and evening shoes and changed the look of "metal" in fashion. A metal thread finely enclosed in plastic, this was indeed an invaluable new material.

There is not much in this era which has not been repeated in later years, or which was not borrowed from earlier periods of fashion, so it is the changes in the fundamentals only which make it different from these other years. Lasts, heels, and toes are seen to be the most important elements in shoe fashion and details and materials are clearly secondary and common to most periods of change.

NEW ELIZABETHAN

Left (1955)
From Balenciaga's collection. Bulk at the top. Black fox collar on a sinuous black tunic dress. Skirt length up.

Right (1958)
Saint-Laurent at Dior. The "trapeze" line. Wedge-shaped silhouette with higher skirt, just below the knee.

The heel was an important feature of this period, and although it varied in shape and height, it remained slim to balance the slim length of the pointed last.

1. The plain court shoe, the basis of many simple shapes whose common denominator was the pointed toe. This toe shape extended beyond the natural toe and was an elongation of the last by about 1 inch.

2. The toe became much longer until it was termed the "winkle-picker" in 1958–61, when it could be as much as 3 inches longer than the foot itself. Pleated kid was a very strong fashion feature of this period. The toe fitted into an A shape and to align themselves with the clothes of the same period, vamps were said to be of the A-line trend also.

3. When the inevitable reaction set in, the first evidence was the "chisel" toe. This was merely the moderate point with its tip nipped off into a square. There were many choices of upper design on this last, which was an acceptable shape of toe for many heel-heights and types of shoes.

4. The next toe-shape in the sequence was the "almond" toe, which had many other names: the petal, the thumb print, the tapered toe. This was a gently-rounded shape on a last with a long forepart, as were the others. Heels were still slim. These last shapes together with their toe variations were applicable to tie shoes and court shoes alike. The height of heel went down to correspond with the roundness of the toe; thus it can generally be said that the rounder the toe the lower the heel.

5. Used on many of these toe-shapes, the ankle-strap court was an important style. Usually open-backed, quite often with an open toe as well which began to appear as soon as the rounder shorter last was used, the shoe had none of the heaviness of the previous version of an ankle-strap.

6. Apart from the high stiletto heel, which remained popular, the lower heel was growing in favour. Called "little" heels or "baby" heels, these were undercut and with very small top-pieces. Even thicker or leather heels were set under the last and not straight-backed.

84. NEW ELIZABETHAN (I)

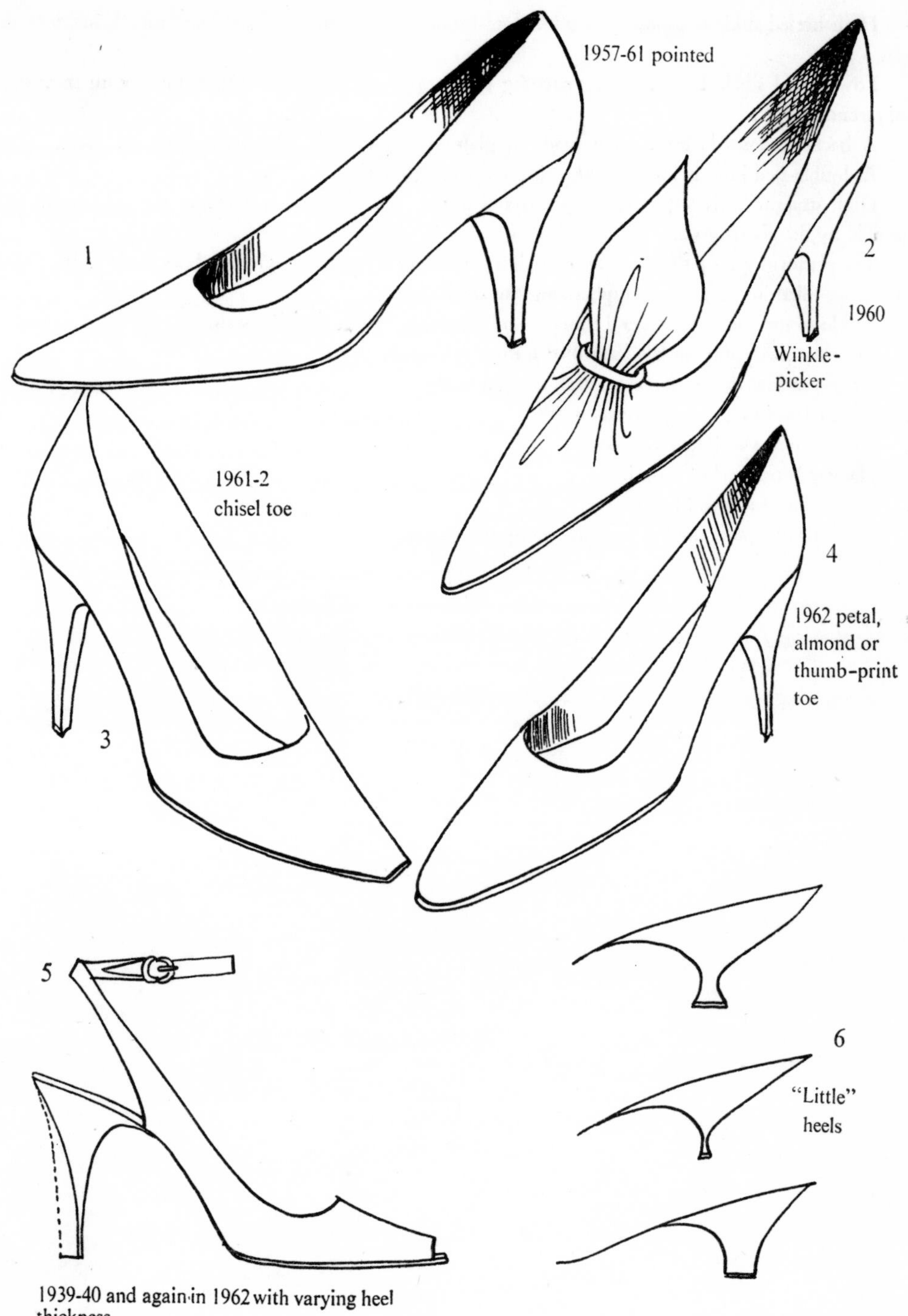

1939-40 and again in 1962 with varying heel thickness

1. High-heeled ankle-hugging boot with close-fitting laced front and deep round toe. Usually made in suede.
2. Low-heeled suede bootee with matching calf facing and platform. Often lined with shearling or wool tartan. (1951.)
3. A back-laced suede boot often made in glamorous glittering fabrics for après-ski wear. (1950.)
4. A double-tied boot in suedes with calf platform. (1951.)
5. High straight heels with matching covered insole. The sling-back becomes the ankle-strap and is adjustable by the elastic gore.
6. The platform was on the wane by 1950, but versions of it remained as in the shoes worn by the Queen. Shell vamps filled in with straps emphasizing the ankle-strap.
7. Ankle-straps criss-cross several times round the ankle. High straight heels.
8. Even flat shoes and sandals use rolled leather ankle-ties.
9. Drop-pearls as decoration on a high straight heel.
10. Stitched and tucked heel-cover of calf.
11. Cross-stitched or inked heel cover.
12. Hand-painted heel of wood.
13. Gilt nailhead-studded heel-cover.
14. Pearls or diamanté used as heel and vamp decoration.

85. NEW ELIZABETHAN (II)

1
2
1951
3
4
1950
5
6
7
1950
8
9
10
11
12
13
14
1951

The 'fifties and 'sixties saw great changes in heels and a wide choice for all. The most popular and the one with the longest history is the stiletto, which came originally from Italy.

1. Casuals were also affected by the pointed toe preference in lasts. This bar court was a popular style. Its low heel was made of leather, real or simulated. Developments in simulated leather heels by covering wooden or plastic blocks with laminated sheets or photographic patterns grew during these years.

2. The stiletto grew higher and thinner until it was less than the the diameter of a cigarette. Made in nylon and plastic, sometimes over a steel core, it was relatively unbreakable.

3. Toward the 'sixties experiments were made with a set-back heel which gave the illusion of a long look to the last, which was shortening in the forepart.

4. From 1949 on, platforms of all kinds were more practical especially on casual shoes of this type.

5. The "no-heel" shoes were a fashion of no lasting value but one which offered opportunity to inventive designers via springs instead of heels, sculptured wedges which cut away the need for a conventional heel entirely, and extended soles which incorporated the use of steel.

6. The toe is already very long in this sketch, but not yet the winkle-picker. Rouleaux trimmings—leather rolled over a spring—used a great deal.

7. The thick stocky leather heel of the shoe typified by the "Country Club" range of the period, from Clarks. A very important contribution to shoe design. This brogued leather shoe with an extended welted edge, typical of the 1950s was to reappear again as high fashion in late 1967, proving again the theory of the 20-year cycle.

8. In profile the stacked heel has altered over the years from an undercut shape to a straight-back shape, but apart from the materials used remains substantially the same.

86. NEW ELIZABETHAN (III)

5
1960
heel-less shoes
1
6
1960
2
3
7
1956
1968
4
8
1958
1949

22

The Atom Age (The Nineteen-Sixties)

IT WILL NOT BE POSSIBLE to trace fully the development and shape of this period of fashion until we have come to the end of it and can look at it dispassionately. When it does come, the end of an era presents itself unequivocally, and with it there comes a change in every aspect of fashion.

There is no doubt, however, that the sixties have been a period of revolution such as has never occurred before, at least in this form. Gathering momentum during the years following the end of World War II, several tendencies were seen to be significant by those skilled in observing such matters. The "Nouvelle Vague" in France, the "way-out," the "beat generation" typified by the Beatles, in Britain and America, can be credited with a great deal of the influence. The "scene" was London, Kings Road and Carnaby Street, the places of significance where fashion was concerned. No longer was it the débutantes' season, Bond Street, Ascot, or any of the once familiar smart places, though all in turn underwent the influences of the "in" crowd.

The privileged classes, as we have seen, are the instigators of new fashion. This is a fact that still holds good although the people who make up those privileged classes are different. These are now the young; not necessarily the rich, upper-class young, but *all* young people.

Fashion, in some of its aspects, must still begin at a high price-level because of the cost of producing goods in the limited numbers in which they usually first appear. But nowadays new fashions do not necessarily begin at the top and frequently articles are produced quite cheaply. Formerly fashion spread downwards but now it often works outwards, among the young, and then upwards as the more conservative take to it.

Communications have speeded up so that ideas move quickly and what was once the "in" thing soon becomes generally accepted and then the "out" thing in much less time than it used to take. This is good for trade and for designers themselves, because it means that ideas are always on the move, and articles are relatively cheap to produce because they are made in large quantities. Television, radio, films, newspapers, innumerable fashion magazines, a thriving trade press, all these things we take for granted were unknown or rare a very short time ago (relatively, in the history of fashion).

The present period takes ideas from all other periods and refashions them for the age in which we live. Fashion of the past comes up new and different, often not immediately recognized as a reincarnation. Compare, for example, the brief length of the mini-skirt and its accompanying long coloured tights, with the same long-legged style (masculine then) of the Middle Ages, and more recently of the twenties. What was the "winkle-picker" but a Plantagenet fashion revived? Following it, came the wide square toe of 1967—was not this a more streamlined version of Henry VIII's favourite shoes? The later stubby-toed low-heeled version came as a reaction to the pointed toe, following exactly the same sequence as before.

Today the younger generation treat synthetics with which they have always been familiar, as part of our age, and they do not compare them unfavourably with the natural materials. They are a material in their own right, not replacing materials such as leather, wool, silk, wood, but adding to them and making possible a wider choice.

Discovery has made shoemaking quicker, easier, and cheaper, bringing new methods which have in turn created a new approach to the craft. It is sad that the old craft does not exist as the original guildsmen would have known it, except in small isolated examples of shoemakers who still produce a certain amount of handwork. But who is to say that machine-work mass production is not a craft in itself, even if it comes to push-button shoemaking, as it undoubtedly will before the end of the century?

After the stiletto heel there came many experiments with heels. Roger Vivier experimented with forward-curving shapes, backward-bending heels, high circular heels, and heels with long prow fronts. There were many versions of the thin, high shape in an effort to give a new look to the heel, which stubbornly would not go out of fashion: the square back, the pointed back, the columnar shape, and many others. But as part of the movement towards freedom the low heel was essential, and fashionable heels dropped from three inches to one inch or lower, and the "little" heel was in. For a period of about three years the low heel remained "high" fashion. The lower heel did not go with pointed toes and these too began to change, tentatively at first, for the pointed toe had had a long reign too.

There followed in succession Rond Point, Thumb Print, Taper toe, and Petal and Almond toes, but it was not until the lower heel looked unbalanced when teamed with the wrong toe that the square toe was born. Initially this was meant only as an interim fashion, but manufacturers and retailers had been so long accustomed to one shape that they could not recognize the coming revolution in fashion and they were too slow in making and buying it. When they finally had the courage to do so, the shape was changing again and many were left heavily stocked with shoes that had gone out of date too soon. The interim lasted a bare twelve months and then the toe began to acquire a rounded shape. Changes came rapidly then, heels thickening and toes rounding until by 1966–7 both were accepted fashions.

Connected with this toe-and-heel development was the powerful influence on both of the shortening hem. Of all the factors in fashion affecting shoes the general silhouette and the hem height are the most important. It was the "sack" or waistless shape of dresses, and the variation called the shift, which produced simple and direct shapes in shoes. Both were indicative of a growing need for non-restrictive clothes, and this has something that shoe designers were also going to feel. The active lives lived by men and women alike cannot be lived in clothes or shoes which hamper movement. The latest male effort to keep women at home and "in their rightful place"—stiletto heels and pointed toes—had to admit defeat. Short skirts helped to bring in low heels, so that shapes became younger-looking, more comfortable, and more suitable to the life women lead in reality. High heels, pointed toes, restrictive shoes and clothes, are part of a fantasy life and women who wear them are perhaps indicating that they live in, or would like to live in this fantasy world where women are the toys and not the equals of men.

We can see that it is rebellion against established ideas which is most contributive to a change of fashion. The rebellion of the young which began after World War I reaches its zenith fifty years later and is responsible for a totally different way of dressing, as regards both shoes and clothes.

It is the fundamentals of shoe design that make shoe fashion. Details become important only when fundamentals have changed and become accepted. These fundamentals derive from the wood, the last, from whose shape come heel heights and toe forms. Heels generally change first, compelling toes to balance the silhouette. Details such as the varying uses of materials new and established, trimmings, the height and shape of tabs, cut-outs or underlays, bars and buckles and straps, even colours and surface textures, are all secondary to this, and do not date a shoe as much as does its shape.

The "leather look" in clothes was an important trend which started with mods and rockers and brought with it the thigh boots of 1967. Said to have psychological undertones significant of the violent age in which we live, this is a far-reaching fashion which includes all ages. Op Art and Pop Art replaced the *art nouveau* movement of the nineteenth century, which came again in these mid-sixties; Op began with Yves St.-Laurent's dresses which brought Piet Mondrian's paintings to the mass market of the rag trade. Such influences as these replaced the Diaghilevs and the Poirets of an earlier fashion. The influence of films has also been important. Colour and clothes as illustrated in *Viva Maria*, *Dr. Zhivago*, and *Bonny and Clyde* bring new influences to change our fashions.

New methods of manufacture also help to change the look of shoes and make them cheaper and more readily available to all at reasonable prices in keeping with the "throw-away" trend that grows in fashion as in everything else. Injection moulding has brought us "instant" boots and shoes, welding has simplified the intricate stitching of the closing room, lamination has brought a new aspect to the problems of lining, adhesives replace tacks, and plastic makes lasts more durable than wood.

Fashion is not the "arty" whim some think it is or a pastime for idle women and empty minds, but a high-powered industry which grows out of necessity, out of man's inventive and artistic mind, and out of scientific development as well.

ATOM AGE

Left (1964)
Courrèges trouser suit of silver lamé. Helmet-type hat.

Centre (1964)
"Mini" dress in geometric design. Patterned tights.

Right (1967)
Synthetic and real hair pieces. "Mini" dress with wide sleeves and bloomers of same material made to show.

The 'sixties could be summed up briefly as the years of the heel and toe, because great controversy raged around them for more than six years. Many wild and bizarre shapes came and went as heels especially became subjects for wide experiment. It is impossible and confusing to list them all.

1. Experiments with new materials for heels produced architectural versions made of steel like this hollow shape in 1967.

2. 1966–7 saw the settling of welts as fashion, and produced both real and mock welts on all kinds of shoes. Some were merely an insertion of coloured piping having more affinity with platforms, others were wide and stitched, some wheeled.

3. These two brocade shoes from Roger Vivier in Paris had heels that were revolutionary both for high and low shapes. But this was only a start and such shapes were to cross and re-cross the fashion scene for many years.

4. 1964 saw the stiletto heel curving forwards as well as backwards in an effort to look different whilst still maintaining height. But this was only a re-creation of what had gone before and it did not stay as a fashion.

5. The Rond Point was the natural reaction to the winkle-picker and the two vied with each other for some time. The forepart of the last was still long although the point was blunter.

6. The Scissor-point was the last decisive gesture of the pointed toe as a fashion; ever since this shape it has remained on the shoe scene but not as a new fashion.

7. The pointed toe at last gave way to the square or rounded-square, which became a fashion on its own and from 1964 on has remained. Heels began to thicken up to balance the new shorter shape.

8. The square toes were accepted for lower heels and more sporty shoes more readily and worn as a lead fashion in the mid-'sixties.

87. THE ATOM AGE (I)

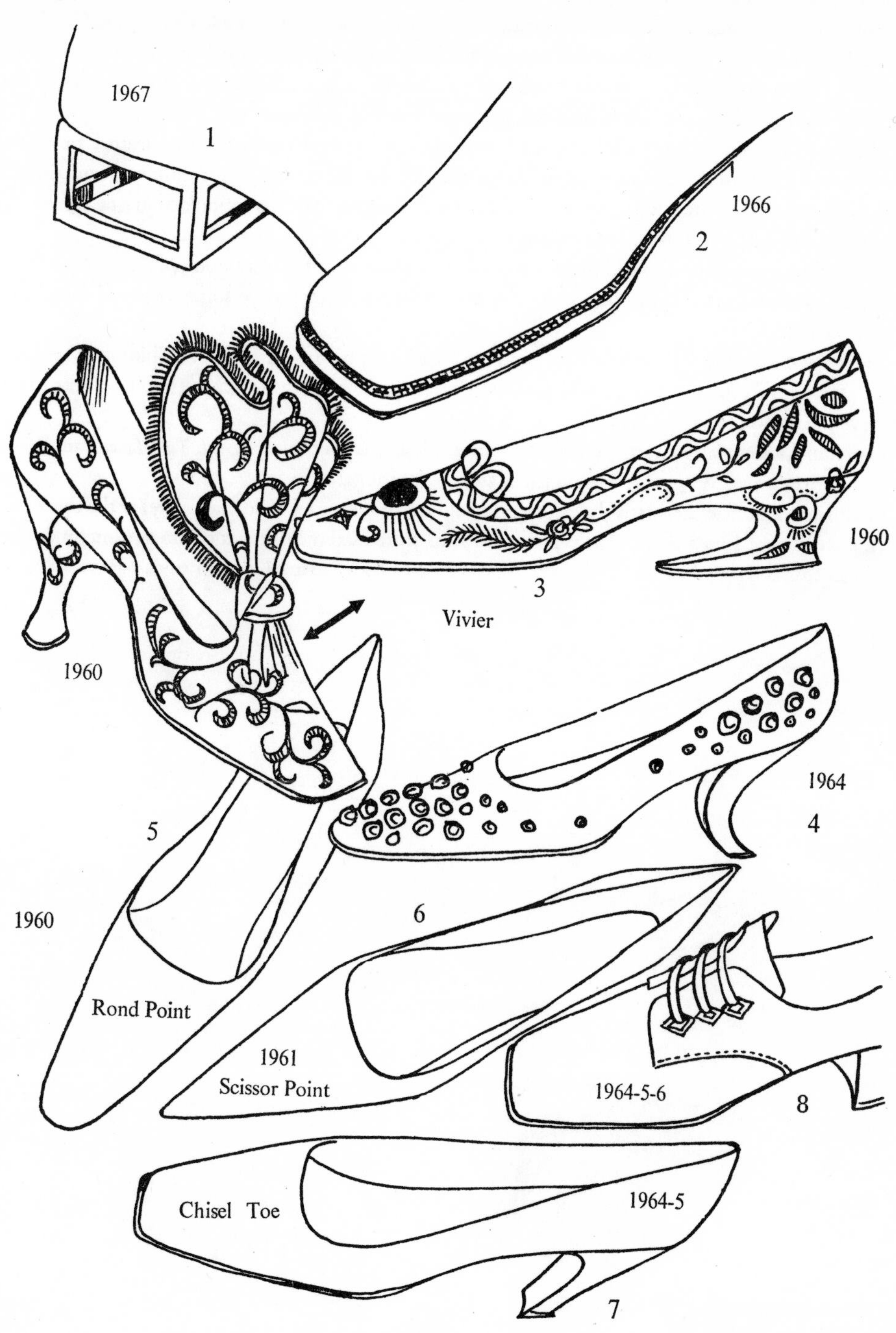
1967
1
1966
2
1960
3
Vivier
1960
1964
4
5
1960
6
Rond Point
1961
Scissor Point
1964-5-6
8
Chisel Toe
1964-5
7

1. The concealed gore shoe came in first for men, but versions of it were used as women's shoes. The leather from the vamp and the quarter were stitched so as to overlap and hide the elastic gore.

2. The high Chelsea boot had many versions but had an exposed elastic gore on both sides for fit and adjustment. First introduced as a popular fashion by the Beatles, it generally had a square or round toe, but there were bastard versions which still used the pointed toe. Was also made as a shoe.

2. Either of the above shoes could be made with the popular unit sole, or with a leather or synthetic sole. Unit soles were made in many styles for men and women, as well as for children, and simplified considerably sole and heel attaching. Made of rubber or a synthetic they were moulded in one piece. These kinds of sole treatment will have a long life into the future.

4. The tabbed gusset shoe also had many versions but was one of the most popular shapes to use the new very square or round toe. Made in smooth or grained leathers it often carried some form of broguing, and was mock welted.

5. The showing of the *Viva Maria* film brought a rush of turn-of-the-century fashions, of which this low-cut court with its flat tailored bow in faille or matching leather, was typical. Bright colours or black patent gave it a wide age-group appeal.

6. Large buckles, metal or leather-covered, or even plastic, were typical of the *Tom Jones* and *Cromwell* revivals. Set over an elastic gore it was high-cut and well-fitting.

7. Platforms came back, tentatively at first via coloured pipings let in as mock welts, then as covered and cork platforms of $\frac{1}{2}$ inch deep. The piping platforms were used on all types of shoes, sometimes in self-coloured calf to match suede, or in vivid contrast. Tabs and fringes attached with studs or rivets.

88. THE ATOM AGE (II)

1965-7
1
2
3
1967
4
5
6
1966
1967-8
7

1. Zips with large rings provided a new form of fastening wich was used on plain shoes made of coloured leathers, suedes or fabrics. Sometimes these rings carried a leather trimming or a Perspex shape as a tag decoration.

2. Op Art was a great influence on fashion, and shoes made good use of it as a black and white theme. The favourite was this checkerboard pattern in black patent and white calf or suede. The scope was tremendous and extended into boots also; later the colours were of a wider choice.

3. High knee-boots became more popular than the mid-calf styles. They were fastened with a zip which was generally on the inside of the leg. They were very close-fitting, and later were made of stretch materials which needed no fastenings. Their toes were square or round, often walled, and toward 1968 became deeper. Main colours were brown and black.

4. A very popular trouser shoe called the Charley Boot, which was made in many types of leathers. It had a high tab concealing an elastic gore and was very plain. Trousers created a need for this type of shoe or boot, as many more women were wearing trouser suits and normal shoes were not suitable.

5. The Courrèges boot, made in white kid, calf or patent, was a mid-calf boot with wide open slots at the top and a matching knot at the front. This boot was widely copied throughout the country, which created a great deal of controversy with the originator.

6. Space Age designs in metal had a great effect on footwear, and in 1966 many shoes were shown which used real metal as an overlay attached by rivets. Metal was simulated by a silver or aluminium finish on leather and other materials for complete shoes and boots.

7. 1967 saw the advent of the thigh boots which rose to meet the mini-skirt's short hem. They had long back zips or were made of stretch materials or leather. Very close fitting, they had deep round toes.

8. Back zips, as on flying-boots, were very popular for all heights.

89. THE ATOM AGE (III)

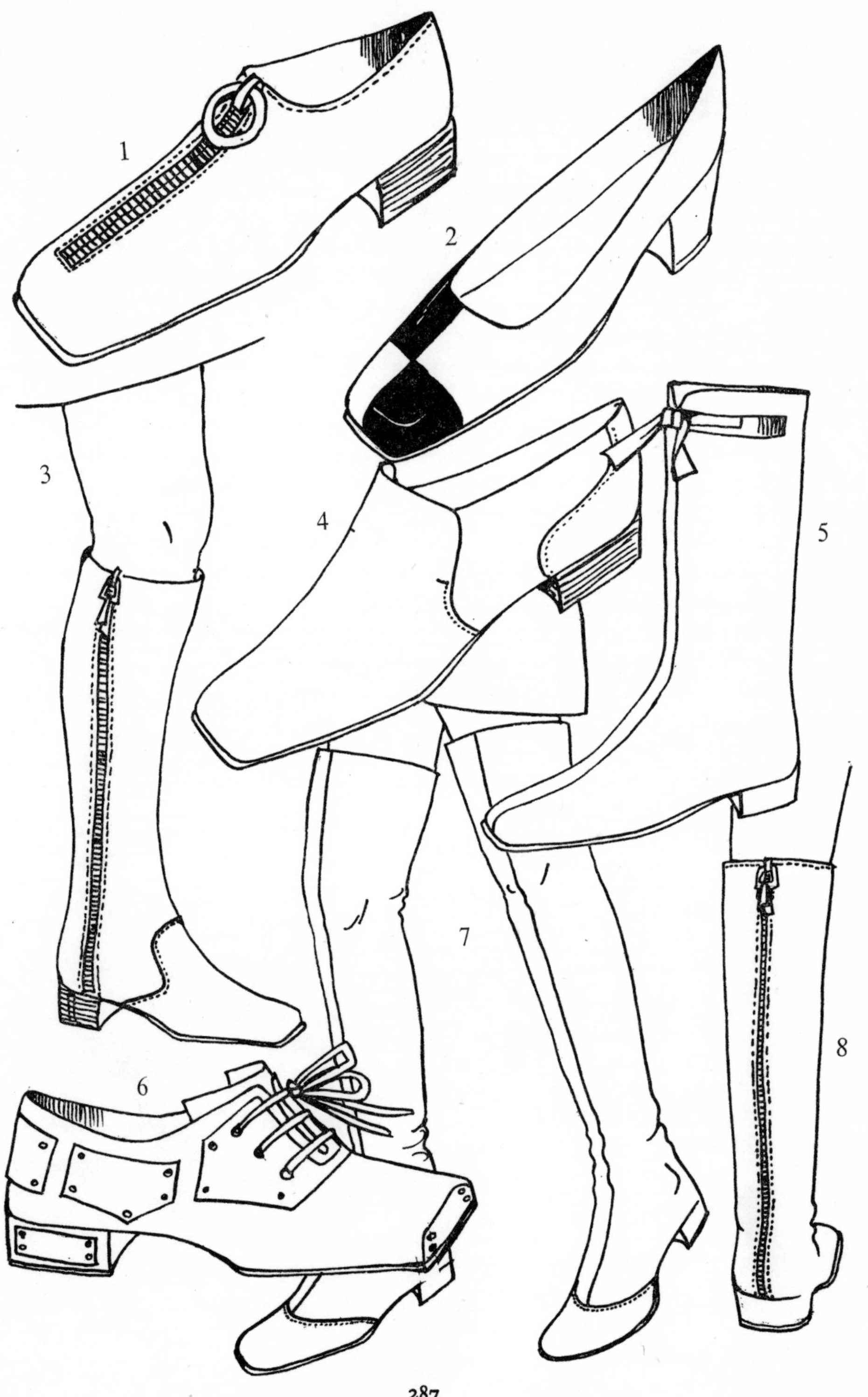
1
2
3
4
5
6
7
8

A GREEK SHOEMAKER

On this Attic black-figure pelike from Rhodes, a shoemaker is depicted measuring a customer's foot for a sandal. He has placed the foot on the leather and is cutting round it with a "clicking" knife. Notice his tools in the rack above his head. Early 5th sentury B.C., by the Eucharides painter.

(By courtesy of the Ashmolean Museum, Oxford)

A SIXTEENTH-CENTURY SHOEMAKER'S SHOP

A woodcut by Jost Amman, published in 1568.

(By courtesy of the Trustees of the British Museum)

(G.3313)

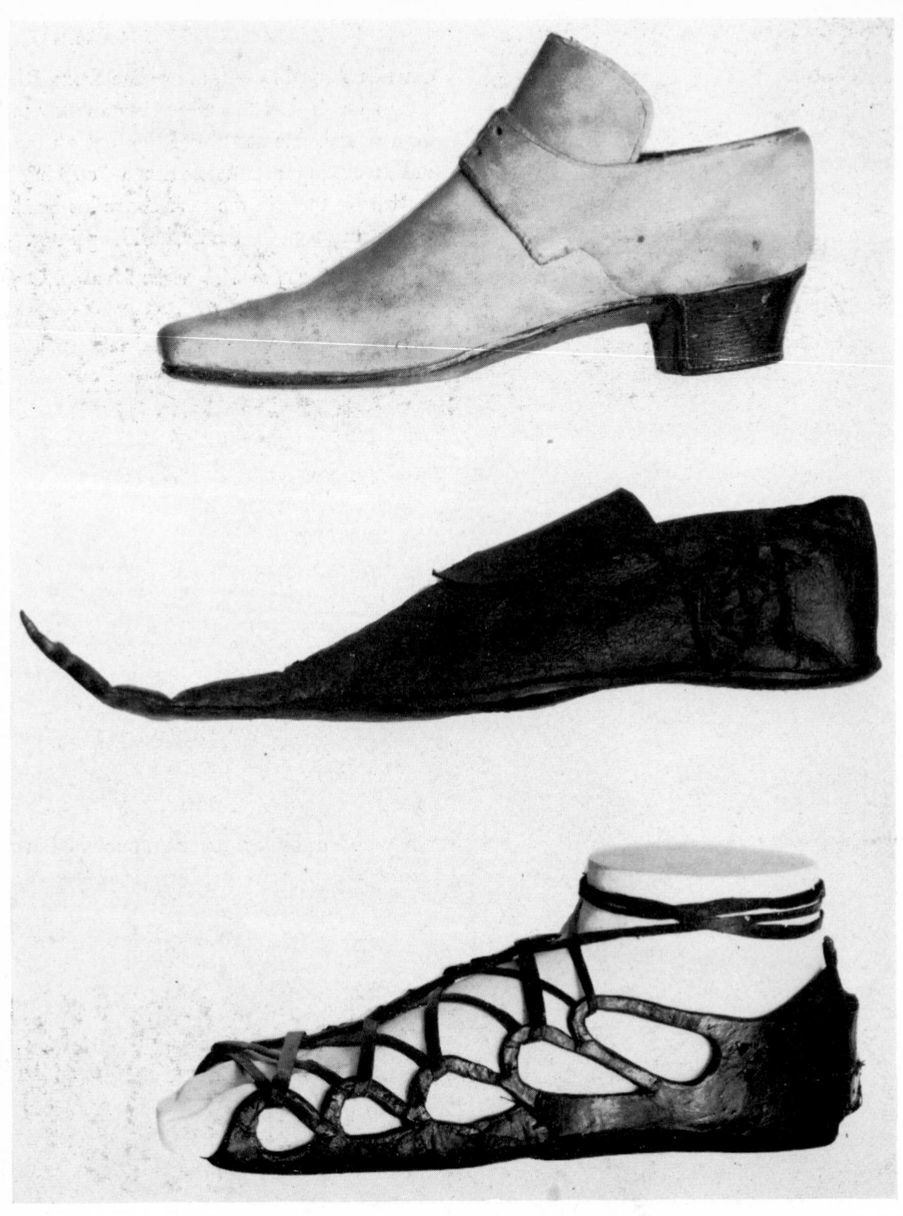

SHOES FROM THE LONDON MUSEUM

Top: Late 17th century shoe

This shoe is a model of an original, probably made for a theatrical production. It is of modern make, but serves to show the style and shape accurately.

Centre: Late 15th century shoe

Bottom: Roman shoe

(By kind permission of the London Museum)

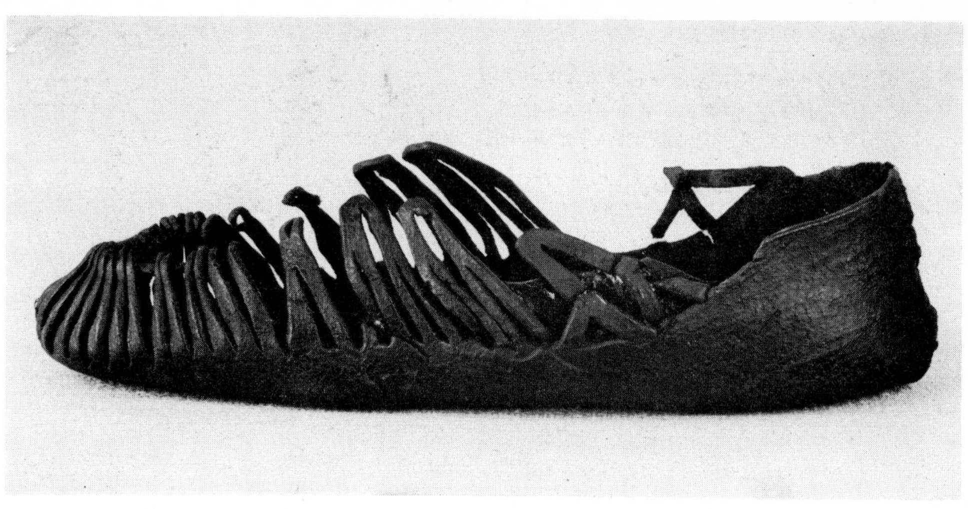

EXAMPLES OF SHOES IN SLIT AND EXPANDED LEATHER

Leather shoe similar in type to those used in early Britain. The slots and loops for the thong fastenings are made by slitting and expanding the wet leather. A style common throughout Europe, and continuing into a much later period among the peasants. Found in Schleswig-Holstein.

(By courtesy of the Landes Museum, Schleswig-Holstein)

Another shoe showing the different designs obtained by using slit and expanded leather among the early shoemakers of Britain and Europe. This is a style that was also used by the Romans. Tied with thongs of rawhide.

(By courtesy of the Landes Museum, Schleswig-Holstein)

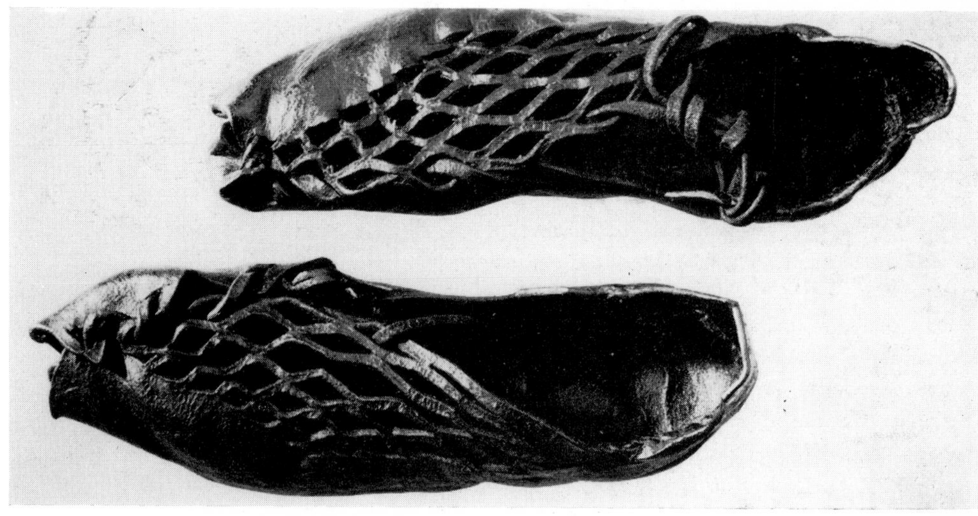

SHOES FROM IRELAND

It is virtually impossible to date, even approximately, any of these shoes, although the one from Craigywarren is probably of the Early Christian Period.

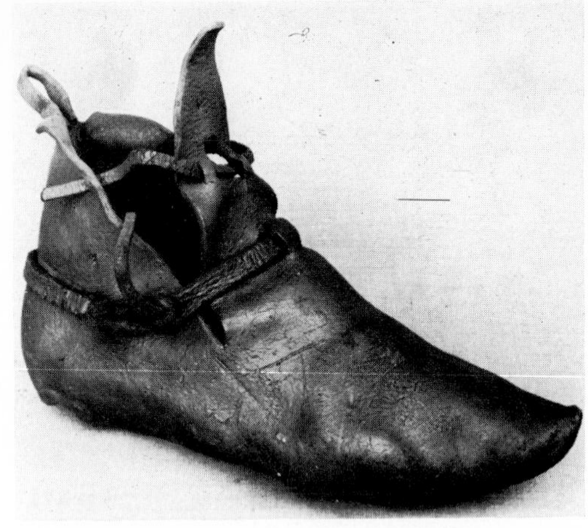

Top: Leather shoe from Kilcummin, Co. Offaly, found in a bog. Made of a single piece of leather. It has a long toe-cap from which runs a triangular tongue 14 cm. long. The back of the shoe is 12 cm. high and slopes down sharply to the instep region. At the top of the back is a loop of leather 4 cm. long, each half of which is continuous with the leather on each side of the heel seam. There is only one seam in the shoe and it runs from the point of the toe longitudinally down the centre of the sole and up the back of the heel. The meeting edges of the leather have been turned inwards and sewn together through a double welt. The fastening thong passed through two holes in the back of the upper and then through two in the upper part of the tongue.

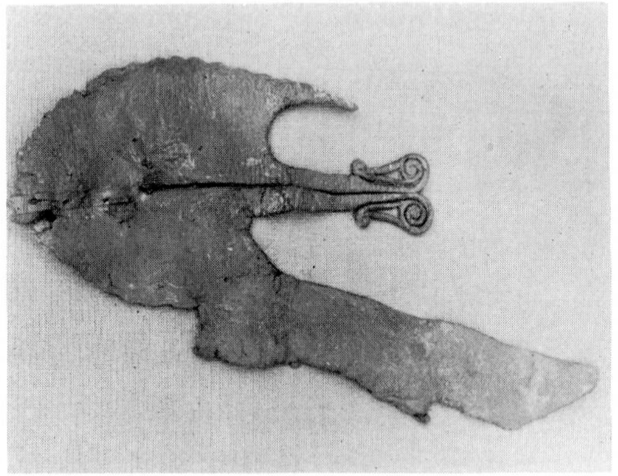

Centre: Upper of decorated shoe from Craigywarren Crannog, Co. Antrim. Consists of the vamp, tongue and portion of side of a single-piece shoe. The tongue is 5·5 cm. long and 1·5 cm. wide at its junction with the vamp. Its upper end is decorated with two symmetrically placed spirals, the whole having the appearance of two birds' heads back to back. The tongue is split for the whole of its length, the halves being joined only for a space of about 2 mm. at the top.

Bottom: Find-place not recorded. A single-piece shoe 24 cm. long. Seams run up the centre of the toe-cap and the back of the heel, both being sewn with gut. There are two lacing holes on each side of the shoe at the instep region and there is a further slit on each side of the toe-cap near the instep. A tongue in the shape of a truncated triangle projects on to the wearer's instep. The heel is decorated with incised patterns. On each side of the back of the shoe are three horizontal bands of a ladder pattern and three similar bands run vertically up on each side of the heel seam. A similar band runs around the perimeter of the toe-cap and one borders the toe seam on each side. On either side of the toe-cap there is incised decoration which is vaguely like foliage.

(*By courtesy of the National Museum of Ireland, Dublin*)

Wooden support of patten

A pair of pattens found at Mucklon, Co. Kildare. Each consists of a two-piece leather upper and a wooden sole mounted on three stilts. At the back the leather is 14 cm. high, sloping downwards on each side to a rectangular tongue 5 cm. long and 6·5 cm. wide. A single decorative line is incised all round the upper edge of the shoe on the outside, including the tongue. It is 7 mm. from the edge of the leather. A small cross is incised in each of the upper corners on the tongue. From the centre of the toe to the top of the tongue there runs a ladder design consisting of four parallel lines with irregular transverse nicks. Each upper was nailed to the wooden sole by 17 nails, none of which survives. The wooden sole is carved out of a single piece of wood from which three extensions were left on the underside. Into these extensions three stilts were morticed. The tip of each stilt bears traces of a protecting cap of some material which does not survive but it was, apparently, nailed on. The wood of the sole is alder (Alnus) and that of the three stilts yew (Taxus). The length of the wooden soles is 28·5 cm., average height 13 cm., maximum width 10 cm. The pattens were found in a bog.

(*By courtesy of the National Museum of Ireland, Dublin*)

General view of pattens

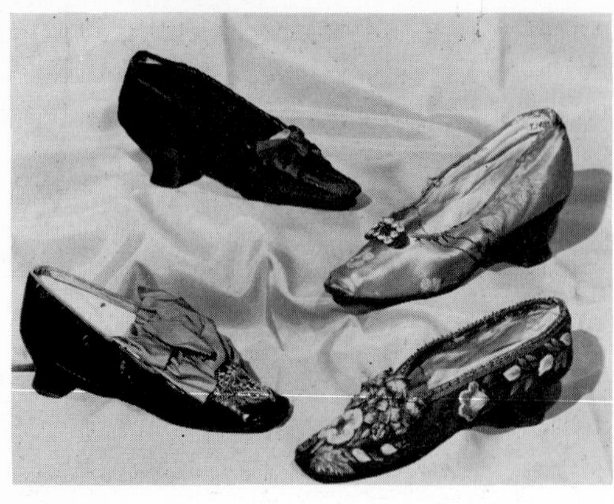

NINETEENTH-CENTURY SHOES

Top left: black silk court shoe with pleated vamp and pleated matching bow. Self-covered knock-on heel. *Top right:* a yellow figured satin shoe for formal occasions with a square diamanté buckle and rounded square toe. Mid-high curved heel covered with yellow kid.
Bottom left: a black kid shoe with a blue silk bow and blue and white embroidery on vamp, lightly tip-tilted round toe and knock-on heel.
Bottom right: red silk slipper with wide rounded shallow square toe. Floppy bow trim made of same ribbon as binding. Many-coloured embroidery.

(By courtesy of the Victoria & Albert Museum)

Left: a kid-topped elastic-sided boot needing a button-hook for its five shank buttons. Thick leather heel and shallow round toe.
Centre: a grey velvet spat on a man's boot with eight stitched buttons and a scalloped top.
Right: a lady's satin boot with scalloped top and scalloped button facing. It has a higher heel, a thick Louis.

(By courtesy of the Victoria & Albert Museum)

A black kid boot with a deep elastic gore on both sides and a tape pull-on tab at back and front. The finely embroidered vamp and toe and detail on the heel are machine-stitched. The edge of the sole and heel are finely stitched in white.

(By courtesy of the Victoria & Albert Museum)

Many of the shoes shown in these Plates were the inspiration of a collection of modern shoes in the Saxone and Lilley and Skinner Collection in July 1964. Tabbed court shoes with gracefully curving heels and mid-calf lace-up boots, all drew on their ancestors to create a "Romano" and a "Grande Dame" look in modern footwear.

QUEEN ELIZABETH I

This full-length portrait of the queen in the conventional Armada portrait pose, with fan in left hand, right hand on the arm of a chair with the cipher ER, is usually attributed to Richard Stevens. However, more probably it is by an unknown painter of c. 1595.

Note the satin embroidered shoes with their square toes and wedge heel and the sole which is almost a platform. The shoes are lavishly decorated with pearls and jewels.

(At Hardwick Hall, Derbyshire, a property of the National Trust. Photograph by Edwin Smith, reproduced by kind permission of the National Trust.)

ROMANTIC STYLE

This elegant gentleman, Baron Schwiter painted by Delacroix (1798–1863), wears plain shoes of a very restrained style to match his clothes. The straps of his trousers are worn inside the shoes which have low straight sides and a wide square toe. Delacroix was hailed as a leader of the Romantic movement, although he regarded it with extreme mistrust.

(By permission of the Trustees of the National Gallery.)

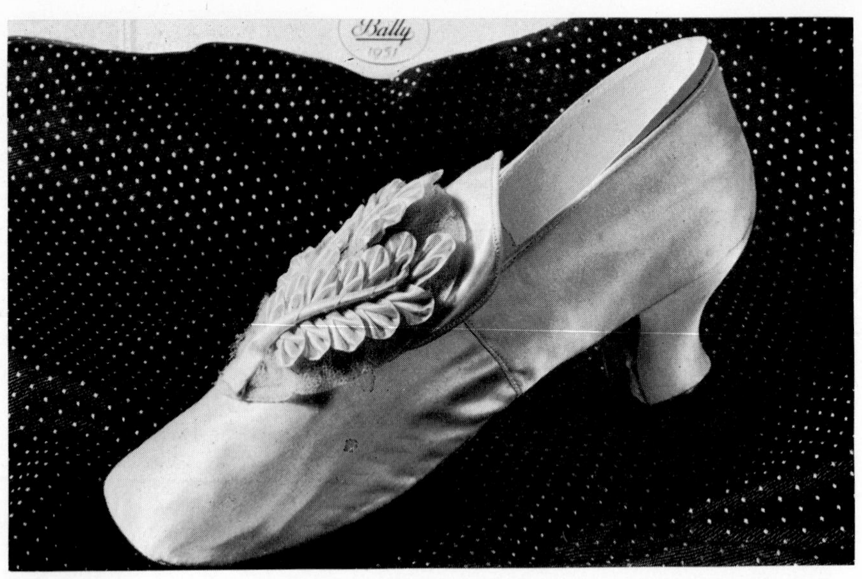

EARLY SHOES BY BALLY

C. 1850. White satin tabbed court with lace and satin handmade decoration. The heel and toe are repeated in the fashions of shoes in 1968.

1851. A glacé kid buttoned shoe with pleated satin buckle trim. Note the curved leather heel.

(By courtesy of Bally Shoe Co., Schönenwerd, Switzerland)

EARLY SHOES AND BOOTS BY LOTUS

1858. Brown cashmere side-laced boot with Morocco leather toe-cap and leather heel. Worn by the grandmother of a late employee of Lotus, at her marriage in 1858.

1901. Kid button-boot with leather heel and lightly brogued toe-cap. The shank buttons need button-hooks for fastening. In 1901 the original price was 10s. 6d.

1905. A woman's hand-welted Derby tie-shoe of 1905. This high-cut six-hole tie was of the usual height for this kind of shoe.

1907. White-kid tie-shoe with gold-kid toe-cap, facing, and collar. The wheeled heel breast is typical of the period.

(By courtesy of Lotus Ltd.)

SHOES MADE BY CLARKS OF STREET, SOMERSET

1906. Black glacé-kid shoe with thick curved heel in the "lavatory bottom" style, with a pointed toe. The steel buckle sits on a pointed tab. Note the fine stitching at the base of the heel.

1900–1914. Cream satin bar-shoe with a self-covered button and straight-fronted heel with deeply curved back. Hand-embroidered vamp, throat and bar with coloured glass beads.

1914. Ribbon-laced evening shoe in coloured brocade with covered Louis heel. The laces fit through beige-coloured eyelets. Later, this type of shoe was to be called a "tango" pump.

Left: made for the Wembley Exhibition in 1924, a beige suede three-bar-shoe with shanked pearl buttons. Trimmed with matching kid. *Right:* satin gusset shoe with pointed toe and kid saddle matched to Louis heel cover. Cut metal studded with paste jewel makes the curved buckle.

(*By courtesy of C. & J. Clark, Street, Somerset*)

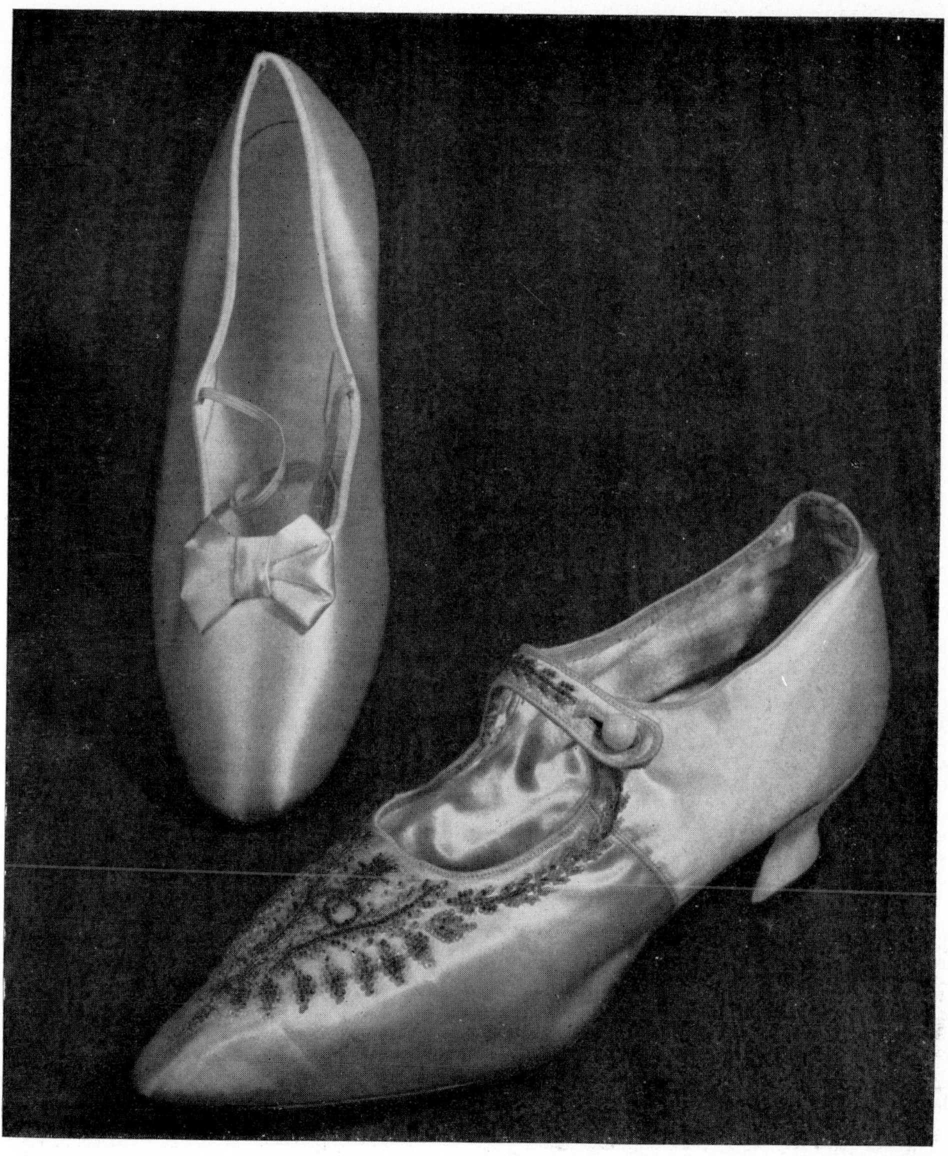

A COMPARISON OF WHITE SATIN

A ballet shoe made by Clarks of Street, in 1941, and a buttoned bar shoe, lavishly embroidered by hand with glass beads, made by the same firm in 1900–1920. Note the difference in the smoothness of the material, brought about by improved modern manufacture.

(By courtesy of C. & J. Clark, Street, Somerset)

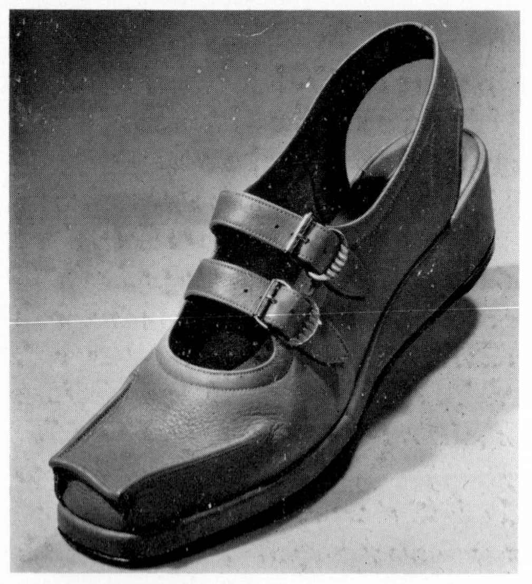

A SLIP-LASTED SHOE IN SOFT UNLINED CALF LEATHER

Showing a square construction of the toe created entirely by seaming. Designed by Eunice Wilson, made by Lotus Ltd., Stafford. The wedge and platform cover are stitched on the flat, one with the upper. The shoes are made without lasts and then re-formed over special lasts for this method of making. Called the "California slip-lasted" method, it is but an up-to-date (1949) way of using an old traditional process. The rands of the Tudor and Stuart period closely resemble this modern version, and were padded in much the same way.

(Reproduced from the author's collection)

1959 A POINTED-TOE COURT SHOE

Showing how the sole leather continues up under the arch and down the front, or breast, of the stiletto heel.

(By courtesy of the Lancashire Tanning Co. Ltd.)

TWENTIETH-CENTURY SANDAL WITH ROMAN AND GREEK AFFINITIES

Designed by Eunice Wilson 1950, and retailed by Dolcis Ltd. This sandal is typical of many of this period, and is almost a classic in any period. Made of gold kid, the straps are slotted through the insole.

23

America

The discovery of America in 1492 was to have a far-reaching effect on fashion in general and on shoe fashion in particular. Social reasons have often been a cause of a new fashion's finding a starting point, and social necessities have often created a "new look." At the beginning, the newly-discovered country opened up vistas of new worlds of which Europe had only dreamed, and brought back to her treasures hitherto unknown.

When the country was fully developed and colonists were going out in large numbers, either as immigrants or as landowners and settlers' shoes were an important necessity. In Europe they had already been established as lefts and rights, although "straights" were still being made. But at that time America had more need of quickly-produced shoes than of fashionable ones, and therefore most of these early shoes were straights. Because of this urgency, when machine-made shoes were becoming more usual America was able to arrive much more quickly at a high standard of mass production than could the countries on this side of the Atlantic. Thus fashion was quickly absorbed into the factories which were created to turn out machine-made shoes by the hundred.

A fashion which arose directly out of America's history, and which still retains its popularity, is the moccasin, which was originally worn by the North-American Indian because of its softness, its silence, and its surefooted tread. Present-day moccasins vary but little from the first hand-made examples. Modern bedroom slippers are often made by this construction, sometimes on "straight" sole pattern also.

This type of shoe is essentially a piece of leather wrapped round the foot from underneath and pleated to the centre, where the skin is drawn together and overlaid with a decorated apron. There are tie shapes, tabbed shapes, and collared step-in shapes, much as there were for the original Indians, but modern creative talent has added many variations to these basic types. Many of these shoes are made without lasts, as were their ancestors.

The United States is the biggest producer, and the biggest consumer, of footwear in the world. Because of its high standard of production development it also exercises a great influence on European footwear fashions. But, as in most countries in the twentieth century, it imports great quantities of footwear to supplement its own. During the nineteen-twenties and -thirties many of these came from Czechoslovakia and Austria, since these countries were centres of fashion influence at that time.

In a great continent, the wide changes of climate and varying ways of life make it difficult to state clearly which is the main influence that it offers to the rest of the world, but it is safe to say that one of the biggest contributions to construction progress was the Californian process of slip-lasting. This was a method of making sandals, developed during the nineteen-forties, which opened up wider possibilities for designers. From America too came the fashion for overshoes which, having developed from plain pull-ons made from rubber, were worn as theatre boots and carriage boots with extravagant collars of fur in the nineteen-twenties, and are now worn as a winter fashion in most countries.

Pumps, known as courts in England, came as a modern fashion from America with the dancing craze. They were cut very much like a man's evening shoe with a flat grosgrain bow, and it was considered very daring for a lady to wear these low-cut shoes when for so long she had been wearing high-laced boots.

Many other shoes, like the saddle Oxford, the co-respondent shoe, the spectator sports shoe, the open toe, the heel-less shoe, all came from America direct. Many other fashions from Italy to America, who with her enormous buying potential was able to help the Italian shoe industry after the Second World War.

AMERICAN

BLACKFOOT INDIANS

Woman

Animal skin dress and shawl richly beaded and embroidered.

Man

Fur collar and beads round neck. Tight trousers with side bands. Apron back and front.

COWBOY

Stetson. Knotted kerchief. Close-fitted waistcoat over shirt. Tight trousers with fur chaps.

1. Beige kid shoe with matching ribbon-bound topline. The inside heel is concave and could be an early example of the concealed heel type of shoe. On the suede-surfaced sole it carries a tape with the maker's name handwritten on.

2. A white satin wedding slipper with bound top-line and ribbon ties. Satin bow held by a metal ornament. The sole narrower than the heel and has a very narrow flat waist. (1820.)

3. Another wedding shoe in cream satin lined with matching linen. Ruched satin double bow. The very curved heel is straight at the front and covered in matching satin. The inside heel concave and the insole covered with linen.

(All from the John Judkyn Memorial.)

90. AMERICAN (I)

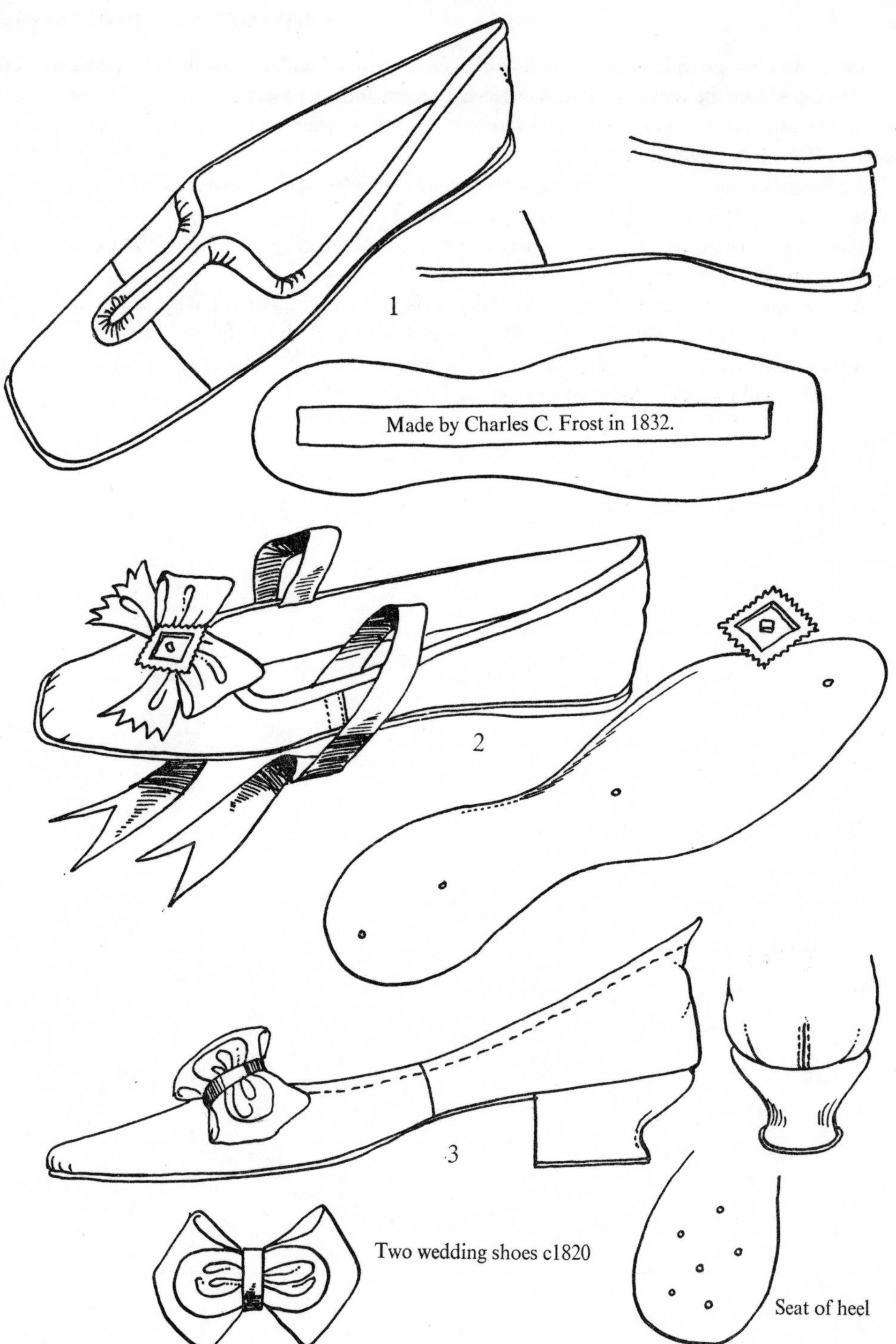
1
Made by Charles C. Frost in 1832.
2
3
Two wedding shoes c1820
Seat of heel

1. 1830. An olive-green kidskin slipper bound in cream silk and with cream-silk ties. Lined with cream linen. The shoes were the wedding slippers of Laura Bartlett, and are 10 inches long with leather soles. The soles are interesting as they build up to a shallow wedge. The opened-up vamp has a pleated silk whorl trimming. (John Judkyn Memorial.)

2. A silk brocade shoe of 1760 with a narrow rounded toe. The brocade is so cut that the rose decoration of the brocade centred on the toe. (John Judkyn Memorial.)

3. The thick shape of the heel is very curved and is $2\frac{3}{4}$ inches high, with a triangular top-piece. (John Judkyn Memorial.)

4. A high heel of 1775, very waisted and curvy. There is a tiny inserted piping of the same kid that covers the heel, as a welt or thin platform. (Museum of Costume, Bath.)

5. Another thin wedge, self-covered to match the shoe in black silk. The shoe has a modified pointed toe and a self-bound top-line. (Museum of Costume, Bath.)

91. AMERICAN (II) (18TH–19TH CENTURY HEELS)

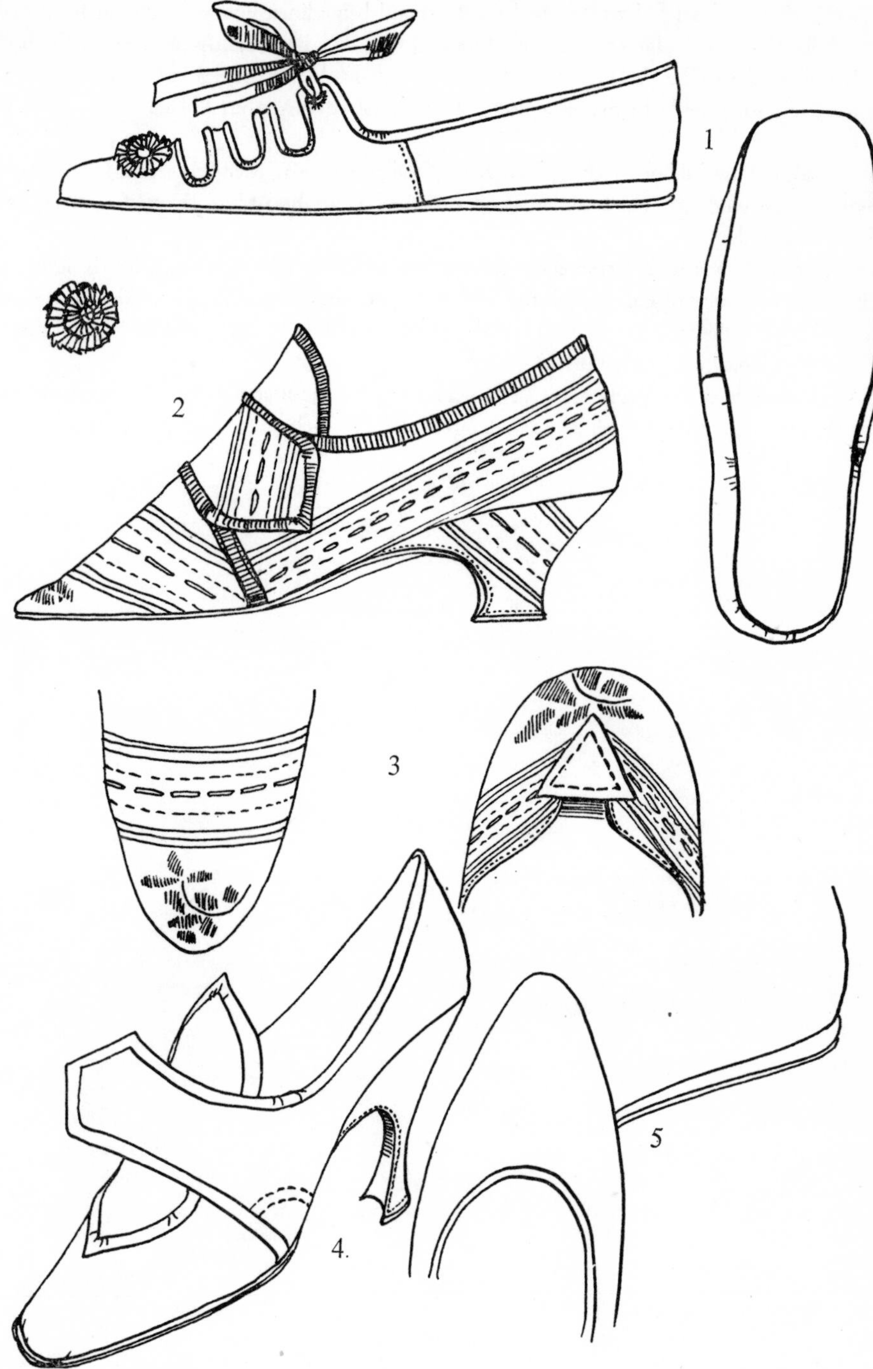
1
2
3
4.
5

1. A Quaker shoe in fawn kid with turned top-lines and beige linen lining. High-cut front tied with self ribbon. A lightly-welted edge and a rounded natural toe. The heel slightly-undercut at the back, and the inside is hollowed to take the heel-ball. The sole is channel-seamed; the last made left and right. A mid 19th-century shoe made to match a dress of the same colour, from Philadelphia. (John Judkyn Memorial.)
2. A shoe made in England but known to have been worn in America. Made on a straight last, in coloured brocades with ribbon binding. Thick undercut heel stitched at the breast and covered with the brocade. (John Judkyn Memorial.)
3. Another brocade shoe with a ribbon-bound top-line and tab. The very thick heel is lightly curved and there is a light inset welt of kid, though the heel itself is covered in matching brocade and is stitched at the breast. The back of the shoe has its seam reinforced with a ribbon covering and the natural shaped sole is channel seamed. (John Judkyn Memorial.)
4. A typical example of the many types of brocade used for shoes at this period. Great use made of stylized flowers and fruit; colour is gentle and unaggressive. (Victoria and Albert Museum.)

92. AMERICAN (III)

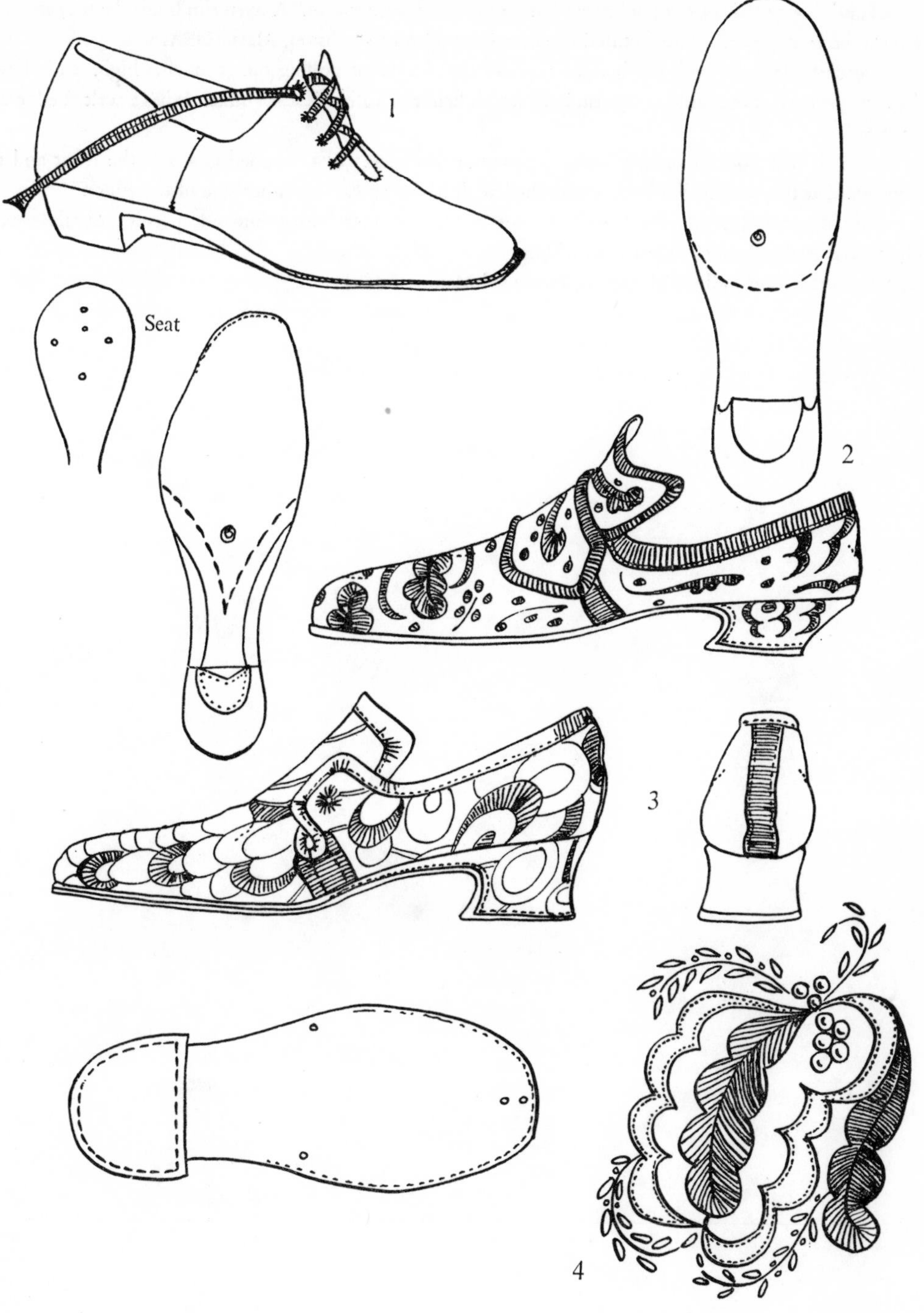
1
Seat
2
3
4

1. Child's boot made in 1840 in brown leather with red leather tops. A brass rim binds the toes and nails attach the heels and toes. Manufactured by John Bacheldor of Holliston, Mass., USA.

2. Seamless felt boot, with red braided top and tape loops for pulling on. 13 inches high, it obviously had a stirrup-guard at one time as the stitching which held the leather is still visible. It has a welted edge and a heavy sole.

3. A Civil War boot in brown leather seamed at the back. The tongued guard at the front and the stirrup-guard at the back of the heel, are stitched with heavy thread on either side of the edges.

4. Contemporary but timeless Cowboy boot in black leather with white side panels and silver nails. High-stacked leather heel is undercut for riding.

(1, 2, 3 from the John Judkyn Memorial, Freshford Manor, Bath.)

93. AMERICAN (IV) (BOOTS)

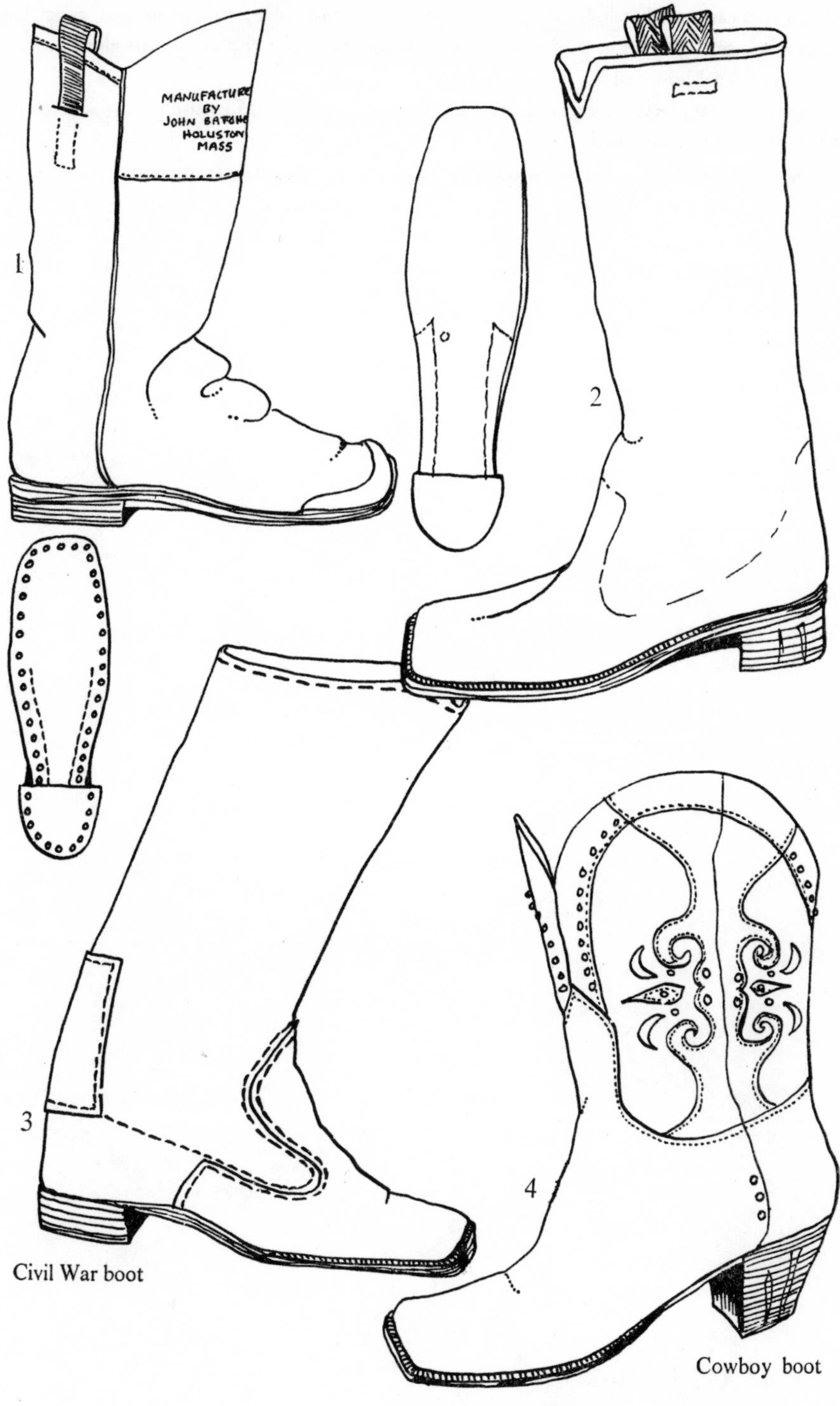

Civil War boot

Cowboy boot

1. Deerskin moccasin with self-leather thongs, decorated with blue, red, white and green beads. The sole is cut from heavier leather and probably covers sole seams similar to that in a modern moccasin. 19th century. (John Judkyn Memorial.)

2. A modern moccasin has various upper styles, but the construction is similar: the leather is wrapped up around the foot from underneath.

3. There are various seaming methods used for drawing together the surplus material from under the foot.

94. AMERICAN (V) (MOCCASINS)

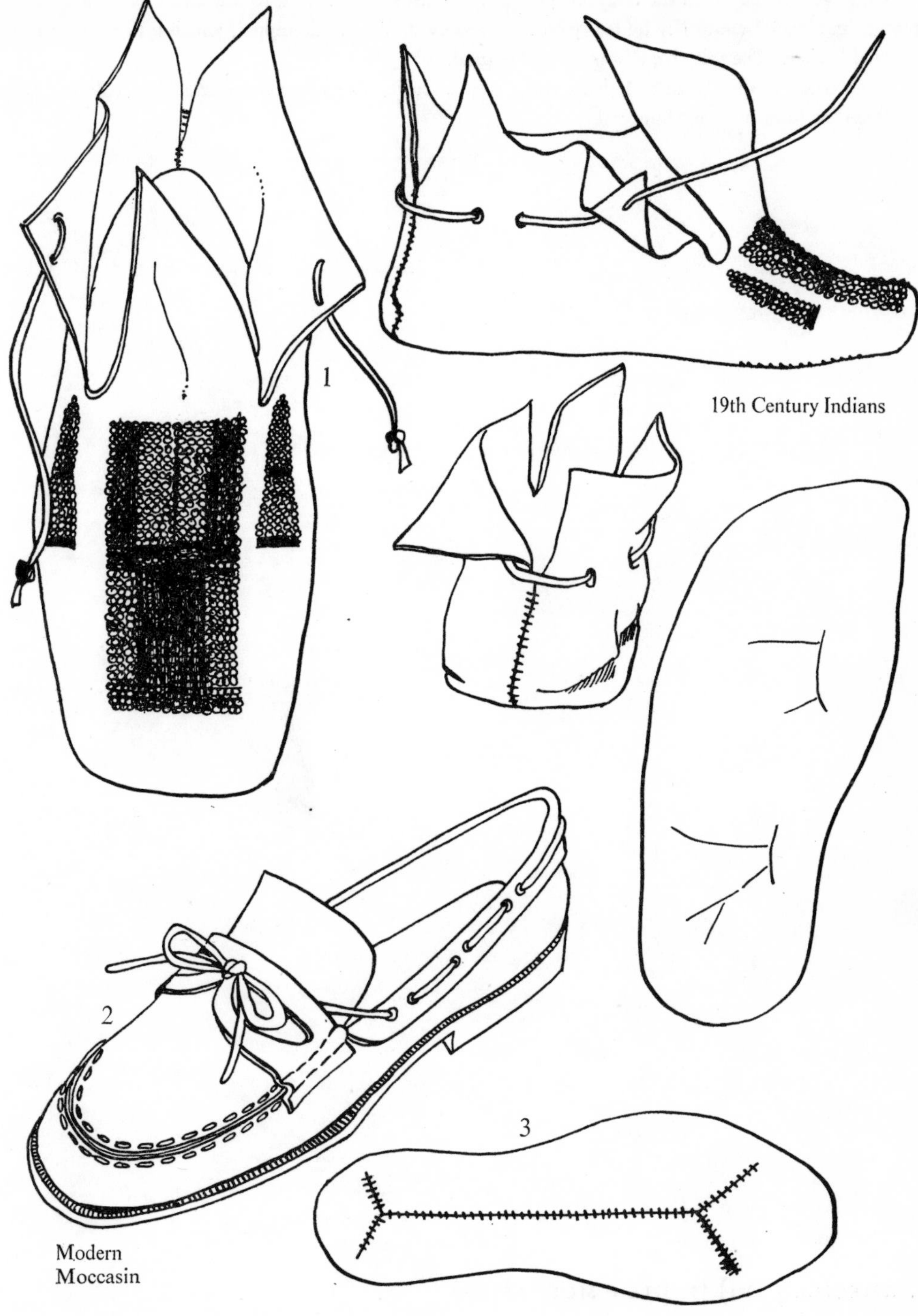

19th Century Indians

Modern Moccasin

1. Child's moccasin from the Arapaho Indians of South Dakota. In soft deerskin embroidered in red and white and black beads. The folded collar is separately stitched to the upper, which is tied with a thong of knotted leather. The sole shape is broad and natural.

2. A moccasin of the Canadian Indians of the 19th century. The vamp embroidery is in coloured raffia. (Both from the John Judkyn Memorial.)

95. AMERICAN (VI) (INDIAN MOCCASINS)

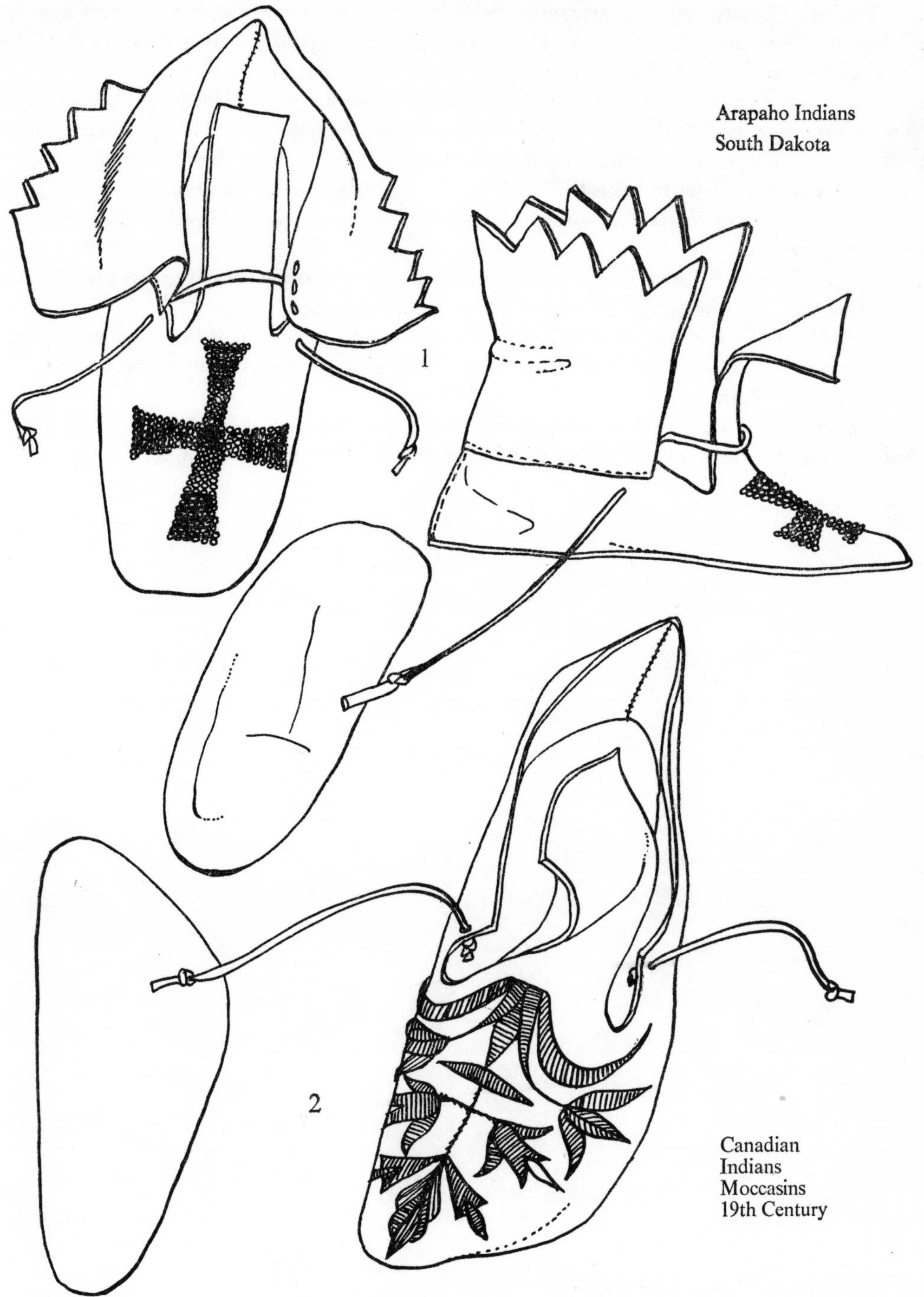

Arapaho Indians
South Dakota

Canadian
Indians
Moccasins
19th Century

1. The leather leggings worn by cowboys are called "chaps." The complete Mexican name is Chaparejos, and there are three main groups or styles. This is of the closed leg type which are sometimes called "shotgun" chaps because they look like twin gun barrels. These were popular in the 1870s.

2. The cowboy's riding boot has two main features by which it is distinguished from boots for other riders. It has a high, thick heel which slopes forward and a narrow square toe. Though the style is traditional these two features are important: the high heel prevents the boot from slipping through the stirrup and the toe enables the boot to be easily slipped into the stirrup. Decorations are often lavish, even today, and inlaid with silver or contrasting colour. This boot shows the spur attached with a thick ornamental leather strap.

3. A black leather boot with heavily ornamented top. The decoration consists of fancy stitching and inlaid white calf. The stitching on the vamp is also an impressed pattern.

4. Two blue steel spurs from Mexico, both with large wheel rowels about 2½ inches across. These are worn at the back of the heel and attached by either a heavy chain or a thick leather strap, or both. The steel is inlaid with silver.

5. Tapaderos are also of Mexican origin and are often called "taps" for short. These are leather hoods which fit round the stirrup and are tied on with leather thongs. They are deeply tooled.

96. AMERICAN (VII) (COWBOY)

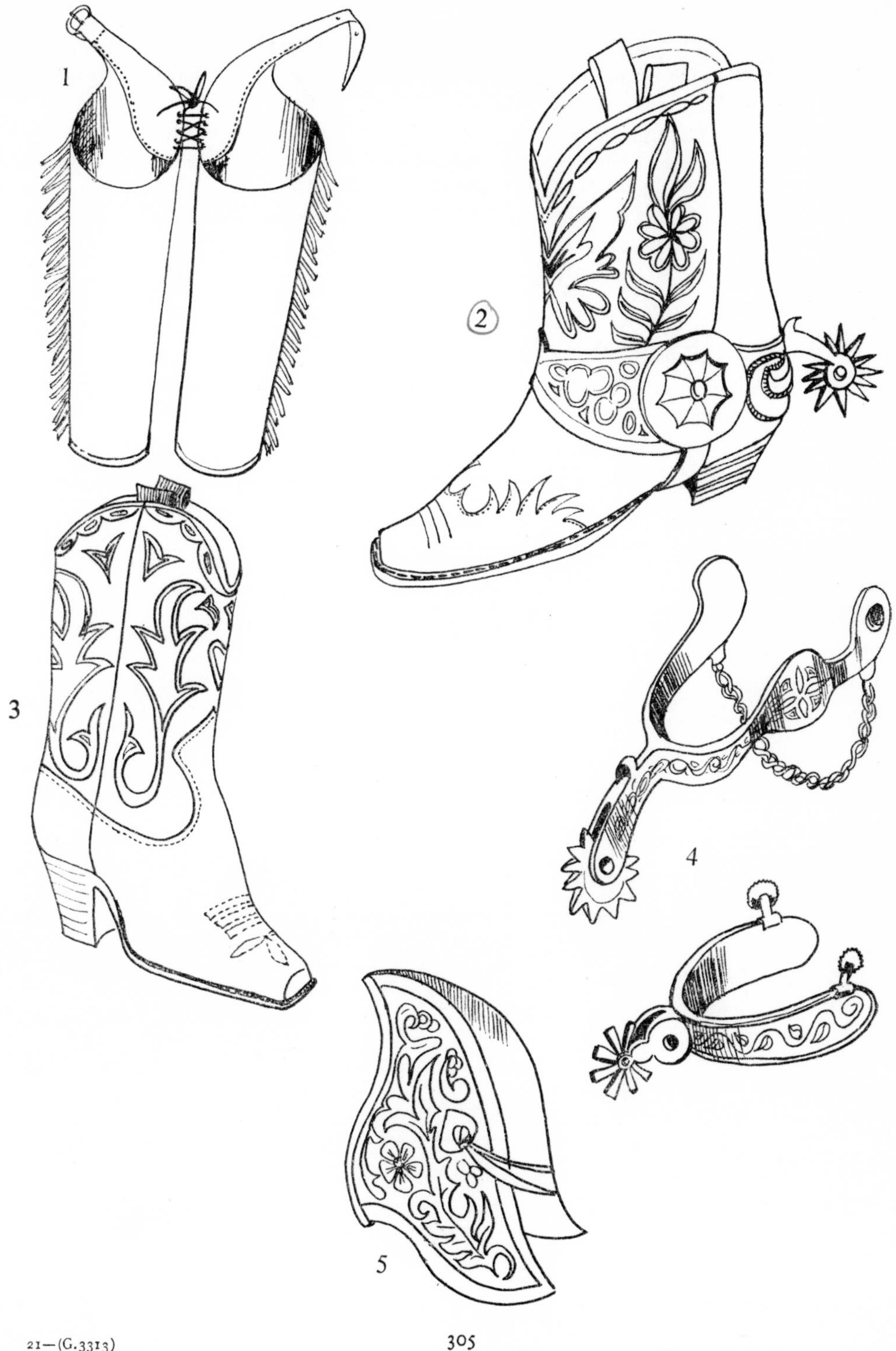
1
2
3
4
5

1. Boot of the Navajo Indians in thick saffron-coloured suede and rawhide moulded sole. The suede has a beige back. Buttoned by coins, leaving the soft flap to fly free at back. The coins are dimes dated 1919 and 1926 and quarters dated 1894 and 1904. (Date 1930.)

2. A Canadian Indian moccasin of the 19th century beaded in black and white with red and green painted decoration. Fringed tab is laced to the shoe with leather thongs which go round the back. The back itself is deeply fringed so that the ends trail behind; it is said to be cut like this to wipe out footprints. (Both from the John Judkyn Memorial.)

97. AMERICAN (VIII) (AMERICAN AND CANADIAN INDIAN MOCCASINS)

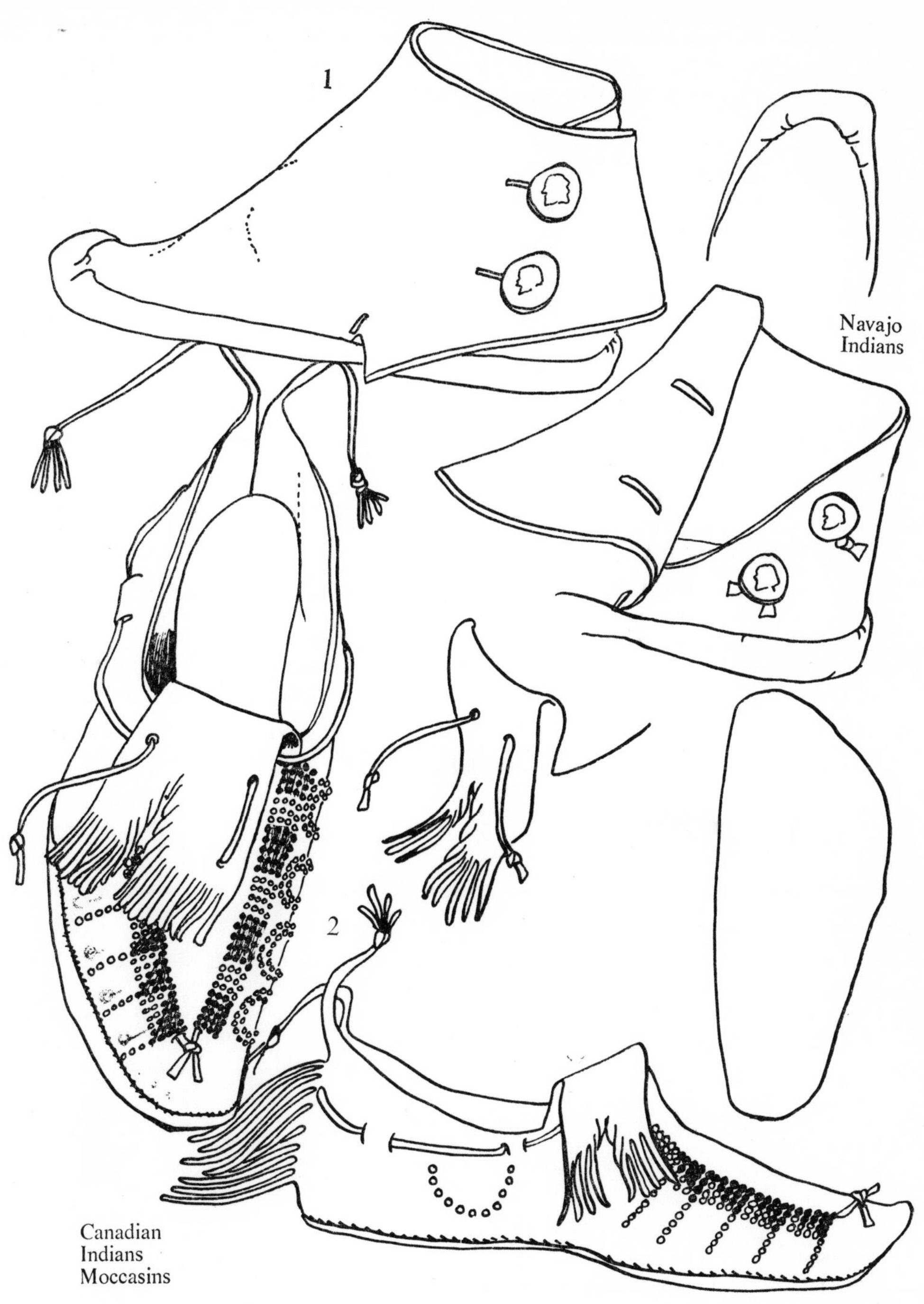

Navajo Indians

Canadian Indians Moccasins

The basic shape for moccasins has not changed a great deal over the centuries. Cut from leather which is placed under the foot, wrapped round it and stitched to an apron vamp, or totally thonged together as in ancient times. The Aran Islander's pampootie, the moccasin of the North American Indian, the casual of modern shoemaking, all have this method in common with our ancestors. Modern moccasins have an outdoor sole added, if meant for hard wear, but retain the same flexibility.

98. AMERICAN (IX) (MODERN MOCCASINS)

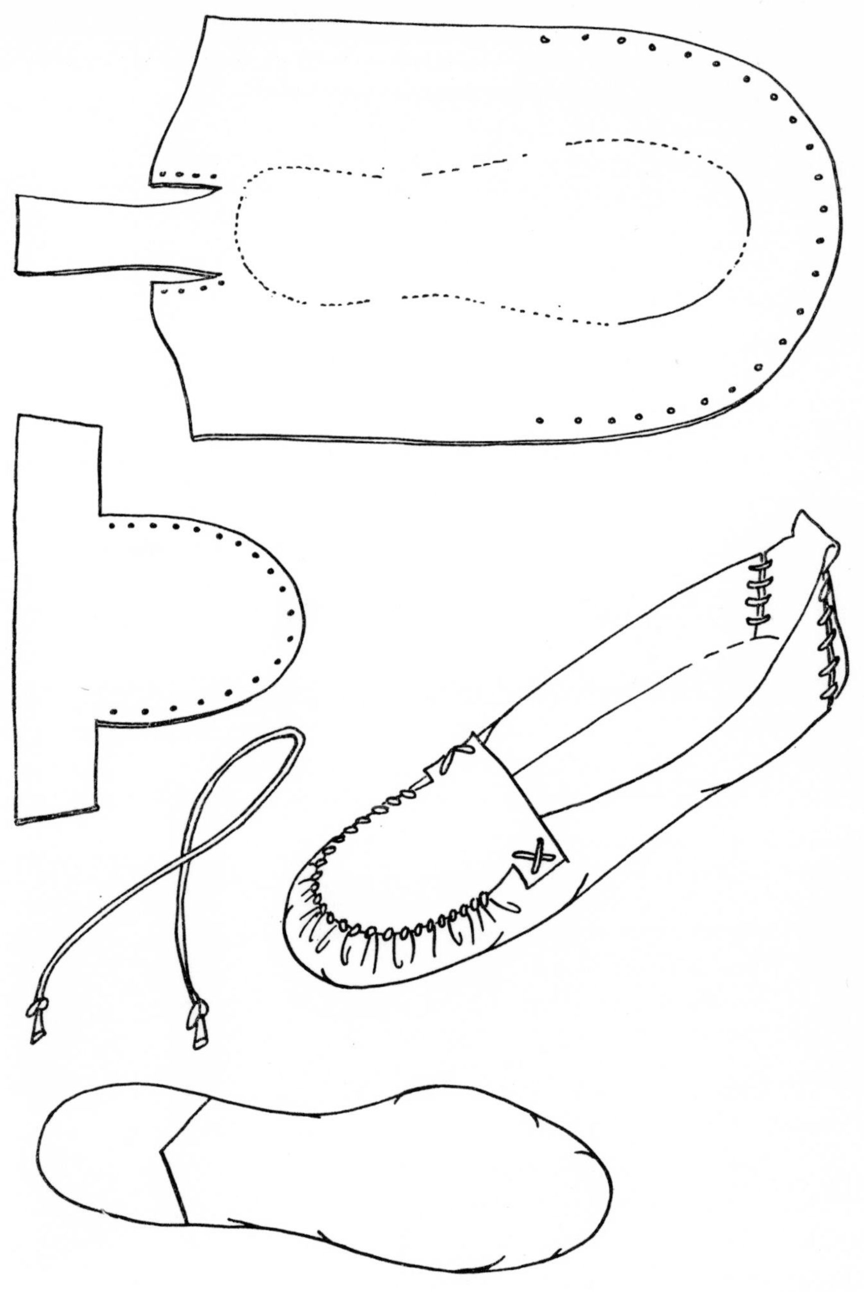

1. Boots were very popular now that they were machine made and the varieties of their design were enormous. They were laced almost to the top and some were then laced round hooks. The toe was almost pointed. There was often a striped lining and a tape pull-tag at the back.
2. Contrast was in evening shoes which were much lighter. Still with a long almost pointed toe and made of black patent. A flat faille bow finished off the high-cut vamp.
3. Black and white sports shoe with crepe rubber sole and deep round toe.
4. Some boots were lightly brogued along the galosh line and had cloth tops.
5. The long slender last was important and set-off by a relatively plain upper.

99. AMERICAN (X) (1890–1900)

1
2
3
4
5

24

Postscript

THERE IS A GREAT DEAL of nonsense talked about design of all kinds, both by those who understand it and those who don't. This especially applies where designing clothes is concerned, but at least it has been proved that Britain's methods of training her potential designers show very good results at all levels of the trade.

Whilst almost every art school of any standing has a dress design department, it is above all to those in the shoe centres of Britain that we owe the success of our shoe designers. To a shoe designer an all-round fashion training plus as wide a study of general art as possible is essential. He should also take advantage of the detailed technical training offered by the very forward-thinking technical colleges, also situated in the shoe-manufacturing centres of Leicester, Northampton, and the Hackney district of London, because a knowledge of the practical side of the industry is important.

It is becoming apparent, however, that fashion training for a shoe designer is as important as the technical side. Since the development of mass production some shoe manufacturers have tended to bury their heads like the ostrich, and seem to be unaware that as shoes are worn with clothes they are therefore influenced by the same trends and developments. Many art schools have realized this and are making their students aware that there are many accessories to fashion, of which shoes are probably the most important. Whatever other accessory we can do without, the circumstances in which we can do without shoes are rare, and the people who go shoeless are becoming fewer.

Top among these schools is the Royal College of Art which takes the cream of the students from other art schools all over the country and from abroad. The R.A.C. Fashion School is one of the most highly thought of in Europe. Here a great deal of attention is paid to the design and appreciation of accessories, so that fashion is designed as a whole and not as isolated items. Students leaving the R.C.A. Fashion School have had a thoroughly practical training and are highly sought after. Though there is no concentration on the technical production of shoes as at the technical colleges, factories are visited in the course of the year, and most of the students have spent some time in one or more of them by the time they have graduated.

More and more attention is being given to design and the interpretation of it in a fashion context in all technical colleges, especially in those which are able to work closely with the industry. This gives a student a down-to-earth approach to the problems of production and marketing, and, whilst not hampering or inhibiting their creative abilities, teaches them that shoes, more than all other items of fashion, have to be practical and wearable.

Industry itself is also providing encouragement by offering prizes, scholarships, bursaries, and other awards to the potential designer. These take the form of money and travel awards, working holidays abroad, and introductory jobs into the trade. Thus the student can gain a great deal of help and experience before actually beginning work. All this helps, because it is very essential to travel these days as fashion moves so fast and is no longer confined to any one country, nor dictated to by any one group of people or nationality, so that unless one is attuned to all that is going on, no matter where, one can miss a great deal.

Fashion always comes from the privileged classes and spreads out in a widening circle of influence to the rest until it is time to change again. The privileged classes now are the young, and the wealthy or "society" classes have no longer the importance in fashion circles that they once had. This is the light in which we must look at the working of fashion nowadays, not exclusively basing our views on the past but making a different interpretation of what has happened before.

It is the way of life, more than anything, which changes fashion, and this is most clearly demonstrated in our own day. We have only to look back on the recent Mondrian craze which was applied to clothes, shoes, hats, handbags, everything to do with fashion, in a way that would probably have shocked the painter himself. Op Art was another influence which when used by fashion was called a theft and a plagiarism by its originators. No doubt they were justified in their accusations, but on looking back through the costume books of any period one sees very clearly that clothes have always been affected by surrounding influence, and this is no more the case in our day than at any other time.

Fashion is not static and can change in a few years, but today's clothes are the clearest interpretation there can be of the freedom of expression and thought which typifies our age. Shoes express this very clearly, for no longer do we wear tight shoes to confine our large healthy feet. Neither do women limit themselves to sombre colours alone to prove that they are "ladies." They need not wear high heels if they do not like or cannot wear them; they can wear flat heels without being called dowdy or eccentric. The price of our shoes no longer betrays our income group, for the titled lady is quite likely to have bought hers in the chain store while the shop assistant bought hers in Paris. We no longer have to make them last for years, because they are relatively less expensive now and we can discard them for a new fashion without a pang of conscience.

Appendix I

Museums holding boot and shoe collections

(Quoted by kind permission of the National Joint Recruitment and Training Council of the Boot and Shoe Manufacturing Industry)

Most museums in the British Isles have period costumes (including shoes) on view. The following have larger collections and those marked with an asterisk have special exhibits of boots and shoes.

Belfast: Museum and Art Gallery.
Birmingham: City Museum and Art Gallery.
Bristol*: City Museum at Blaise Castle Folk Museum, Henbury.
Cardiff: National Museum of Wales at the Welsh Folk Museum, St. Fagans.
Cheltenham: Art Gallery and Museum.
Douglas: Manx Museum, Library and Art Gallery.
Edinburgh: National Museum of Antiquities of Scotland.
Exeter: Royal Albert Memorial Museum.
Glasgow: Art Gallery and Museum.
Halifax*: Bankfield Museum.
Hereford: City Museum and Art Gallery.
Ipswich: Museum at Christchurch Mansion.
Kettering*: Westfields Museum.
Leeds: City Museum.
Leicester*: Newarke House.
London* Bethnal Green Museum.
London* Guildhall Museum (also has the Museum of Leathercraft).
London* London Museum.
London* Victoria and Albert Museum.
Luton: Museum and Art Gallery.
Maidstone: Museum and Art Gallery
Manchester*: The Gallery of English Costume at Platt Hall
Northampton* Central Museum and Art Gallery
Norwich* Bridewell Museum of Local Industries.
Norwich* Castle Museum.

Paisley: Museum and Art Galleries.
Preston: Harris Museum and Art Gallery.
Salisbury: Salisbury, South Wilts and Blackmore Museum.
Taunton: Somerset County Museum.
Tunbridge Wells: Museum and Art Gallery.
York: Castle Museum.
York: Philosophical Society Museum

Reproductions of "cobblers' or cloggers' shops" can be seen in the museums at Leicester (Newarke House); Northampton, the Bowes Museum at Barnard Castle; and York Castle.

Private collections may be seen at Messrs. C. & J. Clark Ltd., Street, Somerset; Messrs. John Shortland Ltd., Irthlingborough, Northants, and at the following Technical Colleges: Cordwainers, London; Kettering; Leicester; Northampton; Rushden. Also the Gorbold Collection of Oriental Shoes, formed and presented by Mr R. Gorbold, can be seen at the British Boot, Shoe and Allied Trades Research Association (SATRA), Kettering, Northants. Prior arrangements should be made to view these collections.

References for Museums: *Museums and Art Galleries in Great Britain and Northern Ireland* (Index Publishers Ltd.); *Victorian Costume and Costume Accessories*, Ann M. Buck (Herbert Jenkins, 1961).

Ashmolean Museum, Oxford
Ludlow Museum
Worcester Museum
Walworth Road Museum, London, S.E.1.
Also, by appointment, American shoes at the John Judkyn Memorial, Freshford Manor, Nr. Bath
and
Bally's Museum at Schoenwerd, Switzerland

Messrs. Lotus Ltd., Stafford, and the Norvic Shoe Company, Norwich, also have private collections of shoes.

There are also extensive collections in Ireland, which deserves a separate volume of shoe history. These are: The National Museum of Ireland, Kildare Street, Dublin; the County Museum, Armagh, N. Ireland; and the Ulster Museum, Stranmills, Belfast.

Many historical houses, open to the public have individual collections or interesting single samples.

Appendix II

Schools and colleges concerned with shoe fashions

There are many schools, art schools, and technical colleges which teach history of costume, dress and shoe pattern cutting, as well as the specialist colleges in boot and shoe manufacture. It is not possible to make a complete list, but of the many which have been particularly helpful to me or to my students I should like to mention the following:

ARS SUTORIA, MILAN, ITALY

Run by one of the most influential and able men in the world shoe trade, Dr. Giuseppe Muggiani, and his son Dr. Giampiero Muggiani, this is a shoe school *par excellence*. Here design and pattern cutting are taught to students who come from all over the world. Their work, and the brilliant ideas of its directors, are illustrated in the well-known shoe magazine *Ars Sutoria*. Many of the best shoe designers in industry today are products of this school.

NORTHAMPTON COLLEGE OF TECHNOLOGY

This college conducts a comprehensive course of shoe design and technical production, whose students are drawn from the industries of the world. Its head, Mr. John Thornton, is probably our ablest and most knowledgeable shoe historian, whose ability to date and identify excavated discoveries is requested on many important archaeological occasions.

LEICESTER SCHOOL OF BOOT AND SHOE MANUFACTURE

Centred in the heart of Britain's shoe industry, Leicester's contribution to the technical training of shoe designers and makers is inestimable.

CORDWAINER'S TECHNICAL COLLEGE, LONDON

Students are prepared for City and Guilds of London examinations here, and receive a comprehensive training for the footwear and leather goods industries.

LEATHERSELLER'S COLLEGE, LONDON, is a school of long-standing repute. It is situated in the heart of London's leather district and there is little to do with the leather trade that is not covered by its courses.

THE ROYAL COLLEGE OF ART'S FASHION SCHOOL

This is a post-graduate school of the university, which, although it has no shoe department as such, has been the fashion background for several well-known shoe designers. There is a first-year course of shoe history and theory.

Many other Art Schools have a course in shoe design. A selection of these is:

HARROW SCHOOL OF ART

LIVERPOOL SCHOOL OF ART

HORNSEY COLLEGE OF ART

WALTHAM FOREST TECHNICAL COLLEGE

These and many others enter for, and win, several of the now well-established competitions for potential shoe designers.

Bibliography

Costume in England, F. W. Fairholt (1885).
History of British Costume, Joseph Planché (1874).

Both these books are invaluable to the student for their references to sources and are the main reasons why I have not listed many of my own. They quote from most of the illuminated manuscripts, and Fairholt in particular gives numerous notes on statues, brasses, windows, etc. He also gives a very extensive list of books available at his own time of writing, and so, though I have referred to many of them myself, I do not feel the need to duplicate his very valuable bibliography.

The Bayeux Tapestry, Eric Maclagan (King Penguin).

There are many books on this subject, the biggest and best of which is one recently published by the Phaidon Press.

Britain's Story Told in Pictures, consisting of six small books by C. W. Airne, M.A. and published by Thomas Hope and Sankey Hudson. These cover several separate periods, and I have found them invaluable for background material.

Everyday Life in Roman and Anglo-Saxon Times, Marjorie and C. H. B. Quennell.

This leads up to their larger book:

History of Everyday Things in England from 1066–1799.
English Women's Costume in The Eighteenth Century, C. Willett Cunnington.

And many other books by this famous costume historian and his wife.

The Woman in Fashion, Doris Langley Moore.
English Fashion, Alison Settle.
Costume and Fashion, Herbert Norris (4 volumes).
The Dress and Habits of the People in England, Notes by Planché, illustrations by J. Strutt.
Ancient Costumes of England, C. H. Smith.
The Mode in Footwear, Turner Wilcox.
Costume Catalogue of the London Museum.
English Costume, Doreen Yarwood.
The Well-Dressed Woman, Georgie Herschel.
Shoemaker of Dreams, Salvatore Ferragamo.
The Age of Worth, Edith Saunders.

Style in Costume.
History of English Footwear, Iris Brooke.
Costume of the Western World (Harrap's Series).
Gallery of Fashion (Batsford Colour Book).
17th and 18th Century Costumes, James Laver.
Dress, James Laver.
Taste and Fashion, James Laver.
Costume in Antiquity, James Laver.

Plus many articles and reprints of lectures by this leading costume authority.

Fashions and Fashion Plates, 1800–1900, James Laver.

Mr. Laver's books also have excellent bibliographies and notes of the various contemporary fashion magazines from which many of his illustrations come.

Costume Through The Ages, Introduced by James Laver.
Always in Vogue, Edna Woolman Chase and Ilka Chase.
Women in Antiquity, James Laver.
The Glass of Fashion, Cecil Beaton.
Paris à la Mode, Celia Bertin.
Book of The Bally Shoe Museum,
All the books of archaeology which refer to finds in tumuli, etc., and all the books on social history you can find.
The King of Paris, Guy Endore.
The Fabulous Originals, Irving Wallace.
Larousse: Ancient and Mediaeval History.
Modern History
Renaissance and Baroque Art
Mythology
And others from the Larousse Reference Library.
Costume Cavalcade, Harold Hansen.
Muffs and Morals, Pearl Binder.
On Human Finery, Quentin Bell.
Reign by Reign, Stephen Usherwood.
Encyclopedia Britannica.
English Ballet, Jane Leeper (King Penguin).
The Gallery of English Costume, A series published for the Art Galleries Committee of the Corporation of Manchester, 1949.
Arms and Armour, Vesey Norman.
A Book of Military Uniforms and Weapons, Karel Toman.
British Costume During 19 Centuries, Mrs. Charles G. Ashdown.

Knowledge, encyclopedia published by Purnell & Sons.
Costume Through The Centuries, Jane Oliver.
The Book of Days, R. Chambers.
Fashion, Mila Contini.
Armbearing Guilds of London, Bromley and Child.
Romance of the Shoe, Thomas Wright.
Histoire du Costume, Francois Boucher.
Dictionaire Du Costume, Maurice Leloir
Le Grand Livre Du Tapis.
Book of The Feet, J. Sparks Hall.
England Before The Norman Conquest, Sir Charles Oman.
The Ashley Book of Knots, W. Ashley.
Textbook of Footwear Manufacture, Ed. Dr. J. Thornton.
Textbook of Footwear Materials, Ed. Dr. J. Thornton.
Royal Shoes and Gloves, W. B. Redfern.
Costume in Pictures, Phillis Cunnington.
Footwear Weekly, British trade press.
Shoe and Leather News, British trade press.
Leather, British trade press.
Boot and Shoe Recorder, American trade press
Shoe and Leather Journal, Australian trade press
Leather and Shoes, American trade press.
Fairchilds Publications, American trade press.
Ars Sutoria, Italian trade press.
Arpel, Italian trade press.

Index